Reviews fɪ

"... the ruins, n
routes held sac

"Foɪ each site,
description of t
getting there." *(Theology Digest* Summer, 2000)

"(Readers) will thrill to the wonderful history and the vibrations of the world's sacred healing places." *(East & West* 2/2000)

"Sites that emanate the energy of sacred spots."
(The Sunday Times 1/2000)

"Sacred sites (to) the ruins, sanctuaries, mountains, lost cities, temples, and pilgrimage routes of ancient civilizations."
(San Francisco Chronicle 1/2000)

"Many sacred places are now bustling tourist and pilgrimage destinations. But no crowd or souvenir shop can stand in the way of a traveler with great intentions and zero expectations."
(Spirituality & Health Summer, 2000)

"Unleash your imagination by going on a mystical journey. Brad Olsen gives his take on some of the most amazing and unexplained spots on the globe—including the underwater ruins of Bimini, which seems to point the way to the Lost City of Atlantis. You can choose to take an armchair pilgrimage (the book is a fascinating read) or follow his tips on how to travel to these powerful sites yourself."
(Mode 7/2000)

"Should you be inspired to make a pilgrimage of your own, you might want to pick up a copy of Brad Olsen's guide to the world's sacred places. Olsen's marvelous drawings and mysterious maps enhance a package that is as bizarre as it is wonderfully accessible. The historical data and metaphysical ruminations make it an intriguing read. So pick a mystical corner of the world, be it Mount Shasta, Delphi or Borobudur, and plan out a pilgrimage real or imagined among the Tungus shamans of Siberian Russia, the ghosts of Mohenjo-daro, the Muslim faithful at the Grand Mosque in Mecca, and more." *(San Francisco Examiner* 1/2000)

Reviews from *Sacred Places North America*

"An interesting book for both the armchair and the adventurous traveler, this (book) is recommended." (*Library Journal* 4/2003)

"The book is filled with fascinating archeological, geological, and historical material. These 108 sacred places in the United States, Canada, and Hawaii offer ample opportunity for questing by spiritual seekers." (*Spirituality & Health* 3/2003)

"A revealing, useful, and enthusiastically recommended guide for the vacationer seeking to fulfill their spiritual as well as their recreational yearnings." (*Midwest Book Review* 2/2003)

"World traveler Brad Olsen has compiled a book that documents 108 destination spots for 'feeling the energy' of our spiritual historical roots. Pilgrimage is one way we can find ourselves and this book will provide a guide." (*Twin Cities Wellness* 3/2003)

"The book's chapters correspond to ten regional sections of the U.S. and Canada, which are further subdivided into specific U.S. States and Canadian provinces. No less than 38 of the 50 United States are revealed to contain sacred sites — some of which are very public and easy to access, such as the House of David in Michigan, and some of which are more obscure, like Shiprock, 'the stand-alone neck of an ancient volcano core' in New Mexico. But never fear: Olsen provides lucid and detailed directions, as well as tantalizing and historically well-informed essay-portraits, for each destination. The book is also peppered with excellent maps, illustrations, and photos." (*Fearless Books* 2/2003)

"For travelers who prefer destinations with spirit ... juxtaposing local folklore and Native American legend with scientific theories to provide context." (*Orlando Sentinel* 2/2003)

"It's an odd lot, the places that have a way of touching your heart: mountains and homesteads, caves and monasteries, lakes and pathways. Author Brad Olsen has recognized that variety in this bringing together of 108 places that stir the soul. Many of the destinations mentioned come as no surprise in a collection of the hallowed: Ohio's Serpent Mound, Wyoming's Yellowstone, Colorado's Mesa Verde, for instance. But other entries serve as a delightful reminder that there is room in our hearts to expand the definition of sacred: Massachusetts' Walden Pond, Michigan's House of David, and Tennessee's (and Elvis') Graceland, for instance." (*Chicago Tribune* 4/2003)

"Olsen maps out obscure destinations brimming with intrigue and history, places where you will not have to fight thousands of tourists. You'll find lots of maps, drawings and photos. It's a travel guide for the individualist." (*Ashley Tribune* 3/2003)

SACRED PLACES

EUROPE

108 DESTINATIONS

Written, photographed, and illustrated by

BRAD OLSEN

CONSORTIUM OF COLLECTIVE CONSCIOUSNESS

www.cccpublishing.com   www.bradolsen.com   www.stompers.com

Sacred Places Europe:
108 Destinations

first edition

Copyright © 2007 by Brad Olsen

Published by the Consortium of Collective Consciousness ™

All rights reserved.

Library of Congress Cataloging-in-Publication Data:

Olsen, Bradford C.

  Sacred Places Europe: 108 Destinations / Brad Olsen

    p. cm.

  Includes index

  ISBN 10: 1-888729-12-0 (Pbk.)

  ISBN 13: 978-1-888729-12-2

  1. Spirituality — Guidebooks. 2. Travel — Guidebooks. I. Title

  Library of Congress Catalog Card Number: 2005904373

Printed in the United States of America.

10 9 8 7 6 5 4 3 2 1

Front Cover Photos: Unknown Statue, Madrid, Spain; Saint Peter's Basilica, Vatican City; Valley of the Temples, Sicily, Italy; Le Ménec alignments, Carnac, France. **Back Cover Photo:** Viking runestone from Forhistorisk Museum Moesgård, Århus, Denmark. **All images © 2007, Brad Olsen.**

ALSO BY BRAD OLSEN

Sacred Places Around the World: 108 Destinations
2004

Sacred Places North America: 108 Destinations
2003

World Stompers: A Global Travel Manifesto
2001

In Search of Adventure: A Wild Travel Anthology
1999

Extreme Adventures Northern California
1997

Extreme Adventures Hawaii
1997

The Dating System used in this text is based upon the modern method of using Before Current Era (BCE) instead of Before Christ (B.C.), and Current Era (CE) rather than "in the year of the Lord" *anno Domini* (A.D.). Those unfamiliar with this dating system should take note that 1 B.C. is the same as 1 BCE and everything then counts backward just the same. Similarly, 1 A.D. is 1 CE with all the years counting forward to the present, or Current Era. To assist in universal understanding, all measurements of length, distance, area, weight, and volume are listed both in the old British standard and the metric system.

108 SACRED PLACES IN EUROPE

FRANCE AND THE LOW COUNTRIES

CENTRAL EUROPE

EASTERN EUROPE

SCANDINAVIA

GERMANY AND THE ALPS

GREECE

ITALY AND MALTA

SPAIN AND PORTUGAL

AUTHOR'S KARMA STATEMENT

If the Success or Failure of this Planet,
and of Human Beings,
Depended on How I Am and What I Do;
How Would I Be? What Would I Do?

—Buckminster Fuller

Conversations with Europeans on the subject of sacred places all seem to follow a similar pattern. First they'd like to know "what exactly is a sacred place?" I point out some obvious worldwide examples: the Great Pyramids, Angkor Wat, Stonehenge, and the Maltese temples. When I try to describe one or two sites in the vicinity where we are having the conversation they almost always respond with a head nodding affirmative: "ahhh yes, I know now what you mean."

I got the idea for this "Author's Karma Statement" entry along the Tagus River in Lisbon, Portugal. Just an hour ago, while developing my recent photos from the last month of travel, I met a clerk named Regina at *Extracolor Fotográficos*, a person who has seen a lot of photographic images in her life. After the opening salvos on the subject of sacred places, I told her of the Portuguese sites I had in mind visiting: Évora, Fátima, Braga, and then over the border to Santiago, Spain. "*Ahhh, sí,*" Regina nodded affirmatively. Unprompted, she related in English some of the sacred sites she knew about in the region. She gave me the directions to a pirate's grotto near Lisbon, a few off-the-beaten-path megaliths near Évora, and something else that seemed peculiar. Regina told me about a popular photograph she develops rather frequently, featuring ambiguous images of the sky. The random shots of the firmament are all taken at Fátima, the famous vision site of the Blessed Virgin Mother in central Portugal. All the photos are taken under the supervision of a priest, along with a large dose of faith. Most of the sky photos Regina has developed revealed absolutely nothing, but a few show a figure of some kind. She could not describe the Fátima sky figure much better than saying it was a constant image, seemed to be of a light origin, and only appeared in a few of the photographs. What is peculiar is that none of the people who took the photos saw anything with the naked eye, yet different cameras, with different lenses, at different times registered a similar image!

10

I told Regina I had a similar picture of my own published in the color insert pages of *Sacred Places Around the World: 108 Destinations*. The photo shows the front row of Vietnamese high priests in the Cao Dai temple with blue colored light images around their bodies. She recognized the similarity to the Fátima figures as we both nodded in agreement. We both understood that there can be strange manifestations at sacred sites. I paid Regina for my photos, she said she'd buy my book, and I told her I'd be back in a week with my new photos of Portugal and western Spain for her to develop. She gave me some coupons so I would return. Of course, I would. For me, it is more than just giving her my business, it is sharing with her a mutual and profound travel experience.

This kind of completely arbitrary encounter is what gives travel its edge. Without random acts of kindness, my trip would have been rather bland. I am grateful to people like Regina, and my older established friends in Europe, all of whom share with me a passion for travel. New acquaintances often took me to locations I never knew existed. Older friends made sure I had a good time, put me up, and showed me their photo albums to offer new suggestions. It should be noted that I am happy to respond in kindness to their travel requests whenever they visit San Francisco. New acquaintances and older European friends truly assisted me in a crucial way to make this book project happen. Over the course of several trips, many European friends became deeply interested in my book project and went out of their way to assist me. I dedicate this book to all my friends, both old and new.

The sharing of knowledge should be universal.

▲ The massive "Monument to the Discoveries" overlooks the Tagus River at Belém. Leading the group stands Prince Henry the Navigator. It was opened to the public in 1960, replacing a temporary model that was erected for the 1940 Exhibition of the Portuguese World.

As I write this passage, I am facing Lisbon's *Rio Tejo*, known in ancient times as the "Port of Gaul." The Portuguese certainly understood the importance of sharing knowledge. Even under the less than altruistic motives of military conquest, resource exploitation, or colonization, information was still being distributed. Literature was published, maps drawn, commodities traded, new languages taught and customs learned, all with the belief in the importance of sharing knowledge. From nearby Belém sailed the galleons of Henry the Navigator, Vasco de Gama, and many other explorers harking from the "Age of Discovery." Remnants of the worldwide Portuguese empire exist today in the former colonies of Macau near Hong Kong and Goa India, along with the countries of Angola and Mozambique in Africa. Today, more native Portuguese speakers reside in Brazil than all the rest of the world combined.

Creating these guide books is my way of sharing information. I feel I lead a blessed life for having the opportunity to do what I love to do. I give thanks everyday. My aim is to visit as many sacred sites as I can, whether or not I write them up or draw them into my map books. Do I reveal every sacred place I discover? No. As much as I believe in sharing information, I also believe there is a zone of communal privacy that should be respected. I believe there are some

▲ This is my earliest drawn map of European sacred places. It emphasizes the Saint Michael's Line spanning across the continent to the Holy Land in present-day Israel.

12

sensitive locations that need not be disclosed to the general public. Therefore all the places I describe in my books are open to all, usually a major landmark or UNESCO World Heritage Site, and certainly an integral part of our human legacy.

Visiting sacred sites should be regarded at the very least as an educational field trip. This can be the most inspiring, intellectual, and spiritual experience of one's life. It should go without mention, but please be very respectful at sacred places. Whisper or avoid speaking, remove litter instead of creating it, and never deface a monument or take anything away. Everyone who arrives after us will appreciate the compliment. It is likely that visitors to a sacred site will take some photos or video, explore the general area, and leave with some interesting stories to tell. This can be your own way of sharing knowledge. Tell your friends and loved ones about your experience. Host a slide show party. Encourage them to make a trip of their own. Similar to sailors of a bygone era setting off to ports unknown, be open to your own experiences and take in as much as you possibly can! These are interesting times in which we find ourselves. The value of sacred sites has never meant so much to all of us. Love them like they are your own.

Yours in Mutual Explorations,

—Brad Olsen

Lisbon, Portugal

August 24th, 2004

FOREWORD BY MARTIN GRAY

Places of Peace and Power in Europe

Every continent has its own spirit of place. Every people is polarized in some particular locality, which is home, the homeland. Different places on the face of the earth have different vital effluence, different vibration, different chemical exhalations, different polarity with different stars: call it what you like, but the spirit of place is a great reality.
—D. H. Lawrence

Since the dawn of civilization people have visited, venerated and used sacred places. This is certainly the case in Europe, where from at least 4500 BCE a mysterious people began erecting stone temples and celestial observatories. Known as the *megalithic* culture (meaning "great stone"), its' sages positioned various types of stone structures at particular places on the land. Where, and what, were those places? They are places of power and they are located everywhere upon the earth. What makes these places of power, what is the nature of their powers, and where specifically are they located in Europe? These are the fascinating subjects you will find well discussed in this book.

Some 25 years ago I began a serious study of the sacred sites and pilgrimage traditions of the world. My travels to those places took me to more than 100 countries and 1,000 holy places. The second region of my long pilgrimage was Europe. For nearly a year I bicycled through a dozen countries in order to visit and photograph hundreds of power places and sacred sites of the different European cultures. It was a wonderful journey, full of learning, and during it I began to understand the nature of the power places. For a number of reasons there are particular sites that have a special energy, a charged field, a sense of another realm. These places, first discovered in the long-ago megalithic era, were used and reused by a constant succession of other cultures, including the Celts, the Romans and the Christians.

Each of these different cultures often used the very same locations for their religious structures as had the cultures before them. One on top of another, different people built various types of structures to use the powers of those places. Those powers were extraordinary and they brought many benefits to the pilgrims who visited them. There were places of healing, places where oracular visions might occur, places of wisdom, peace and love. That is precisely why our ancestors honored these places.

And the various types of structures they erected at the power places were intended to gather, concentrate and radiate the powers of the places. The megalithic people built earthen chambered mounds and stone rings; the Romans great temples with elegant white columns; and the Christians their cathedrals soaring to the heavens.

A fascinating, though little known, fact about the megalithic structures is that nearly all of them were positioned to indicate particular celestial objects and their cycles of movement over many years. Gazing at the stars and the sun, the moon and the planets, our ancestors became the first real astronomers of deep antiquity. From their solar observations they determined those periods in the year known as the solstices and the equinoxes. These are the times when the sun is furthest north or south, and two times a year when it is at the midpoint of the sky. Archaic people, ignorant of the findings of contemporary science, interpreted celestial objects and their movements as being the actions of the gods and goddesses. Over uncounted millennia sun gods, moon goddesses and star deities appeared all throughout the world. To understand these sky beings far, far back in prehistoric times, Europe is a very good region to explore. At many sacred sites in that area you will find an unbroken tradition of use stretching back 5,000 years or more.

How would I suggest you approach and experience these places of power? For me, a parallel journey through the mythology, history and folklore of the holy sites is a wonderful way to begin. In this study you will come to notice a similarity of character, or persona type between the ancient mythic beings and those deities of later cultures. Those beings lived at the same places and did much the same things. Healing springs

▲ Croagh Patrick in Ireland is the perfect example of a pagan festival site that changed emphasis to a medieval pilgrimage location with the coming of Christianity to the Emerald Isle.

of the great mother became sacred springs of the pagan goddess Brigid, which then became, in Christian times, the holy springs of Saint Brigitte. You may still visit these sites today. Traveling to them, especially in Europe is quite easy; there are buses going nearly everywhere and you can also hitch a ride with safety. Accommodations, often in quaint cottages and small hostels, are also plentiful. The food is delicious and the people friendly. I suggest you go upon a pilgrimage, for you will be happy you have done so.

What can these places do for us today? Besides the particular energetic frequency found at each site, be it for healing or vision or empowerment, is there another effect, something even larger than our own personal experience? Yes, there is. In every country of the world there are a growing number of people participating in the evolution of consciousness and the betterment of the world. We are becoming united, across national borders, unhindered by languages, as a family of love. The more you travel, the more you will find people like you everywhere.

This phenomenon will bring joy to your heart while encouraging you to live life to its fullest. Therefore, to gain a measure of power and healing and wisdom from the ancient holy places, go upon a pilgrimage. Such a spiritual journey will make your passage through life all the more beautiful.

—Martin Gray
SacredSites.com & MagicPlanet.org

▲ Sometimes shopping at sacred sites can be just as enjoyable as the visit. These icons are representative of the priceless objects that can be found inside Russia's famous Sergiev Posad monastery.

INTRODUCTION TO THE EUROPEAN CONTINENT

When you go in peace, when you move in peace, exist in peace, the mind is still, the soul serene, and the heart is tranquil; and you move in harmony with the rhythm of the spheres, partake of the sense of oneness of all that is, and realize the connection between yourself and the divine.
—*Pythagoras*

Due to its wide appeal, the European continent offers something for everyone. Europe is especially ideal for travelers seeking adventurous destinations in close proximity. Begin a first-time European adventure in Ireland or Great Britain, where English is spoken. The British Isles are filled with ancient history and history in the making — more crop circles appear every summer in southern England than in any other place in the world. Plan a visit during July or August when the crop circle season is in full bloom.

Mainland Europe can sometimes seem like a world apart. Hundreds of individual cultures and languages remain crammed together in Europe, each taking on unique characteristics that have evolved throughout time. Travelers from large homogenous countries like Canada, Australia, and the United States are routinely amazed at how quickly everything can change in such a very short distance. From the earliest cave painters to modern-day artists, Europe remains a treasure-trove of diverse Western culture featuring a dazzling array of beautiful sacred places.

Neolithic Foundation

Although Europe was host to earlier Paleolithic cave artists and Mesolithic hunting tribes, the continent reached a pinnacle of prehistoric sophistication during the Neolithic Era. The engineering techniques of the late Stone Age still puzzle modern experts. The most common Neolithic monument is the dolmen, consisting of two portals with side and end stones, creating a single large chamber. The portals are usually pronounced and the chamber is roofed by a cap-stone, usually an enormous slab of rock. Dolmens are frequently found on hillsides and usually feature an easterly orientation to capture the rising sun. Sometimes dolmen structures are accentuated by large, single standing stones called menhirs. The menhir may stand alone as a sighting stone or part of a long row, or processional avenue, of erect standing stones.

Another ingenious invention of the late Stone Age is the henge. The Neolithic henge is a round ritual enclosure made of earthen mounds, wooded structures, or standing stones surrounded by an outside ditch. The most famous henge is Stonehenge, located in southern England. The modern science of archaeoastronomy has demonstrated that Neolithic henges served an astronomical purpose, and may well have been the source of our "sciences" to observe the heavens and predict the seasons. Our Neolithic ancestors made the profound realization that the world was also a vast clock. Rotations of time, like the circular henge, were viewed as cyclical. Winter thawed into spring, which warmed into summer. Then summer surrendered to cool autumn, until the first freeze of winter descended and the cycle renewed itself. Knowledge of the heavens kept time with the earth. The sun dependably marked off sequential time as it made its yearly march across the sky and back again. Capturing the predictability of the sun, moon phases, and star sightings within the henge was perhaps the greatest advancement of knowledge for prehistoric people.

The Neolithic Era flourished from 3300 BCE until 2000 BCE. The sphere of influence stretched from the tiny Maltese archipelago in the Mediterranean Sea, around the Atlantic coastlines of Spain, Portugal, France, Holland, Germany, and north into the British Isles and Scandinavia. Because the megalithic architecture is usually

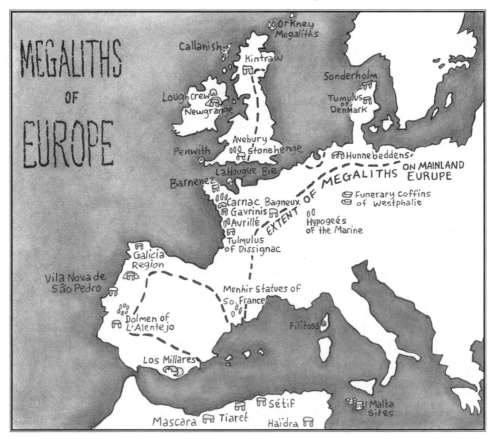

located near the ocean or a waterway, it can be surmised that the Neolithic people were skillful mariners. They were also prolific stone carvers. Lending credibility to the theory of cultural diffusion, via watercraft travel, distinctive spiral carvings repeat as a pattern throughout Neolithic Europe. The dolmen structure design is also universal. Unfortunately, most of the dolmens of Europe have lost their original covering of smaller stones — called cairns. What usually remains is the skeleton of the structure, the dolmen. The slowly-eroding forces of nature took far less of a toll on the Neolithic monuments than the early Christians did, who superstitiously viewed the monuments as work of the devil. What could be carted off or destroyed almost always was. The sheer size of the enormous stones used in Neolithic architecture became their only saving grace.

European Pilgrimage

The European continent has long been a crossroad for countless generations of wanderers and mystics. From a Paleolithic artist painting animals in European caves, to the rise of indigenous pagan rituals and eventually the monotheistic faith of Christianity, European paths became the interchange for Western cultures and religions. A select group of historians believe that Jesus Christ himself traveled from the Holy Land to Glastonbury, England with his merchant uncle, Saint Joseph of Arimathea. This would have been when the pagan Roman and Celtic religions ruled the land. After Christianity swept the continent a few centuries later, pilgrim routes converged on sacred cathedrals all across Europe.

The earliest form of non-warfare travel in Europe was pilgrimage. The Church encouraged its adherents to take a pilgrimage as penitence or as a spiritualized form of extradition. The goal of a pilgrimage was to view holy relics and thereby receive heavenly rewards. Medieval pilgrims believed that praying in front of a reliquary containing the body part of a saint would persuade that particular saint to intercede with God on their behalf. The medieval pilgrim also believed that by visiting a famous place of pilgrimage a faithful individual could be cured of an ailment, come into closer contact with the divine, or even be exonerated for a crime committed in the past. The most important place of Christian pilgrimage was Jerusalem, located in present-day Israel. As is the case today, travel to that part of the world was unpredictable and at most times unsafe. It was better to stay in Europe, or one's own home country, and receive equal rewards. The most famous European pilgrimage was along the Compostela Route bisecting France and northern Spain. Another popular road was to Rome where the Pope presided. But many other lesser known pilgrimage destinations are scattered across Europe.

The golden age of medieval pilgrimage was not to last. The Reformation period of the 16th century was a time of intense fearfulness for both Protestants and Catholics. There were violent repudiations of the past, bitter condemnations, the terror of heresy due to doctrinal deviation, an obsession with hell, and a hyperactive awareness of personal sin. It was a period of extreme anxiety and anguish. It pitted countryman against countryman. Lines were drawn all across the European continent. Many great works of art were destroyed. Priceless church frescoes were whitewashed over to protest the "idolatry" of saint worship. Yet after the terrible years of the Reformation a new kind of society was beginning to emerge, one based on reason, technology, and science. Europeans blossomed beyond their own continent and began to colonize and influence the rest of the world.

With the advent of international sea travel a new type of pilgrimage emerged. Riding along with the merchant ships to faraway ports were the priests and ministers, who sought to convert "heathen" nonbelievers. The Puritans of Britain and Holland crossed the Atlantic to settle in New England. Jesuit missionaries traveled even farther: the Spanish Francis Xavier (1506-1552) converted thousands in India and Japan, Matteo Ricci (1552-1610) evangelized China, and Robert de Nobili (1577-1656) took the Gospel deep into the jungles of India. The Jesuits also conducted widespread missionary work in Africa, other parts of Asia, and North and South America. Since the Jesuits were (and are still today) headed by a "superior general" in Rome, they encouraged their newly converted brethren to make a pilgrimage there, to the holy city of the Pope. Suddenly, European pilgrimage redefined itself and has since included parishioners from the nearly 100 nations where the Jesuits established their schools and monasteries.

CHRISTIAN   PAGAN   OTHER

CHRISTIAN	PAGAN	OTHER
Monastery	Viking	Muslim
Cathedral	Dolmen	Sacred Mountain
Chapel	Goddess Site	Pilgrimage Routes
Marian Site	Greek	
Grail Site	Roman	Jewish
Early Christian	Celtic / Druid	Petroglyph
Byzantine	Burial Mounds	Hot Spring / Holy Well
Eastern Orthodox	Standing Stones	Sacred Cave or Grotto

EUROPE ICON SET

Travel Evolution

Whether conscious or not, the human spirit tends to follow the same paths long venerated by our ancestors. Travel is food for the soul, especially when those trips help us grow. Journeys to sacred places open our minds to the world around us, our collective history, the cosmos above, and to each other. The openness to regenerate oneself at a sacred site can be the first step. When we arrive at a spiritual destination, we find ourselves closer to our own individual reality, not only in time, but in space. Something magical happens that triggers an unconscious memory. To learn about sacred places is to learn about ourselves.

> Sacred places help us to understand our own existence and the universe around us.

Ancient wisdom combined with recent scientific discoveries help transform the way we attune ourselves at sacred places. By understanding our relationship with the cosmos we can comprehend the eternal rhythms of nature and the very order of existence. The old maxim "as above, so below" might also mean "once ancient, now modern." For example, consider how modern crop circles have profound similarities with ancient stone circles. Both emit high frequencies of ultrasound that include healing properties to all living things. Hundreds of people have reported spontaneous healings at newly created crop circles. Such is the case at ancient stone circles, standing stones, and earthen rings. The universe appears vastly complicated, yet also very simple. Scientists tell us there are at least 13 dimensions surrounding us, but in our limited capacity we can only perceive three. Just because something is invisible to the naked eye doesn't mean the space is void.

Ley Lines

The concept of ley paths appear in this book for several reasons. Many Europeans, especially those with progressive beliefs, can visualize the earth as being surrounded by energy lines connecting it to the universe. Indeed, the concept of planetary energy flows was first articulated by Europeans: the "gaia hypothesis" as developed by the ancient Greeks, ley lines as described by Englishman Sir Alfred Watkins, and the noosphere or "mind layer" as advanced by Frenchman Teilhard de Chardín. A similar concept developed by the modern residents of Damanhur, Italy describe "Synchronic Lines," or energy rivers, that can modify events and carry ideas, thoughts, moods, and intentions, thereby influencing all living creatures.

Finally, it appears that almost all sacred sites worldwide are linked together by the planetary grid of energy lines. The precise placement of sacred sites is no accident. Whether very old like Stonehenge or the Great Pyramids, or contemporary like Damanhur or the crop circle phenomenon, the very location of these sacred sites is now considered as energy acupuncture points on the face of the earth. In Europe, it is apparent that successive shrines, temples, churches, cathedrals, and monuments were built on intersecting ley lines. Morphogenic resonance predicts that where certain practices are routinely continued, they become imbued with a force field and a certain "spirit" then resides at the location. Hence, the earliest prehistoric shrines were adopted by European pagans, which in turn were replaced by the churches and cathedrals of Christianity.

Geomancy is the art of divining earth energy and detecting ley lines. Modern geomancers describe two kinds of electromagnetic energy lines that the earth uses as part of its nervous system. The first is a straight line, or "yang" line, which intersects the planet much like the latitude and longitude lines on a globe. The second type is curvilinear, or a "yin" line, which resemble the twists and turns of the natural environment. Geomancers have discovered that most of the sacred sites in Europe are built upon the intersection of yang lines. Where three or more yang lines cross, one can almost always find a sacred well, place of pilgrimage, cathedral, temple, or Neolithic stone circle. It is believed by geomancers that where yin lines cross, there is an accumulation of negative energy. People staying for an extended period of time over intersecting yin lines can feel nauseous or worn down. However, there is really no such thing as good or bad energy lines. They are all part of the same system of the earth's regenerating living power.

In the 1920s, the aforementioned Alfred Watkins coined the term "ley lines" in his book entitled *The Old Straight Track*. Watkins discovered a huge grid of flowing energy lines connecting ancient sites, pathways, and geographic markers (mounds, holy wells, ponds, depressions in hills, etc.) all over southern England, primarily in Herefordshire. Some of these ley lines, Watkins noted, dated from the Neolithic period and they denoted the location of Britain's many churches, shrines, villages, and town squares. Although called lines, Watkins and other geomancers began to perceive these lines as three dimensional, similar to tubes. Sometimes the lines would interact and combine with stronger vortex energy.

The World We Live In

We are not only the custodians of the priceless monuments of antiquity, but we are also guardians of the planet. Because humans are living longer than ever before, the world population grows by 80 million people per year. In the early 21st century, people over 60 years old now make up a whopping one-third of the population, as opposed to a mere 10 percent in 1995. France alone has over 8,000 centennials (those over 100 years old), expected to swell over 150,000 by the middle of the 21st century.

The burgeoning human population is taking its toll on the animal kingdom. Today, about one-quarter of the planet's mammal species and one-eighth of all known bird species face extinction. Something close to 90% of all commercial fish stocks are gone, verging on total collapse in the coming decades. The atmosphere is suffering too. The current content of carbon dioxide in the atmosphere is higher than it has been in 160,000 years. This data is from the strata of melting ice chunks breaking off from the polar ice caps at an alarming pace due to global warming. Also troubling is the warming of the planet's oceans, creating atmospheric instability and fierce weather patterns. Some call the new era we are entering the "Age of Storms."

Despite planetary growing pains, human civilization in the 21st century is defined by diversity and duality. One-fifth of the world's population is Chinese, another fifth Muslim. A hundred million are homeless children living in extreme poverty. There are over 10,000 spoken languages. Yet, around 95 percent of the global population believes in some form of God. In essence, many believe that all religions of the world are valid, as each one shares a unique insight into the divine. This communing of humans with the "oneness" of the universe has led to the building of countless places of worship around the world. Some of the European sacred places described in this book are especially relevant only to Catholics. Some are "universal" sites recognized as holy by all religious persuasions. About half are ancient pagan sites worshipped in the time before Christ. Some are museums, World Heritage Sites, national parks, or tourist destinations on private land. Some are fenced off and can only be viewed from a distance. Nevertheless, as we collectively ascend from polarity consciousness into unity consciousness, the relevance of these spiritual sites become even more profound.

GREAT BRITAIN

When Britain first, at heaven's command,
Arose from out the azure main,
This was the charter of the land,
And guardian angels sung this strain:
'Rule, Britannia, rule the waves;
Britons never will be slaves.'
—*James Thompson*

THE FIRST PEOPLE TO CROSS THE ENGLISH CHANNEL and settle in Briton were small bands of hunters from Europe. This initial migration took place around 4000 BCE; however, little remains of these earliest arrivals. Another wave of immigrants came around 3000 BCE, bringing with them basic stone tools and a mysterious new religion. This religion focused on the sacred henge — a circular megalithic structure constructed of either wood or stone. There are seven known timber temples and about 3,000 stone circles throughout Britain from this era, most located in southwestern England. These Stone Age monuments, including the awesome Stonehenge, served as religious meeting centers, as well as astronomical observatories.

The next great influx of culture began with the Celts, who introduced the skill of using bronze and iron. Their unique artistry and designs never went away, becoming a source of inspiration to the Romans and early Christians. In addition, the Celts brought diverse languages, which can still be heard today in Wales (Brythonic), and Ireland and Scotland (Gaelic).

In 43 CE, the Romans crossed the English Channel to rule Britannia for 370 years. The Roman legacy still exists through some of their old roads and structures. Located just south of the Scottish border the 71-mile (115-km) long Hadrian's Wall extends across the country. The wall began construction in 122 CE, under Emperor Hadrian, in order to protect Roman territory in Britain from the Picts — a fierce pagan tribe that has long inspired Scottish freedom fighters.

Afterwards, Christianity arrived in the third century CE with a new Germanic immigration, filling the vacuum left by the Romans. These Germanic tribes called themselves the English.

After a period of relative calm, the next invaders came between the 7th to 10th centuries. The brutal Vikings from Scandinavia were a purely pagan people who briefly ruled various parts of the country. To ensure richness in the next life, several Viking kings were buried inside their ships on eastern British beaches. The relics excavated there are some of the finest that survive today.

Taking advantage of a fractured nation, the Normans of France crossed the channel and conquered England in 1066. The Normans were descendants of Normandy Vikings who had certain allies in the country. Incidentally, they were the last invading foreigners to ever successfully conquer Britain. The Normans established the feudal system which divided Britain into small territories. Imposing castles were constructed all over the country for individual protection of autonomous kingdoms. Eventually the Normans, like all the invaders before them, assimilated as Christians and helped define British society.

During the Middle Ages, numerous power struggles took place between English kings, overseas nations, and small dynasties. Henry VII became the first Tudor king. Great cathedrals were constructed, and the Bible was translated into English. The 16th century became a golden age; Shakespeare wrote his plays, Francis Bacon laid the foundations for modern science, and the European powers explored the planet. The British were especially good at colonization and they soon became extremely rich through their global trading network. The foundation of an English or British Empire began in 1649 when Oliver Cromwell assumed dictatorial powers and modernized the army and navy.

The Empire was at its height in 1770 when France ceded all of their colonies in Canada and all but two trading stations in India. Also at this time Captain Cook sailed the world and claimed Australia and several other new colonies for the Crown. A decade later the Industrial Revolution began in Britain. Soon, Midland country towns became industrial cities. When Queen Victoria took the throne in 1837, Britain was the greatest power in the world. Factories were set up around the globe, all linked by its dominating fleet of ships. This virtual monopoly on world trade made the United Kingdom enormously wealthy, and literally thousands of monuments, palaces, and stately buildings were constructed worldwide as a testament to this period.

ENGLAND

Many argue that there is no greater concentration of sacred sites in one place than southwestern England. Here can be found ancient megaliths, henges, barrows, stone circles, mounds, holy wells, dolmens, chalk geoglyphs, and many famous cathedrals. Although Stonehenge captures the world's attention, the larger complex at Avebury is equally fascinating. Unfortunately, many stones at Avebury (and many other prehistoric sites in Europe) were destroyed by Christian fundamentalists, who misinterpreted the Druidic religion with devil worship. Recent discoveries at West Kennet Long Barrow associate this monument with worship of the Great Goddess. Although hundreds of Neolithic sites exist in England, some of the best known and most accessible are the Boscawen-un, Rollright Stones, Hurlers, and Cheesewring stone circles, Lanyon Quoit and Trethevy Quoit dolmens, and the holy Madron Well. In northern England notable sites include Castlerigg Circle in Cumbria, and Long Meg and Her Daughters.

Avebury

The assorted monuments around the small village of Avebury are among the most important Neolithic ruins in England. They include Europe's tallest artificial hill, the skeleton of a monumental stone circle much like Stonehenge, several underground passage chambers, and the remnants of two 1.5-mile (2.4-km) long stone avenues. One menhir-lined avenue reaches out southeast and terminates in another stone circle called the Sanctuary. Viewed from above, the Sanctuary circle on Overton Hill and the avenue leading to it resemble a serpent. The Avebury monuments were not just a concentration of elaborate ruins, but also a prehistoric staging ground for seasonal rituals and courting dramas. An underground stream, two rivers, and a bubbling spring were also part of the ritual-religious structure. Depending on the season and festival at hand, each ritual moved from location to location during the course of a year.

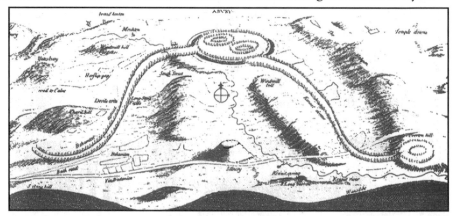

▲ An 18th century map depicts stone avenues connecting Avebury henge to other important ritual sites in the countryside.

The Neolithic monument surrounding Avebury village is the largest and greatest stone circle in the world.

The scale of the Avebury henge is breathtaking. Covering 28 acres (11.3 hectares), the henge is defined by a boundary ditch 50 feet (15 m) deep, which runs between two high banks. The original henge once contained 100 massive standing stones, of which only 27 remain. Much later, the village of Avebury expanded inside the henge, conflicting with its unique structure and design. However, after many centuries, this foundation has continued to endure along with other religious sites in the area. This includes another major Neolithic monument — Stonehenge — which lies 17 miles (26 km) due south on the Salisbury Plain.

Perhaps the most extraordinary monument near Avebury is Silbury Hill — the largest artificial mound in England. Most archaeologists agree its shape was chosen because it resembles a pregnant goddess. Her mound is the womb, 130 feet (40 m) high and measuring more than 550 feet (165 m) in diameter. The rest of her body is defined by a water-filled moat suggesting she is squatting, ready to give birth and complete the life cycle. From her head to her thigh, the Mother measures almost 1,400 feet (420 m). On the flat top of the mound, fertility rituals were likely performed to ensure the longevity of the tribe. Built by hand thousands of years ago, Silbury Hill was put together in sections of chalk-mud, much like a pyramid. Centuries after its construction, a Viking bride was laid to rest just

below the summit. In 1723, these remains were discovered and led archaeologists to believe Silbury Hill was intended as a burial mound. This view has changed in modern times.

Two powerful ley lines intersect underneath the hill, producing a node of very strong energy. Some of the first contemporary crop circles were discovered near Silbury Hill, and continue to manifest nearby on a regular basis.

▲ Avebury village is within the famous henge.

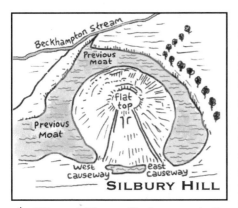

SILBURY HILL

▲ Silbury Hill was likely a symbolic effigy of the Great Goddess Mother. At this site several fertility rituals were performed over the course of a year.

The greater Avebury region includes many unique gems from the Neolithic ritual staging area. The West Kennet Long Barrow is England's largest prehistoric passage chamber, extending 340 feet (104 m) in length. The Devil's Chair is a huge stone that was one of the few carved megaliths to survive the near-destruction of Avebury by the Puritans in the 17th and 18th centuries. Windmill Hill is a causeway camp built in 3350 BCE before Avebury was constructed. The main sites of Avebury proper, including the Processional Avenue, the Sanctuary, Avebury Henge, Silbury Hill and several long barrows are all within a few miles of each other. The surrounding countryside makes for splendid hiking and discovery. Many mysteries remain, but certainly Avebury was a known center of intense religious activity in prehistoric times.

Getting to Avebury

The mighty Neolithic ruins of Avebury are located on the beautiful rolling downs of southwestern England, near Bristol. Avebury is on the A31, 9 miles (15 km) south of Swindon and the M4. From Salisbury the #5 bus to Swindon passes through Avebury several times daily. Avebury was once linked by a sacred track to Glastonbury, which is now a narrow country highway.

Canterbury

The intellectual and emotional lives of the English changed in the 11th and 12th centuries. Until then almost everything in their lives were inspired and directed by the Church in Rome. By offering pilgrims another destination Canterbury became the catalyst for that change, and Rome would have a heavy hand in its early development. The traveling churchman Anselm came from Aosta, Italy, via Normandy, to become Archbishop of Canterbury. Next was Lanfranc, who made an almost identical journey, but started from Pavia. It is almost inconceivable today to imagine two consecutive archbishops of Canterbury being Italian. Today the cathedral is a potent symbol of England's independence from Rome.

The Canterbury Cathedral we see today is one of the oldest and most famous Christian structures in Great Britain. Part of the building dates back to Roman times, but most of it was ruined during the Saxon reign. Lanfranc, the first Norman archbishop, oversaw most of the construction in the 11th century.

After the Dissolution of the Monasteries in 1539 it became the Cathedral of the Anglican Archbishop of Canterbury. Since then it has housed the bishop of highest rank (Primate) in England, who is leader of the Church of England. Not only is the cathedral the mother church of the Diocese of Canterbury (east Kent), it is also the focus for all Anglican churches worldwide. The Archbishop of Canterbury, religious head of the Church of England, has no formal authority outside that country; however, he is the recognized symbolic head for the worldwide communion. Among the other primates, he is *primus inter pares*, or "first among equals." If the Archbishop of Canterbury is compared with other religious leaders, such as the Pope, it is only because the media has elevated him as a prominent figurehead.

Aspects of the Canterbury Cathedral span the lifetime of Christianity in England.

Critical to the history of Canterbury was the murder of Thomas Becket. He was killed inside the Cathedral by four knights of King Henry II in December, 1170 — the second of four murdered archbishops. The crime brought its own revenge. Becket was revered by the faithful throughout Europe as a martyr and canonized by Alexander in 1173. The next year, in the midst of the Revolt of 1173-1174, Henry II humbled himself to do public penance at the tomb of his enemy. It remained one of the most popular places of pilgrimage in England until it was destroyed in the 16th century Dissolution of the Monasteries by King Henry VIII. The income from pilgrims visiting the Becket shrine, which was regarded as a place of healing, largely paid for the subsequent reconstruction of the Cathedral and its associated buildings.

Canterbury was the central focus of one of the greatest works of medieval literature — Geoffrey Chaucer's *Canterbury Tales*. The collection of stories features several tales, each told by a different character as they pilgrimage to Canterbury. In fact, the word "canter" came into the English language from the pace of the horses headed there, called the "Canterbury gallop." Characters include a pardoner, who sells papal indulgences, and a Franklin, who relates an account involving standing stones. The tales highlight the challenges of 14th century pilgrims as they make their way to Canterbury to visit the shrine of Saint Thomas à Becket. The beloved shrine was removed by King Henry VIII when he broke with Rome and subsequently established the independent Church of England.

▲ Becket's shrine containing the "holy blissful martyr" was one of the busiest pilgrimage destinations in medieval Europe.

Getting to Canterbury

Canterbury is an exit along the main A2 Highway from London to Dover. Canterbury is about 45 miles (72 km) from the junction with the M25 London orbital motorway, and 61 miles (98 km) from central London. The other main road through Canterbury is the A28 from Ashford to Ramsgate and Margate. A bus service leaves hourly to and from Victoria Coach Station. The bus trip from London typically takes about two hours. The formidable cathedral is easy to locate on the east end of Canterbury.

crop circles

Despite decades of research and inquiry, the origin and purpose of genuine crop circles remains completely unknown. Although scientists have tried to come up with logical explanations for the phenomena — including random atmospheric whirlwinds or teams of hoaxers, who somehow defy gravity and leave behind no footprints — the fact is crop circles remain a modern day unsolved mystery. Unfortunately, the groups who should be giving us answers, namely government-appointed scientists from the U.S. and U.K., spend more resources debunking crop circles than investigating them with unbiased intent. Having the media ignore the phenomenon or report every crop circle as a hoax is not a tenable explanation. Hopefully the leaders of world governments and major media outlets will soon realize that humanity does not need to be protected from the existence of mysterious phenomena.

The worldwide phenomenon known as crop circles first came to the world's attention sometime in the mid-1980s. Although hoaxers claimed to have started the phenomenon in 1978, the circles have been around much longer. Their origins are first recorded in the 17th century, have appeared in dozens of countries, but it is in southern England that they occur at their most spectacular and their most frequent. Beginning in the spring of 1990, the patterns of English crop circles changed dramatically. From simple geometric shapes they have evolved into elaborate and complex designs. The patterns frequently feature multiple circles with key-shaped, or otherwise abstract-shaped objects, protruding from a center point. Some of the newer crop circles measure 420 feet (126 m) across, much larger than a football field.

England is not the only country to receive this natural phenomenon, nor is it only a contemporary occurrence. Over 10,000 formations have been cataloged worldwide in nearly 50 countries. The large geometric designs appear mostly in mature fields of planted crops — over 100 have been reported in Japanese rice fields alone. An English journal entry from 1678 reports the first known crop circle. Many U.K. farmers recall simple circles appearing on their farmland for generations. Dozens of English eyewitnesses describe crop circles forming in a matter of seconds as far back as 1890. Other word-of-mouth testimonies spanning several centuries acknowledge similar phenomena occurring on mainland Europe.

> Some believe genuine crop circles materialize in order to direct information into the earth's subtle energy grid. The patterns thus enable people who visit them to become inspired and achieve their highest potential.

Hoaxed crop circles are easy to spot because the stalks get trampled and broken. Genuine crop circles appear flattened and intricately interwoven in a near instant, yet none of the stalks are bruised or broken. The anomalous features of genuine crop circles continue to defy human explanation or replication. Some of the best clues are within the plants themselves: their stems are lightly burned around the base, the bend is about an inch above the soil, and their cellular structure is altered. What's more, the electrical discharge that creates genuine crop circles escapes through the plant via small "explosion cavities" in the stem joints, leaving behind yet more tantalizing clues. Groundwater evaporates immediately following a crop circle formation, and the local electromagnetic field of the surrounding area is discernibly altered. Geomancers and dowsers detect long-lasting energy patterns, not to mention the measured effects on the human biological field.

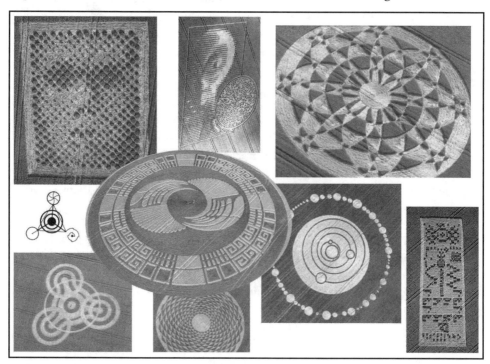

▲ Although a worldwide phenomenon, southern Britain receives by far the most amount of crop circle formations every year.

Eyewitness accounts describe the formations materializing within seconds, usually accompanied by strange lights, crackling sounds, and debilitating or enhancing energy fields. Farmers usually report hearing a low humming noise on the nights they materialize. Their appearance is usually accompanied by military helicopters, which apparently can track their electromagnetic movements on radar. Videotaped footage shot in broad daylight shows small, metallic-like balls of bright white light quickly maneuvering in and around the crop fields just before a pattern emerges. The weightless objects clearly move with purpose and intelligence.

A leading researcher, U.S. biophysicist Dr. W. Ievengood, measured both magnetic and microwave energy effects involved in the circle-making process. Shortly after a formation occurs, compasses placed in the center of a circle will spin randomly. Interestingly, the whole pattern process seems to interact with the human mind. Some of the symbols reflect ancient patterns derived from the Celtic religion, Hopi culture, hieroglyphics, Eskimo petroglyphs, and Tibetan thankas. Patterns featuring modern discoveries depict recent DNA discoveries, musical ratio scales, elaborate faces that appear extraterrestrial, and the ever-popular fractals of chaos theory, which display a mathematical precision that appears to be beyond the realms of human capacity.

New research suggests that sound may be one of the energy sources capable of creating genuine crop circles. It may seem farfetched to think sound waves could render a plant flexible enough to bend, intertwine, and then lie down by applying firm and gentile pressure. Combine this process with the complexity of enormous patterns precisely arranged by sound, or more exactly ultrasound, and one part of the puzzle begins to emerge. Scientists know ultrasound applied at very high frequencies can be directed at physical elements and make their molecules move. This requires frequencies in the high MHz range, such as those detected for decades inside crop circles. If sound is one of the formative principles behind these formations, it is not surprising that crop circles leave such a profound impression on those who are receptive to their tune. Tens of thousands of people who have come into contact with crop circles have taken away with them a more positive view of the world and the cosmos above.

Getting to the crop circles of England

Genuine crop circles often manifest within short distances from known sacred sites in England, especially Neolithic sites. Most crop circles appear in the southwestern Wiltshire and Hampshire regions, with Stonehenge as the apparent center of activity. From this book, follow directions to Stonehenge and the Salisbury Plain, or Avebury. The Silent Circle information center and cafe at Cherhill Wiltshire, close to megalithic Avebury, is a good place to start. Crop circle season starts in late spring and ends in the autumn when the fields are harvested by farmers.

geoglyphs

From the earliest recorded time humans have felt an intrinsic need to artistically create sacred images. Animals, either mythical or real, were common themes in prehistory. Sometimes the subject matter was a larger-than-life chieftain or a supernatural being with tremendous powers. Other times abstract or straight lines were represented. Subjects or symbols that seemed larger than life were created with a magical totem quality in mind. If the ground could be scraped away to reveal a different mineral content or rock color it could serve as a marking board. Ritual locations for the living would not be far away.

A "geoglyph" is an artistic rendering, on a massive scale, carved onto the landscape of the earth's surface. Most prolific in Europe are the white chalk geoglyphs of southern England. The majority of experts believe these large-scale carvings had associated religious meanings. By marking the landscape, these images could evoke power and dreams for a clan of people. It is likely they denoted the location of special ritual places used by the ancient dwellers. Some researchers believe they were simply commissioned decorations for the edification of a wealthy noble. Others attribute them to mythical beasts that supposedly roamed the English countryside. Whatever they were created for, and whoever carved them, their purpose remains a mystery. Also a mystery is why crop circles regularly appear in farmer fields near geoglyphs.

> The geoglyphs of southern England mostly represent white horses, but some are clearly male figures. Others may be mythical beasts.

Scattered throughout southern England are at least 56 known hill figures cut into the abundant chalk downlands. The most famous of these is the White Horse of Uffington on the Berkshire downs, Oxfordshire. The White Horse of Uffington is 365 feet (111 m) wide at its longest point. It is carved into the chalky side of a hill near the ruins of the Uffington Castle. The abstract silhouette of a horse in motion is similar in design to those found on Celtic coins. Most experts believe the Uffington geoglyph is the work of Iron Age Celts, carved around the year 100 BCE. Ask a local and they might say it represents a dragon, drawn in homage to Saint

▲ The Bratton Horse is just below the defensive ramparts of an ancient Celtic hilltop fort.

George, who supposedly killed one on a neighboring hill many centuries ago. Another theory is the lord of the Uffington Castle commissioned the design based on the Celtic goddess Epona, who is usually depicted with horse features. In the neighboring Wiltshire region are a dozen other white horse carvings etched onto the hillsides. All are carefully preserved, but some are located on private land and may be inaccessible.

The origins of the Long Man of Wilmington, or the Wilmington Giant, remain unknown. The figure may be Roman, Bronze Age, or even depict King Harold from the 11th century. One theory speculates that the Giant was cut for amusement by the monks from the priory in Wilmington village. This theory is supported by the Cerne Abbas Giant, which also had a religious house at its base. Other than amusement, it has been suggested that the monks constructed the Wilmington Giant either because they were heretical, part of a secret occult society, or they were inscribing the image of a pilgrim. Going further back in time, another theory suggests the Giant represents the Anglo-Saxon hero Beowulf, fighting Grendel with a spear in each hand. Regardless of its true origins, the Long Man of Wilmington is a sight to behold, appearing 226-feet (68-m) high on Windover Hill's 28° slope. The Giant is one of the largest such representations of a man anywhere in the world, being second only to the Giant Of Attacama in Chile, which stands 393 feet (118 m) high.

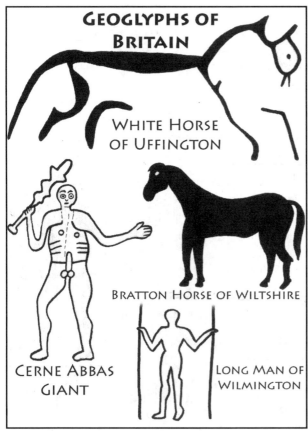

GEOGLYPHS OF BRITAIN

WHITE HORSE OF UFFINGTON

BRATTON HORSE OF WILTSHIRE

CERNE ABBAS GIANT

LONG MAN OF WILMINGTON

▲ Horses and giant men constitute the most famous geoglyphs of southern England.

Cerne Abbas is another massive geoglyph with unknown origins. The earliest record of the giant is mentioned in a text from 1694 and there is a very tenuous reference to the giant in a 13th century manuscript, which supports its antiquity. For centuries, the giant hosted maypole celebrations inside an earthwork located adjacent to the geoglyph. It is believed that the Cerne Abbas giant represents a fertility symbol because of the figure's erect penis. There is a theory that Cerne Abbas is a pagan god, cut by the Saxons, which would indicate a date earlier than the 13th century. This pagan god may be a representation of Hercules, which could indicate a date as early as the 1st century BCE. Another theory dates its carving in the 2nd century CE during the Roman revival of Hercules. This dating does not correspond with the other giants near Plymouth, Cambridge which were cut during the 14th-16th centuries CE. The Cerne Abbas geoglyph is 180 feet (54 m) high and of similar width to other human figures. The giant is cut in outline with more detail than the Long Man of Wilmington. The Cerne Abbas giant wields a 120 feet (36 m) long club over his head.

Getting to the geoglyphs of England

The Uffington White Horse can be found 1.5 miles due south of Uffington village on the Berkshire downs (although now in Oxfordshire). It is situated facing NW near the top of a very impressive steep escarpment below the Ridgeway Long Distance Footpath. The Wilmington Giant is one of two hill figures in Sussex, the other being a white horse near Litlington. The Wilmington Giant is currently owned by the Sussex Archaeological Society. The Cerne Abbas Giant is cut on a large hill northeast of the village called Cerne Abbas. The figure is in good condition because it is preserved by the National Trust. The figure is fenced in and the grass surrounding it is cut regularly.

Glastonbury

The tiny hamlet of Glastonbury was not only an important Neolithic site, but also the reputed home of King Arthur's Camelot. Although little remains physically of either, prehistoric religion and Arthurian legend are just another aspect of Glastonbury, which makes this small town in Somerset so spiritually magnificent. In fact, many proponents of the New Age regard the entire area as an acupuncture point of the Earth body — the crown chakra — and one of the most powerful energy centers on the planet.

The charming atmosphere of Glastonbury and the surrounding countryside has encouraged much folklore and legend. King Arthur, for example, was probably a prominent chief who helped to defend this part of England against the pagan Saxons. It is believed the bones of King Arthur and his Queen Guinevere are buried in the Glastonbury Abbey. This is speculation because the stories of Camelot and the Round Table came many years after their deaths. Glastonbury lore also relates that among the many esteemed visitors to this holy place was Jesus Christ. Jesus was a prolific traveler who may have gone along with his uncle, Saint Joseph of Arimathea, on at least one trading mission to Glastonbury.

> Glastonbury has been a recognized religious
> center since pre-Christian times.

Christian pilgrims have made their way to Glastonbury from the earliest times. It is said that the oldest Christian shrine in England was erected in Glastonbury. Remains of an old wattle (twigs and poles) church date back to 633 CE. Successive churches were built on the exact site of the wattle church, later to be surrounded by a medieval abbey which is now in ruins. On the Abbey grounds is the Glastonbury Thorn, which allegedly sprang from Saint Joseph's staff and blooms every Christmas. Throughout history Christians have yearned to make a pilgrimage to the Holy Land where Christ was born and died. Yet, most had to be satisfied with a pilgrimage to one of the Stations of the Cross. The Glastonbury Abbey is one of the 14 Stations. Each Station represents part of Christ's journey to his execution on Calvary Hill. His name "Jesus Christ" is engraved outside the Abbey, marking the pilgrim's final destination point.

▲ The Pilgrim's Path extends along the spine of the Glastonbury Tor.

Rising above the flat plains of Somerset Levels is the Glastonbury Tor, an unmistakable landmark hill with a ruined church tower at its peak. Excavations atop Glastonbury Tor in the 1960s revealed evidence of earlier timber buildings, metal-working hearths, animal bones, and pieces of pottery with traces of Mediterranean wine stains. The 500-foot (150-m) Tor could have served as a fortress, perhaps the location where Queen Guinevere was held captive by Melwas before King Arthur came to rescue her. The remains of the tower seen today were part of a medieval church dedicated to Saint Michael the Archangel. Monks built Saint Michael's church atop of an existing church, which was later left in ruins by an earthquake. A medieval fair was held at the foot of Glastonbury Tor every year from 1127 until 1825 in honor of Saint Michael. The Chalice Well between the Tor and the Abbey

▲ The "Abbot's Kitchen" is a still intact octagonal museum found within the abbey grounds of Glastonbury.

was said to contain the Holy Grail, the elusive chalice used by Christ during the Last Supper. It was sought in vain by the Knights of the Round Table.

Although Glastonbury was an ancient pagan and Christian center rich with folklore and history, it has taken on a new role as the heart chakra of the planet by New Agers. Accordingly, the cosmic vibration the New Age community celebrates is marked by a massive Zodiac surrounding the Glastonbury area. Similar to the Nazca Lines in Peru, the 10-mile (16-km) wide earthworks are only visible from the air. Hedges, woods, ditches, and ancient footpaths were laid out in the Age of Taurus, to form a ring of the twelve Zodiac signs, and may have been used as a Temple to the Stars. The Zodiac is also representative of King Arthur's Round Table. The Arthurian legends and the Zodiac signify our quest for "the eternal self," also identified as King Arthur's Holy Grail. Grasping its significance requires much patience and imagination due to the Zodiac being largely based on associations and legends rather than known historical facts.

Getting to Glastonbury

The small town in Somerset is most easily reached by car. Glastonbury is on Route 4 from London, and can be accessed from the M5 out of Exeter. The ancient Roman town of Bath is about 30 miles (50 km) from Glastonbury. Tour groups frequently visit Glastonbury from London. Because several transfers are needed, local buses and trains can be difficult to navigate.

Lindisfarne

In the 7th century, the first priests of a new faith were making their way to the north of England. The pagans they wished to convert were sometimes reluctant recipients to the word of Christ. A Benedictine priest named Aidan started to build an abbey, on the isolated "Holy Island" of the pagans. He called his new settlement Lindisfarne. He was succeeded by Cuthbert, who became both the bishop and abbot. After his death Saint Cuthbert was renowned as the apostle of the north, the main figure who is credited for bringing the Christian faith to northern England. His popularity is based on his efforts of caring for the sick during the plague, working miraculous cures, and caring for the needy.

> Little remains of the Lindisfarne monastic settlement on Holy Island. It became an easy target for marauding Vikings two centuries after it was founded.

The isolation of the Holy Island would prove to become its downfall. Located directly across the North Sea from Denmark, it was among the first locations in England to be attacked by the ruthless Nordic raiders. In 793 the Anglo-Saxon Chronicle recorded the event: "In this year dire portents appeared over Northumbria and sorely frightened the people. They consisted of immense whirlwinds and flashes of lightning, and fiery dragons were seen flying in the air. A great famine immediately followed those signs, and a little after that in the same year, on 8 June, the ravages of heathen men miserably destroyed God's church on Lindisfarne, with plunder and slaughter." Abbeys were an easier target than villages, because the monks professed nonviolence and refused to protect themselves. After the Vikings pillaged and burned the monastery, Lindisfarne elders decided to remove the treasury for protection.

In the 9th century, the exhumed body of Saint Cuthbert, which was already attracting pilgrims, was taken to Durham Cathedral near Lindisfarne. His shrine became a popular medieval pilgrimage destination, even becoming more renowned when Henry VIII's agents came to remove the treasure. The body of Cuthbert was found uncorrupted, causing the shrine and treasure to be saved.

The Lindisfarne priory was built in 1093, but it too was eventually destroyed. Only partial walls remain. Despite the repeated Viking attacks, the monastic settlement continued to function until the Dissolution of the Monasteries. The tombs of Saint Aidan and Saint Cuthbert remain empty. Only the 13th century parish church remains intact. Nevertheless, medieval pilgrims continued to come

▲ The Holy Island as seen from the mainland.

to Holy Island via the Pilgrim Route, designated with wooden poles which disappear under the tide. Today the island serves as a nature reserve and continues to attract 50,000 visitors annually.

Getting to Lindisfarne

▲ The Lindisfarne ruins are evocative of its turbulent history

The remains of Lindisfarne priory are located on Holy Island along Britain's northeastern Northumbrian coast. Holy Island lies 5 miles (8 km) east of the A1 road at Beal, located 6 miles (11 km) south of Berwik-on-Tweed, which has the nearest railway station. The island is 3 miles long (5 km) with a village, a ruined priory, and a castle on a rock. The site can only be visited at low tide when there is enough sand to travel across the channel. The North Sea can be unpredictable so caution should be made before attempting a crossing. The island is privately owned but access is not restricted.

Liverpool

The four members of the Beatles — John Lennon, Paul McCartney, George Harrison, and Ringo Starr — grew up in the northern working class city of Liverpool. The Beatles were born during the horrific World War II Nazi air bombings of Britain. Having experienced a world war and reconstruction as children, then living through the Vietnam era as young men, the Beatles, especially John Lennon, came to embrace and embody pacifism. Theirs was the vision that powered such songs as *All You Need Is Love*, *Let It Be*, and *Come Together*. In little more than a six-year studio recording career the Beatles elevated pop music from teenage sock hops to a sophisticated art form. Liverpool will always be remembered for shaping the lives of the "Fab Four," who became known the world over as socially conscious musicians with a message of peace. Their hometown is a modern pilgrimage destination for multiple generations of Beatles fans.

> The Beatles have been dubbed "The Sons of Liverpool," but most of us know them as the most popular rock group of all time.

As popular as the Beatles became, they were not without controversy. In the summer of 1966 John Lennon made an off-hand comment that the Beatles were more popular than Jesus Christ. Taken out of context, the pronouncement created a firestorm of criticism and led to many radio stations pulling the Beatles from their play lists. Lennon apologized for his remarks several times, including

▲ The Beatles are practically synonymous with Liverpool.

at a Chicago press conference where he tried pointing out that he was merely commenting on the Beatlemania phenomenon and not literally equating the group to Jesus. Many feel he was pressured into apologizing against his will, especially when he continually insisted "it was wrong, or it was *taken* wrong." In hindsight the Beatles *were* bigger than any religious movement of the 1960s, at least in terms of their rising popularity. Certainly the tongue-in-cheek Liverpudlian style, to which John attributed his sarcastic wit, never held the comments against their favorite sons. Whatever they said, or whatever they believed in, nothing could diminish their popularity. Only the Beatles could stop the Beatles, which they did in April, 1970.

Now, many decades after the Beatles disbanded, their persona still remains larger than life — especially in the English city of their birth. Liverpool has commissioned sculptures of the Beatles and commemorates their lives with public events. For example, on the 25th anniversary of John Lennon's 1980 shooting in New York City, more than 1,000 tributes to the pop icon were attached to balloons and released. Lennon's image was projected at Liverpool's Albert Docks and flowers were laid at his statue outside the Cavern nightclub, where the Beatles honed their craft and launched their career. Lord Mayor Alan Dean of Liverpool said at the 2005 commemoration: "John Lennon's influence on future generations is immense. Not only did he help change perceptions of Liverpool around the world — he and the Beatles changed the aspirations of young working class kids all over the world, showing that if you've got ability you can go anywhere. Few people in his position used their fame to stand up against injustices and to spread the message of love and peace in the way he did."

Getting to the Beatles' Liverpool

Liverpool is easily accessible by air, land, and sea. If driving, take the M62 Motorway to the city center. By train, the nearest rail line to the Beatles' sites is Liverpool Lime Street. Or a devout fan can fly direct to the Liverpool John Lennon Airport from a dozen cities. Several tour companies lead groups to the myriad of Beatles-influenced locations around Liverpool. A good place to start any city tour is at "The Beatles Story" museum at the Albert Dock. Among the stops is 20 Forthlin Road, the former home of Paul McCartney's family where the Beatles met, rehearsed, and wrote many of their earliest songs. Both the Cavern Club and the statue of John Lennon are located on Mathew Street, near the intersection of North John Street.

stone circles

The United Kingdom contains some 1,000 ancient stone circles scattered across the countryside. Most are located in the southwest quadrant of the country, with the famous Stonehenge as the apparent center. Upright stones, in a circular formation, are usually associated with the sun as a supreme deity, because of the life-giving power it bestows upon the planet. British Isle henge circles were devoted to sun worship, symbolized as the giver of light in our solar system and the ultimate source of information. Incorporated into the stone circles are sophisticated astronomical alignments.

Within a five-mile (8-km) radius of Stonehenge itself lie more than 500 stone, wood, and earthen monuments. Construction of these huge monuments continued for almost 3,000 years, from the 5th to the 2nd millennium BCE. Two miles from the solar capital Stonehenge is Woodhenge, a wooden circle whose timber has disappeared long ago. But a large circular ditch and embankment still exists. Woodhenge is believed to have been aligned with the constructs of Mercury, the nearest planet to the sun, and connected to Stonehenge in this respect. 17 miles (27 km) north of Woodhenge is the famous stone circle at

▲ The Boscawen-un stone circle near Land's End was one of the three main assembly places of bards and augurs in the whole of Britain.

Avebury called Sanctuary. Its two circles of sarsen stones were likely erected during the building phase of Stonehenge and could represent another planet in our solar system. Also within a few miles of Stonehenge are more than 350 barrows, or ancient passage chambers that often contained tombs.

> The stone circles of Europe represent a prehistoric culture brimming with great skill and energy, plus a profound understanding of our solar system.

Almost all the stone circles of Britain are enclosures that share a curvilinear plan: circles, "flattened" circles, ellipses, and egg-shaped rings. All consist of freestanding stones, except the two inner rings of Stonehenge, which include "trilithons," meaning two standing stones supporting a lintel stone. Recently mathematicians and astronomers have deduced, much to the chagrin of archaeologists, that many of the British stone enclosures were laid out with a sophisticated standard unit of length according to the rules of geometry. Furthermore, it is conclusively acknowledged that the builders used a solar calendar and recorded some of the movements of the moon.

The triple alignment of standing stones of Mid Clyth, near Caithness in the Scottish Highlands, is arranged in a fan shape along a median north-south axis. Not a stone circle in the true sense, Mid Clyth may be a precursor to the round pattern with early alignment calculations. Archaeologists have sometimes compared this site with the Kerlescan alignments at Carnac, France.

The stones used at Duloe are rather crudely cut, yet Duloe is unique because it is the only circle in Cornwall made entirely from white quartz crystal. Eight protruding boulders create a circle with intense energy, perceptible to attuned

people. Modern dowsers claim there is a natural psychedelic larder within this site, which keeps food preserved longer than normal. It is also interesting to note that many standing stone circles, especially Duloe, naturally emit ultrasound at very high frequencies. When tuned into this MHz range, ultrasound prevents damage to sensitive tissue — the associated healing properties are used today in the treatment of muscular ailments.

▲ The Pipers is a pair of menhirs aligned to a larger stone circle called the Merry Maidens.

As with other ancient sites, the Rollright Stones are believed to aid with female fertility. Barren women would go to the King Stone at night and embrace it with their naked bodies. Today the King Stone is surrounded by a fence which could make this a little difficult. Nearby, the Whispering Knights were visited by girls and young women, who could hear the stones whispering to them the name of their future husbands.

▲ The eight white quartz crystal stones of Duloe are set close together in an oval formation.

Getting to Britain's important stone circles

Mid Clyth, a hamlet in Latheron parish near the village Caithness, is on the coast 3.2 miles (5 km) northeast of Lybster. The biggest town with a post office is Wick. The site is called "Hill O' Many Stanes" or the "Mid Clyth Stone Rows." The best time to visit the Highlands of Scotland is the summer months. Map reference ND/295384. By car look for the signpost off the A9 where there is a car park. Duloe is rarely visited and finding the site can be difficult. The best way is to arrive in the town Duloe, Cornwall, and then inquire about directions in a pub or petrol station. Check reference SX/235583 on an England map or travel to the south end of the B3254 and ask the first person you come across. Everyone in the immediate region knows where the Duloe circle is located. Duloe village is located in the Bodmin Moor area between Liskeard and Looe. The Rollright Stones are located just north of Chipping Norton in Oxfordshire. The nearest village is Long Compton. Map reference is SP/296308.

Stonehenge

The impressive Stonehenge is one of the world's most famous sacred sites. Built approximately 4,200 years ago on the Salisbury Plain in Wiltshire, it is the best example of a megalithic circular-cross arrangement. Wealthy Wessex chieftains reportedly built the sophisticated megalithic construction as an agricultural calendar and worship center. Stonehenge originally consisted of one perfect ring of horizontal lintel stones on top of erect sarsen stones. Within the sarsen circle are the five impressive trilithons, forming a horseshoe-shaped ring of huge stones. A free-standing trilithon "archway" consists of two upright stones supporting a horizontal lintel. Both the inner and outer rings were arranged in concentric circles. Outside the sarsen ring was another ring of "blue stones" and a ditch. An odd stone to the northeast aligns to the exact point where the sun rises on summer solstice, illuminating the inner sanctum after it rises over this "Heel Stone." When the sun rises on the shortest day, the winter solstice, the sun again enters the inner sanctum, this time through the largest trilithon archway. Most people gathered at the big mid winter celebrations at Stonehenge would call this "the supernatural doorway." On these significant mornings, the rays of the sun stream through the arches to the inner circle where in prehistory high priests would bless the coming and going of the seasons. Also calculated by this monumental observatory are eclipses of the sun and moon, the northernmost setting of the moon, the midwinter sunrise, and indications of the phases of the moon from new to full.

> Stonehenge is the most famous prehistoric megalith in Europe. As one of humanity's greatest monuments, Stonehenge functioned as a sophisticated astronomical observatory, a precise calendar, as well as a religious gathering centre.

What remains of Stonehenge today is a mere shell of its former glory, yet the full understanding of its alignments and computations continue to be revealed. For example, the 19 huge Blue Stones around the inner horseshoe are now thought to represent the 19 years between the extreme rising and setting points of the moon. This may also suggest the 19 years before another full moon occurs on the exact same day of the calendar year. It should be noted that there are 19 eclipse years (or 223 full moons) between similar eclipses when the sun, earth, and moon return to their same relative positions. It is exactly 29.53 days between full moons and in the outer Sarsen Circle there are 29-and-one-half monoliths.

Discovered recently, 56 is the number of Aubrey Holes set around the outer circle. The number 56 is significant because it corresponds to a 56-year cycle of the full moon rising nearest the winter solstice over the Heel Stone. By knowing this lunar cycle of 56 years, astronomers can always successfully predict an eclipse. Interestingly, less than half the eclipses that Stonehenge predicts can actually be viewed from England! Finally, the five large trilithon archways are now thought to represent the five planets visible to the naked eye: Mercury, Venus, Mars, Jupiter, and Saturn. The other planets' positions may factor into even larger cycles.

ALIGNMENTS AT STONEHENGE, ENGLAND

It is speculated that the first Stonehenge consisted of a

circular ditch dug sometime between 2,600 and 2,200 BCE. This was followed by the construction within the ditch of two concentric circles of 60 Blue Stones, believed to have been quarried in the Presili Mountains of southern Wales. At least 200 years elapsed before the two great inner circles were constructed. The outer circle and inner

▲ The outer ditch surrounding Stonehenge is clearly visible from the air.

horseshoe sarsen stones were cut from a local Wiltshire quarry. How these 20-foot (6-m) upright slabs — topped with perfectly fitted horizontal slabs (lintels) — were put into place at such a distant time in history remains a mystery. The Druids, an order of priests that began in the age of the Gauls, continue to worship at Stonehenge during the summer and winter solstices. This communing with nature and the cosmos represents one of the longest preserved religious traditions in the world.

The Salisbury Plain around Stonehenge is equally mysterious. Dozens of round mounds covering long barrows are scattered in all directions around Stonehenge. Ancient footpaths once connected Avebury and other potent ritual centres in the surrounding countryside. From the air, two avenues can still be detected leading into Stonehenge where the monument is aligned with the two solstice sightings. Geomancers report several powerful ley lines intersecting at Stonehenge, with the ultimate power days falling on the longest and shortest days of the year. Also curious is that most English crop circles appear in the Wiltshire and Hampshire regions of southern England, with Stonehenge at the presumed center of activity. In July, 1996 a famous crop circle called the "Julia Set" appeared across the street from Stonehenge. Many others have materialized near Stonehenge since then.

Getting to Stonehenge

Stonehenge is on the Salisbury Plain in southern England. It is easily reached by road from the nearby towns of Amesbury or Salisbury. Public buses leave from Salisbury to Stonehenge on an hourly basis every day. In recent years, Stonehenge has been fenced off and the Druid rituals are permitted only on the winter and summer solstice. From London take the M25 (called the Ring Road as it goes in a circle around London) then get on the M3 which goes southwest from London. The M3 will intersect the A303 which passes right by Stonehenge. It is just over an hour's drive from London. Stonehenge is located 8 miles (13 km) north of Salisbury village.

SCOTLAND

No record of human habitation in Scotland preceded 10,000 BCE, concurrent with the end of the last Ice Age in Europe. The oldest known Neolithic settlement can be dated to around 8500 BCE, near Edinburgh. Many Scottish pilgrims consider the Neolithic Clava Cairns site a must-see stop on the Scottish mainland. Of the three cairns here, two feature passageways aligned to the midwinter sunset. Of the Stone Age, Bronze Age, and Iron Age civilizations that existed in the country, many artifacts remain, but few left any written records. One curious leftover of prehistory are the vitrified forts of Scotland. Stones that are vitrified have been exposed to extreme heat so hot that it fuses rock into glass, similar to the heat produced by a nuclear explosion. Those who believe human warfare destroyed Atlantis point to the vitrified forts of Scotland as evidence.

The written history of Scotland largely begins with the arrival of the Roman Empire beginning in 44 CE. The Romans occupied what is now England and Wales, administering it as a Roman province called *Britannia*. To the north was a territory not governed by the Romans — called *Caledonia*, peopled by the Picts. As mentioned earlier, the famous Hadrian's Wall separated the two provinces. From a historical viewpoint, Scotland appears a peripheral country, slow to gain from the advances of Mediterranean civilization. It eventually merged with England, Wales, and Northern Ireland to comprise the United Kingdom.

Callanish

One of the most outstanding stone circles in the British Isles, also one of the best preserved and most difficult to reach, is the Callanish ring in the Outer Hebrides. Callanish consists of 13 primary stones forming a circle about 43 feet (13 m) in diameter. The 4,200 year-old site features a long approach of standing stones to the north and shorter rows of erect stones to the east, south, and west. These rows have been described as celestial alignment markers or, perhaps, incomplete avenues. If viewed from above, the overall layout of the monument resembles a distorted Celtic cross.

> Outside the Callanish circle, several rows lead away from the monument, indicating the four cardinal compass points.

The first written reference to Callanish is John Morisone, a Lewis native, who in 1680 wrote that "great stones standing up in ranks were sett [sic] up in place for devotione." Local tradition says that these standing formations were once giants, who were turned into stone by Saint Kieran because they refused to convert

▲ Most of the long stone avenues that once connected the greater Callanish region are now lost.

to Christianity. Others recall the legend of a great priest-king, who had the stones raised by an army of black slaves. Another local belief says that at sunrise, on midsummer morning, the "shining one" walked along the stone avenue, "his arrival heralded by the cuckoo's call." This legend could be a folk memory recalling the astronomical significance of the stones.

The Callanish circle lies at the center of three single and one double set of stone rows, which protrude outward like a compass. The central stone stands over 14 feet (4.5 m) tall and may have been the sighting stone used for astronomical calculations. The northern line is the most prominent row of menhirs. It is a double row forming a processional approach to and from the center. The double row, perhaps an avenue, extends 230-265 feet (70-80 m) to the north. As mentioned, the Callanish arrangement resembles a Celtic cross when viewed from above; although, it predates Christianity by thousands of years. Pottery finds suggest a date of 2200 BCE for the construction of the circle. It has been speculated, among other theories, that the stones form a calendar system based on the position of the moon. One scholar observed that 4,000 years ago the alignment of the southward facing stone avenue pointed to the setting of midsummer full moon behind Clisham — a distant hill. Callanish has several known astronomical alignments, including one with the Pleiades star cluster.

Despite the fact that the inner circle consists of a modest diameter, the stones are unlike other circles in Great Britain. Callanish stones are tall and thin and made of local Lewisian gneiss stone, quarried only a mile to the northeast. The central henge surrounds a mound covering a passage barrow. The tallest of the stones indicate the entrance to a burial cairn, where human remains have been discovered. An excavation in 1980 and 1981 concluded that the burial chamber

▲ The Callanish standing stones are among the tallest menhirs in Europe.

was a late addition to the site and had been modified a number of times. A mile or so from the main Callanish site are several other stone circles, called *Cnoc Ceann a'Gharaidh* (Callanish II), *Cnoc Filibhir Bheag* (Callanish III), and *Ceann Hulavig* (Callanish IV). Each of these stone circles is found close to megalithic funerary monuments. The tapering standing stones on the Isle of Lewis are perfectly integrated into the landscape. This collection of monuments may indicate that the greater area around Callanish was a major Neolithic ritual site.

Getting to Callanish

The Callanish site is situated just outside the village of Callanish (spelled *Calanais* in Gaelic) on the west coast of Scotland's Outer Hebrides island chain. The amazing Callanish circle and avenue of standing stones can be found 12 miles (20 km) west of Stornoway village on the Isle of Lewis. A regular ferry service from Stornoway on Lewis to Ullapool in Ross-Shire, Scotland takes about 2 hours and 45 minutes.

Iona

The religious community of Iona was founded by Saint Columba, who came there in 543 CE from exile in Ireland. Along with 12 fellow Irish companions, Saint Columba founded the first monastery on Iona. From here they set about the conversion of pagan Scotland and much of northern England to Christianity. Iona's fame as a place of learning and Christian mission spread throughout the far reaches of Europe. In medieval times the small and remote island became a major pilgrimage destination. Iona took on a new meaning as a holy island in the early Christian era. The island was so renowned that several kings of Scotland, Ireland, and Norway had their bodies transported to Iona for burial after they died elsewhere.

> Iona is regarded as a holy island, where many famous illuminated manuscripts were created.

Already a sacred island to the pagans of Scotland, Iona grew to become the center of Celtic Christianity for four centuries. Iona is a perfect example of the blending of two cultures. Christianity clearly overlaps with one of the great spiritual locations of the Celtic world. Columba was a powerful figure in Irish politics and is said to have founded his monastery as repentance for a civil war he instigated earlier.

The story says he was sent into exile on Iona with instructions to convert as many heathens to Christianity as had been lost in battle. Therefore, Iona became a thriving religious community of Irish monasticism, governing 42 parishes in Ireland and 57 in Scotland until the 9th century. There are said to have been 360 large stone Celtic crosses on the island. Nearly all of them were thrown into the

▲ The great Celtic cross of Iona still stands close to the church of Iona in the Hebrides founded by the Irishman, Saint Columba. Carved during the 9th century, it is one of the few surviving outdoor monuments dating back to the Viking Age.

sea, along with 400 Benedictine monks, during the Protestant Reformation of the 14th century.

Several surviving Celtic manuscripts were produced in Iona. They are beautifully written in clear, round lettering that helped spread Christianity throughout the Western world. Although the manuscripts are gospel books, they are nearly devoid of Christian symbols, except for the fierce, Eastern-looking beasts symbolizing the four Evangelists. The books are elaborately decorated, yet reveal little awareness of classical or Christian culture. Instead, the pages of pure ornamentation are some of the richest and most complicated pieces of abstract decoration ever produced. For the illiterate peasants these manuscripts must have had an almost hypnotic effect. The last illuminated manuscript produced in Iona was the famous Book of Kells. Before it was finished, the Abbot of Iona was forced to flee to Ireland due to a sudden invasion. The new invaders were not of the land, but of the sea. In the 7th and 8th centuries, Norsemen began invading the undefended Christian settlements of the British Isles. In the year 806 CE, 68 monks were massacred by invading Danes and in 814 the headship of Iona was transferred to Kells in Ireland, stripping Iona of its power and prestige.

Shortly before his death Columba prophesied, "Before the world comes to an end, Iona shall be as she was." The raids of the invading Vikings helped fulfill his vision with brutal attacks in the years 795, 802, and 806. The small island of Iona had the misfortune of being located along the Viking's sea route to Ireland and mainland Europe. By 807, the community within the monastery was devastated, along with all their libraries. In the centuries following the abandonment of the monastery to Kells, with further destruction from the Reformation, pilgrims slowly started coming back to Iona. Many who visit today think the muted light of Iona, the wine-dark sea, and the solemn hills of Mull continue to radiate a sense of peace and inner freedom.

Getting to Iona

The small, storm-swept island of Iona is located about a mile off the southwestern Scottish coast. To reach Iona travelers need to make the lengthy journey to Oban in the West Highlands of Scotland, then take the ferry to the Isle of Mull, cross the isle overland to the ferry port at Fionnphort. Throughout the summer months the ship M.V. Volante operates a scheduled ferry service between Iona and Fionnphort. The service is for passengers only and operates in the evening, after the Caledonian MacBrayne (Cal-Mac) ferry is finished for the day. The Cal Mac ferry services Iona year round.

Rosslyn

The Rosslyn Chapel was designed by William Sinclair of the Saint Clair clan, a Scottish noble family descended from Norman knights and, according to legend, directly linked to the Knights Templar. The enigmatic chapel has been described in many terms and by many people over the centuries. Some consider it a Templar mausoleum or the cradle of Scotch Masonry. To others it is a sacred chapel and the terminus of a Freemasonry initiate pilgrimage route. New Agers call it a geomantic focal point on a powerful ley line linked to the seventh crown charka. More recently Rosslyn Chapel has been made famous by Dan Brown's wildly successful book *The Da Vinci Code*, associating the chapel with the Holy Grail.

Construction of the chapel began in 1440 (completed in 1480), but was officially founded in 1446. The builders of Rosslyn, the Clan of Saint Clair (*Sancto Claros*), were members of the Royal Order of Scotland and supposedly descendents of the Rose Lineage. Rosslyn was designed as a mausoleum for the Sinclair family, whom — it is alleged — are descendents from the Jesus holy bloodline. In medieval times, Mother Mary was known as *Santa Maria Della Rosa*. In at least one account, Jesus himself was called the Rose — the Rose of Sharon — of Is-uren. Indeed, the predominant symbols of Rosslyn are the fleur-de-les, the rose, and the sunflower. Upon the roof, above the aisles, is a depiction of the cross within a grail (supplanted with roses) of the Saint Clairs — the founders, who were once hereditary Grand Masters of Scotch Masonry. Can all this suggest the

▲ The Rosslyn Chapel is ornately decorated, inside and out.

Rose Lineage is associated with the Sinclair family at Rosslyn or, more specifically, a *Rose*line going back to Jesus Christ himself?

> The Rosslyn Chapel is associated with many legends. Speculating on what lies beneath it only enhances its lore.

Because of its purported connections with Freemasonry, the chapel has inevitably become listed as one of the final resting places of the Holy Grail (supposedly taken

▲ Hidden imagery and secret symbols supposedly abound in the Rosslyn Chapel.

from the Temple of Jerusalem by medieval Crusaders). Based on the many legends of "secret vaults" underneath Rosslyn Chapel, possibilities do exist that something important is buried there. Like a page out of *The Da Vinci Code,* the White Lady of Rosslyn Castle is said to hide a secret worth "millions of pounds" — and some have suggested that this could be the Holy Grail or instructions on how to locate it.

An old Saint Clair legend suggests three big medieval chests are buried somewhere on the property and this has inevitably led to various theories as to what could be found in the chests. Past scanning and excavations in or near the chapel have not yet produced any conclusive results. Sealed chambers under the basement of the chapel, however, have yet to be excavated since the digging might collapse the entire structure. The chambers are known to be filled with pure white Arabic sand — rumored to have been brought to the chapel by the Knights Templar from the Dome of the Rock — and ultrasonic scans have revealed six leaden vaults within the sand.

In addition to the theory of the chapel being used by Freemasons and the Knights Templar is the claim that those groups, stationed at Rosslyn Chapel, journeyed to North America and returned several decades before the Columbus voyage of 1492. This claim is based on several pieces of evidence, both in the Rosslyn Chapel and across the Atlantic. In Canada's Atlantic Province of Nova Scotia (which means New Scotland in Latin) some very old tombstones have been found with Masonic symbols and Crusader crosses on them, in what appears to be the oldest European graveyard in North America. In Massachusetts, the Westford Knight is a rock engraving supposedly showing a Scottish knight with Clan Gunn markings, linked to the Henry Sinclair exploration party. In the Rosslyn Chapel are stone carvings of plants native only to North America, such as aloe and maize. How could the builders of Rosslyn Chapel have known about these plants from the Western Hemisphere several decades before the Columbus voyage? Such are the many tidbits of fact and legend that, year after year, only enhance the lore of Rosslyn Chapel.

Getting to Rosslyn

Rosslyn Chapel, originally named the Collegiate Chapel of Saint Matthew, is a 15th century church in the village of Roslin, Midlothian, Scotland. Roslin is 6 miles (10 km) south of Edinburgh's Princes Street. By road take the Edinburgh bypass to the "Straiton Junction" A701 to Penicuik/Peebles. Follow A701 3 miles (5 km) to the sign for Roslin. Once in Roslin village the chapel is signed and easily located. Edinburgh is 30 miles (48 km) from Glasgow, which has an international airport.

Skara Brae

The age-old settlement called Skara Brae is located adjacent to the Bay of Skaill on the west coast of mainland Orkney, off northern Scotland. The level of preservation is one of the finest for a Neolithic settlement and has thus earned the site a UNESCO World Heritage Site listing. Until the 19th century, however, Skara Brae lay undiscovered, buried beneath the sand dunes near the bay. Rough seas and high winds in 1850 stripped away the grass, revealing several prehistoric structures. In 1924, another storm uncovered the remainder of the settlement. Although there were several phases of occupation, all that can be seen today is the last phase. The settlement of eight similar dwellings, linked together by a series of low alleyways, was fully excavated between 1928 and 1930 by Vere Gordon Childe.

Skara Brae is believed to have been occupied for about 600 years, starting about 3100 BCE. The settlement was abandoned by its inhabitants around 2500 BCE, after the climate changed, turning much colder and wet. Archaeologists determined that the Skara Brae inhabitants would number only 50 to 100 at any given time. They were skilled artisans of a pottery style called "grooved ware," because their pots and urns featured a decorative groove at or near the top. The houses used earth sheltering but, rather than being sunk into the ground, they were built into mounds of pre-existing rubbish hills known as "middens." Although the midden provided the houses with some stability, its most important purpose was to act as a layer of insulation against Orkney's harsh winter climate. On average, the houses measure 132 square feet (40 sq. m) in size with a large square room containing a central hearth which would have been used for heating and cooking. As few trees grow on the island, the people of Skara Brae used

▲ Skara Brae was uncovered with cooking utensils, furniture, and tools still intact.

▲ Whatever prehistoric rituals were performed within the Standing Stones of Stenness are now lost to the march of time.

driftwood and whalebone, with turf thatch, to cover their homes. The dwellings were found to contain a number of stone-built pieces of furniture, including cupboards, dressers, seats, and box beds. A sophisticated drainage system was even incorporated into the village design, one that may have included a primitive form of toilet in each dwelling.

> The area around Skara Brae holds many prehistoric structures in the British Isles, from stone circles to still intact Neolithic houses and mound tombs.

It is known that the seaways were very important in Scottish history and prehistory. The ancient Orkney inhabitants likely copied the style of chambered cairns from other Neolithic traders. The cairns were sometimes built with astronomical alignments incorporated into the structure, while others seem to have been designed specifically as communal burial places according to tribal status. The history of chambered cairns in Orkney spans thousands of years, during which time a variety of designs developed.

One of the most mysterious cairns is a mound called Mine Howe, which contains a nearly vertical shaft of 29 stone steps leading down to a dry masonry chamber. The circular room at the bottom measures about five feet (1.5 m) in diameter, but its corbelled ceiling towers 13 feet (4 m) overhead. What activities occurred in the vault of Mine Howe remains a complete mystery. Unfortunately, the farmer who discovered the entrance in 1946 removed "hundreds of bones and other relics," including cockle shells, teeth, and "curious polished stones," whose whereabouts are unknown today. Researchers compare the ditches encircling Mine Howe to the large ditch that surrounds the nearby Standing Stones of Stenness and many other stone circles in the British Isles. Such comparisons date Mine Howe at 5,000 years or older.

Mine Howe and other sites around Skara Brae were likely built for mystical or religious functions. The Mine Howe steps led down into the earth, suggesting an entry into the underworld. Also, the subterranean chamber likely served as a shrine or oracle site where Neolithic people could communicate with the spiritual realms. Similar to Newgrange and Loughcrew in Ireland, or Stonehenge in England, the ritual centers around Skara Brae incorporated celestial information into the megalithic construction design. The solstices, equinoxes, and lunar events were recorded in stone to preserve this information for all time. It is believed elaborate celebrations took place on these auspicious dates, along with deeply mystical rituals of a more somber tone. The Maes Howe passage chamber is aligned to the winter solstice, a day largely recognized as opening the ritual season in prehistory. Other locations worth noting include the Knap of Howar, the oldest house remains in Orkney, dated at 3,600 BCE. The Standing Stones of Stenness and Maeshowe attest to the sacred value of these megalithic structures in the far northern reaches of the Orkney Islands. The Ring of Brodgar is considered one of the finest stone circles to be found anywhere. Of the original 60 stones, 27 remain standing in this 340-foot (103-m) diameter circle, dating from the third millennium BCE.

Getting to Skara Brae

The Orkney Islands are a grouping of windswept islands off Scotland's northern coast. Mine Howe and the parish of Stenness are both designated as a UNESCO World Heritage Site and are located on the island called Mainland Orkney. Regular passenger and vehicle ferry services operate on the following routes: Lerwick (Shetland) to Kirkwall; Aberdeen to Kirkwall; Scrabster to Stromness; Gills Bay (Caithness) to St Margaret's Hope and a summer only walk-on service from John O' Groats to Burwick in South Ronaldsay. There are also daily flights from Glasgow, Edinburgh, Aberdeen, Inverness, and Shetland to Orkney.

WALES

The Druidic religion supposedly had its stronghold in Wales until the Roman invasion. The Welsh were among the first to convert to Christianity by the time the Romans vacated. Wales continued to be Christian when England was overrun by the German and Scandinavian pagan invasions. The Patron Saint of Wales, Saint David (or *Dewi Sant* in Welsh), is known to have undergone a pilgrimage to Rome in the 6th century and was serving as a bishop in Wales — well before Augustine arrived to convert the King of Kent and establish the diocese of Canterbury. All the while, many older Celtic beliefs and customs survived among the Welsh people, including the Welsh language called Brythonic, which is still spoken today.

Saint Winifred's Well

The multi-versioned legend of Winifred comes down from the 7th century. Winifred is also referred to as Gwenfrewi, Saint Gwenfrewy, Guinevere, Saint Winefride, or Winfred of Wales. All versions begin with a nearby prince named Caradog taking a liking to the beautiful Winifred. Caradog pursued her relentlessly, but she always resisted his advances. He was gravely displeased because her decision to become a nun would not allow her to marry him. In a fit of rage Caradog had her head severed. In the decapitation version her head rolled down a hill and where it stopped, a healing spring appeared. This location is known as Saint Winifred's Well in the village of Holywell. Another version tells of Winifred's head being rejoined to her body, due to the efforts of her uncle Saint Beuno, who managed to restore Winifred back to life. In a final story, Saint Beuno places a curse on Caradog, which causes him to melt into the ground — allowing Winifred to become a nun at Gwytherin in Denbighshire. Each version of Winifred's tale relates several details of her life, including Winifred's pilgrimage to Rome. Despite few historical records for this period, there does appear to have been a real Winifred. One surviving record has Winifred's brother, Owain, killing Caradog as revenge for an unknown crime. Another document has Winifred replacing Saint Tenoi as abbess of Gwytherin. Saint Tenoi is believed to be Winifred's aunt.

Winifred reportedly died around 660 CE when her body was interred at the Gwytherin abbey. In 1138, her relics were carried to Shrewsbury, England, where an elaborate shrine was erected. Winifred's shrine at Shrewsbury became a major pilgrimage destination in the Late Middle Ages, but the shrine was destroyed by Henry VIII in 1540. Because Holywell did not contain the relics, it was spared the widespread destruction of the Reformation. Although mostly lost, some of Saint Winifred's relics were returned to Holywell. Nevertheless, Holywell holds the distinction of being the only pilgrimage destination in Britain that continued through the Reformation period to the present day.

> Saint Winifred's Well, also called the
> "Lourdes of Wales," has long been known for
> its healing and renewal qualities.

The present shrine at Holywell was erected in 1505 under royal patronage. Elegant pillars surround a star-shaped basin at the center of the crypt. Above the crypt is a large chapel. The source of Saint Winifred's Well emanates from a star-shaped well, similar in shape to a mandala pattern from the East. The frigid water flows from the crypt and into a large pool in an open air courtyard. Those who visit attest to the well's potency for restoring psychic wholeness, along with ailing the physical self. Testaments of the well's curative power can be found scratched or carved on the walls and pillars surrounding the pool.

The Catholic shrine is open throughout the year and accommodates pilgrims of any faith. Around the well, a constant current of whispered prayers activates the site; otherwise only the murmurings of the water can be heard. Anyone who visits Saint Winifred's Well is encouraged to collect water from the outdoor pool below the chapel. A pilgrim's hospice at Holywell is also open year round. Between Pentecost and September

▲ Saint Winifred's Well was the only pilgrimage allowed after the Reformation. It remains sacred to both Catholics and Protestants.

30th a service, including veneration of the relic of Saint Winifred, is held near the spring every day at 11:30 am, or 2:30 pm on Sundays. The annual National Pilgrimage takes place on the Sunday following the 22nd of June. A procession makes its way through town to congregate poolside for Mass. Another annual pilgrimage, called the Pan-Orthodox, occurs on the first Saturday in October. Bathing is by appointment only and is arranged by the Saint Winifred custodians. If allowed to bathe, the pilgrim follows the protocol from centuries past: pass through the bath three times, circle the source three times, and finish prayers kneeling on a stone near the outdoor pool. Lighting a candle, whether bathing or not, is another way to win the favor of Saint Winifred at her potent healing well. Over 500 years of spiritual favors obtained, including physical cures, has given Saint Winifred's Well an endearing reputation among the faithful.

Getting to Saint Winifred's Well

The shrine of Saint Winifred is located in the town of Holywell — also called *Treffynnon* in Welsh. Holywell is just over the northeastern Welsh border with England, about 20 miles (32 km) west of Chester. Many who visit choose to start their approach at the ruined Basingwerk Abbey, located one mile (1.6 km) north at Greenfield, also in Flintshire. This route follows the last stage of a medieval pilgrim's route through the woods and into the quant village of Holywell.

IRELAND

A man travels the world over in search of what he needs, and returns home to find it. *—George Moore*, Irish novelist

FOR A COUNTRY ABOUT THE SIZE OF MAINE, Ireland is a destination rich in history. Scattered across the Emerald Isle are impressive stone circles, megalithic ritual sites, solitary round towers, Middle Age monasteries, and romantic castles. Tourists flock to the Blarney Stone at Blarney Castle, known for the eloquence it supposedly imparts on all those who kiss the famous rock. Sacred mountains, hermitages, wells, dolmens and large stone crosses enhance the charm of the Irish countryside. About 70% of the Irish people profess Roman Catholicism as their faith, with most of the others belonging to the growing Muslim populations or various Protestant denominations.

The period before Christianity in Ireland is largely prehistoric, with little or no written record. It has always been assumed that the Irish people were of Celtic origin, although recent genetic evidence shows that both the Irish and the Welsh (and to a lesser degree the English and Scots) have many genetic

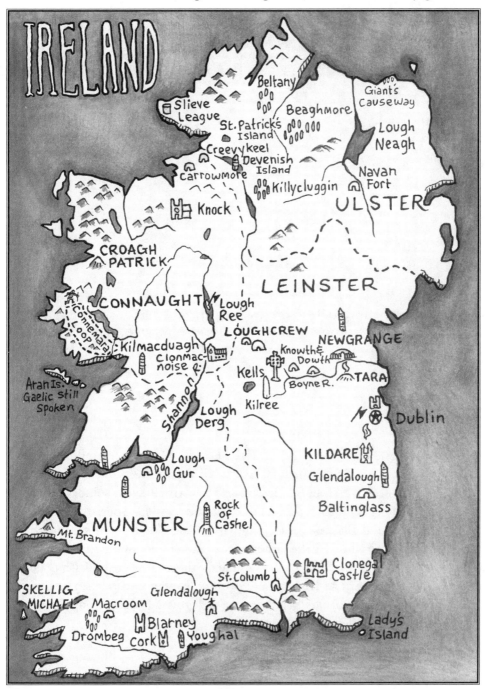

traits in common with the people of the Basque region of Spain. Some theorize that although Basque is certainly not a Celtic language, there may have been a Celto-Basque link or, perhaps, the pre-Celtic population of Ireland may have had Basque origins. Others equate the Celto-Basque connection as a direct link to the common survivors of Atlantis. All positions are difficult to prove, as the information is relatively new. Culturally, however, Ireland is undeniably Celtic.

The Stone Age inhabitants arrived about 10,000 years ago, eventually to develop into the Mesolithic and Neolithic people. The Neolithic builders are remembered for the huge stone monuments they left behind, many of them astronomically aligned. The Bronze Age, which began around 2500 BCE, ushered in the manufacture of elaborate gold and bronze ornaments. The Romans never ventured to Ireland as an invading force as they did in Britannia, leaving the Emerald Isle isolated and purely Celtic until the arrival of Christianity. Tradition maintains that in 432 CE, Saint Patrick returned to the island and, for the rest of his life, worked to convert the pagan Irish to Christianity.

The Druid tradition collapsed as the new faith swept the island. Irish scholars excelled in the study of Latin learning, thus preserving Christian texts during the early Middle Ages. The artistic crafts of manuscript illumination, metalworking, and sculpture flourished. Middle Age art also produced such treasures as the Book of Kells, ornate jewelry, and the many carved stone crosses that dot the island. This golden age was interrupted in the 9th century by 200 years of intermittent warfare with waves of Viking raiders plundering monasteries and towns. Eventually many Vikings settled in Ireland and established towns, including the modern cities of Dublin, Cork, Limerick, and Waterford. The Normans from northern France also contributed to the gene pool mix, but these were small additions. Most of the Irish population descends directly from the original inhabitants who came to Ireland after the end of the Ice Age.

Croagh Patrick

The rounded dome of Croagh Patrick is made of pre-Cambrian quartzite stone. The hard crystalline rock is known to absorb and refract light, as well as attract other unseen forces. The physical property of white quartzite was recognized by the megalith builders, who quarried the stone in northwestern Ireland to build their cairns and stone circles. Beyond the aesthetic value and geological features of Croagh Patrick, the mountain has been a pilgrimage destination longer than any written testament or oral history can record.

Originally associated with Lugh, the god of light, the pagans of Ireland annually flocked to the mountain at the end of July to correspond with the first fruit harvest. The cycle of fertility and a new harvest were celebrated as the sun rose in the east. This Lughnasa site was also shared with Crom Cruach, the dark figure who is associated with the last harvest. Early legend says Crom Cruach would take a sheaf from the people and bring it underground in the form of the corn maiden. Then that seed was planted to ensure fertility for the coming year. Pagans worshipped Lugh and Crom Cruach as balance to the same cycles of light and dark, but the coming Christians forced an end to these celebrations. Crom Cruach was associated with evil and fear, while Lugh was replaced by Saint Patrick as the symbol of light.

> Devout Catholics climb to the summit of
> Croagh Patrick, Ireland's holiest mountain,
> where pilgrims gather at dawn on the last
> Sunday of July to celebrate Saint Patrick's fast
> in 441 CE.

It is interesting that the timing of the pagan festival of Lugh would also become the same date commemorating Saint Patrick's fast that lasted for 40 days and 40 nights. The only difference is the pagan date was the last Friday of July, which was Crom's Day, and now the Christian pilgrimage is the last Sunday of the month known as "Garland Sunday." The Reek, as the mountain is known locally, has been a Christian pilgrimage destination ever since Saint Patrick spent the days of Lent on the peak, fasting and meditating. Patrick was said to have beaten off black demon birds that attempted to disturb his communiqué with God. The birds failed and Patrick successfully persuaded God to allow his personal evaluation of all the Irish people during the Last Judgment.

Croagh Patrick is of course named after Saint Patrick, one of the first Christian missionaries in Ireland. His life has been of keen interest to the Irish people. Saint Patrick was born somewhere along the west coast of Britain, according to his autobiographical *Confessio*. At 16 years old, raiders captured him with "many thousands of people" and sold them as slaves in Ireland. Although he came from a Christian family, he was not particularly religious before his capture. His enslavement to a Druidic chieftain markedly strengthened his faith. He escaped at the age of 22 and spent the next 12 years in a French monastery, where he adopted the name Patrick. One night he heard voices begging him to return to Ireland, which he did. Patrick wrote that he expected to be violently killed at any time or enslaved once again. Not one to be intimidated, he established the Church in Ireland by traveling throughout the country preaching, teaching, building churches, opening schools, and establishing monasteries. His specialty was

▲ The majestic Croagh Patrick has been a recognized sacred mountain for thousands of years.

converting chiefs and bards to Christianity, all the while supporting his preaching with miracles. Patrick gathered many followers, including Saint Benignus, who would later become his successor. His main objective was the establishment of native clergy, along with the abolishment of paganism, idolatry, and sun-worship.

Legend credits Patrick with the banishment of all snakes from Ireland, although the island never supported snake life in the first place. One suggestion is that the snake symbolized the serpent motif of the Druids, or the pagans themselves. Legend also credits Patrick with teaching the Irish about the concept of the Trinity by exhibiting the shamrock — a three-leaf clover common in Ireland — and using it to highlight the Christian dogma of "three divine persons in the one God." Saint Patrick died a very old man on March 17th 493, a yearly holiday that continues to be venerated in Ireland and around the world. Patrick is the patron saint of Ireland, along with Saint Brigid and Saint Columba.

Climbing Croagh Patrick

The most sacred mountain in Ireland is located 2 miles (3.5 km) from the city of Westport in County Mayo. Croagh Patrick can be climbed anytime during the year, but on Saint Patrick's Day and Garland Sunday prepare for huge crowds and a religious service at the summit. At 2,500 feet (758 m) the climb up Croagh Patrick takes about 3 hours round trip without stopping. Most pilgrims opt to take their time and spend the day on the mountain. There is a transport service for pilgrims on Reek Sunday — the last Sunday in July and the official pilgrimage date. At the trailhead is Campbell's Bar, the traditional post-pilgrimage hostelry.

Hill of Tara

In times of lore, the Hill of Tara was famous as a pilgrimage destination where the High Kings held supreme reign over Ireland. In the long pagan epoch, devotees arrived bearing gifts from all over the island nation to join celebrations, coronations, or simply for devotion. The Hill of Tara was most familiar in Irish history as the seat of the High Kings until the 6th century CE. This role extended until the 12th century, yet the earlier splendor was diminished by a changing religious preference to Christianity. The Hill of Tara predates Celtic times, with a known Neolithic structure factoring into the long drama. By the 12th century the Hill of Tara was all but destroyed and left to ruin.

> For many centuries pilgrims traveled from afar to witness the crowning of Ireland's High Kings at the Hill of Tara.

There are a multitude of remains on the hill, including a passage mound, two wells, round trenches surrounding artificial mounds, and various other earthworks and structures. Most of Tara's features were given fanciful names by 19th

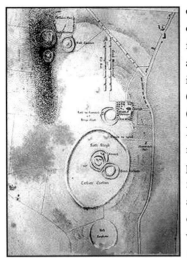

▲ A map from 1837 shows more features on the Hill of Tara than can be found there today.

century antiquarians, who were inspired by the exploits of the Celts. Though it only stands 300 feet (90 m) above sea level, the Hill of Tara is quite a magnificent structure. At the summit of the hill is a circular Iron Age hill fort, almost 3,300 feet (1,000 m) in circumference, known as *Ráith na Ríg* (the Fort of the Kings, also known as the Royal Enclosure). It is within this enclosure where Tara's most significant remains can be found. The most prominent earthworks here are two linked ring forts known as *Teach Chormaic* (Cormac's House) and the *Forradh*, or the Royal Seat. In the middle of the Royal Seat stands an erect standing stone, which is an Irish menhir identified as the *Lia Fáil*, or the "Stone of Destiny." Some think the original Stone of Destiny was taken to Scotland and is now the Stone of Scone. Whichever stone stood in pagan times, it was at the base of this phallic rock where the High Kings of Ireland were crowned.

To the north of the ring forts is a small Neolithic passage chamber known as *Dumha na nGiall* (the Mound of the Hostages), which dates to between 2500-3000 BCE. To the south of the Royal Enclosure lies another ring fort known as *Ráith Laoghaire* (Laoghaire's Fort), where a king of the same name is said to have been buried in an upright position. Half a mile south of the Hill of Tara is another hill fort known as Rath Maeve — the fort of either the legendary queen Medb, who is more usually associated with Connacht, or the less well-known legendary figure of Medb Lethderg, who is associated with Tara. Still another ring fort with three banks called *Ráith na Seanadh* (the Rath of the Synods) is located north of Tara, just outside the bounds of the Ráith na Ríg. Excavations of this monument have produced Roman artifacts dating from the 1st-3rd centuries CE. Further north is a long, narrow rectangular feature commonly known as the Banqueting Hall, although most researchers now view it as a ceremonial avenue leading to the site. Along the avenue are two circular earthworks known as the Sloping Trenches and Gráinne's Fort.

Many generations of historians and archaeologists have worked to uncover the mysteries of Tara. Scholars at first disputed Tara's importance as a pre-Celtic site, but there is one known structure dating to around 5,000 years old from the Neolithic period. This monument, the Mound of the Hostages, is an ancient passage mound reminiscent of those found in the Boyne Valley and Loughcrew. The Mound of the Hostages has a short passage which aligns with the setting sun on the true astronomical cross-quarter days of November 8th and February 4th — significant dates that also corresponded to the ancient Celtic festivals of

Samhain and Imbolg. The mound's passage extends 13 feet (4 m) into the cairn, enough for a sunbeam to adequately determine specific days of the year. The backstone is illuminated on the first days of the winter quarter and again with the coming of spring. The backstone is carved with arcs and circles.

The Tuatha Dé Danann, pre-Celtic dwellers of Ireland, are the legendary first occupiers to use the Hill of Tara as their capital. This half-mythological, half-historic people became ancestor deities to the Celts, influencing their earthly lives from the Otherworld. The Tuatha Dé Danann embodied the spirit of Tara and all who occupied the hill. Tara became a symbol of royal power with deep roots into the past. When the Celts established a royal seat, the hill became associated with the concept of a high king: whoever ruled at Tara ruled over Ireland, thus the kings of Meath gained a sort of godly status. Legend suggests that the Irish Stone of Destiny was required to roar three times if the chosen one was indeed the true king (similar to the Scottish *Lia Fáil*). The Hill of Tara as a Celtic capital enjoyed tremendous political and religious influence, which gradually diminished upon the arrival of Saint Patrick who condemned the site. After it was banned, King Diarmuid Mac Cerbhaill incurred the wrath of Christian clerics by celebrating the Bán Fheis in 560 CE. This event marks the final conflict between paganism and Christianity. Tara was cursed by Saint Ruadhán of Lorrha and legend tells us it was stripped of all power and prestige. The 1169 invasion of Englishman "Strongbow" Richard de Clare lay to waste all that was left of Tara. A grave found near Tara is supposedly that of King Laoghaire, who was said to have been the last pagan king of Ireland.

According to legend, Saint Patrick was the first Christian to confront the pagans at their annual vernal fire called Samhain. The High King always lit this fire when all the fires in the country were extinguished just before twilight so they could only be renewed from the sacred flame at Tara. After the fall of night, the Druids assembled on the Hill of Tara, the symbolic heart of the country. A new fire was created from the sacred oak, and from this fire all the hearths of Ireland could be relit. Samhain was a deeply symbolic ceremony that reenacted the creation of the world by the primordial gods, including animal and human sacrifices. In the 5th century Saint Patrick lit a rival fire on the Hill of Slane at the opposite end of the valley. Patrick's Christian bonfire was miraculously inextinguishable. By Patrick's account in *Confessio*, the season was associated with Easter, also a major pagan holiday. According to the 8th century Christian monk and historian Bede, the time around the spring equinox was dedicated to the pagan fertility goddess Eostre. The Easter Bunny is often identified as a remnant of this fertility festival; however there is no evidence to support this claim.

Getting to the Hill of Tara

The world famous Hill of Tara archaeological complex is located 30 miles (48 km) northwest of Dublin. Currently the best route is the N3 Motorway. Follow signs off the N3 west to the site. There is a controversy about building the new M3 Motorway through the archaeologically rich Tara-Skyne Valley, potentially destroying many sites associated with Tara along the way.

Kildare

The word "Kildare" is derived from the pagan name *Cill-Dara*, meaning the "Church of the Oak." Kildare was a famous pagan sanctuary where a sacred fire burned for centuries into the Christian era. In a clear act of assimilation, the tradition of 19 virgins keeping the fire alive carried on until 1220, when the archbishop of Dublin finally had it ordered extinguished. In 1993, the flame was re-lit and has been burning ever since. Brigid's Fire House is located in the churchyard of Saint Brigid's Cathedral in the center of Kildare. Inside the cathedral there is a Sheela-na-Gig sculpture (a female figure displaying her vagina) on the 16th century tomb of Bishop Wellesley. The pagan-influenced "sheela" has her legs parted and her pubic hair showing.

Brigid's Well, also called Tobar Bride, is about a mile away from the fire sanctuary. Many feel the site represents both the Catholic saint and the pagan goddess. The holy site contains a statue of Saint Brigid (sometimes spelled Brigitte) in her nun's regalia alongside a natural well of remedial waters. Since Neolithic times, the water of certain wells was known for their ability to heal. Other examples are Clonegal in Ireland and Chartres in France. These wells, now devoted to the Virgin Mary, continue to have a miraculous reputation. Certain sacred wells are believed to help women become fertile or cure the sick.

> Kildare was a renowned pagan site before
> being associated with Saint Brigid.

Christianity was slow to be accepted in Druidic Ireland, taking several centuries before the transition was complete. Even with the wane of paganism in Ireland, many practices were eagerly assimilated. Christianity effectively superimposed itself on Celtic tradition as celebrations of pagan importance became associated with Christian worship. A good example is Imbolg on February 1st, a date very sacred to the Druids. This springtime pagan festival eventually became replaced by Saint Brigid's feast day.

Examining the life of Saint Brigid is not so easy, since many questions arise of exactly who she was and what time period she came from. Brigid (meaning the "exalted one") was the name of a pagan goddess long before Christianity arrived. The Celts regarded her as a powerful female deity, who imparted upon followers her enhanced learning abilities, along with artistic and poetic skills. She could be called upon for assistance in childbirth or healing. The pagan Brigid had power

▲ Saint Brigid has at least eight sacred wells devoted to her throughout Ireland, but none are more popular than her shrine at Kildare.

over the animal kingdom as well. Thus, the name Brigid was popular among girls at the time of Christianity's arrival. To further complicate matters there are said to be no less than 15 saints in Ireland with the name of Brigid!

The Brigid who became the Abbess of a nunnery at Kildare is the popular saint commonly worshipped today. However, it should be noted that others with the same name likely preceded her at Kildare. The commonly told story of her life speaks of a girl who was born to a pagan Irish king named Dubhtach. She was baptized and began living with other Christian nuns. Around 480 she founded a Christian double monastery (nuns and monks) at Kildare by either converting the Druidic sanctuary or by building a new site on top of the old, depending on which story is consulted. The attributes of the pagan Brigid were readily perceived in the saint, who established a convent at Kildare. The monastery she founded featured a school of art, where the Book of Kildare, a famous illuminated manuscript, was created. By the time of Saint Brigid's death, claimed to be on February 1st 525 CE, Kildare had become an important center of learning. She is buried at Downpatrick with Saint Patrick, whom she co-shares the title of Ireland's patron saint.

Getting to Kildare

Kildare is located 32 miles (51 km) southwest of Dublin and easily accessible by train, bus, or private car. If driving, take the N7 Dublin-Limerick Road to the center of the town of Kildare, where the Saint Brigid Cathedral is located.

Brigid's Well can be found one mile (1.6 km) south of Kildare. Take the signs out of town toward the Japanese Gardens and turn about 900 feet (270 m) before you reach the Gardens. There will be a sign to direct motorists toward the "Tobar Bride" down a small road to the right. About 300 feet (90 m) further will be another sign that points visitors to the well.

Loughcrew

The cluster of megalithic mounds in eastern Ireland, known as Loughcrew (or *Sliabh na Cailli*), is one of the oldest sacred places in Europe. The largest of the megalithic mounds (cairns) at Loughcrew contain narrow passages, with small chambers, under hills of stones and dirt. Some cairns have been dismantled with only the internal megalithic stones remaining. The site is spread out over a ridge of hills extending for several miles. The Loughcrew cairns, some over 5,000 years old, may represent the oldest calendar ever devised and, perhaps, could be the world's oldest existing dwellings.

The most famous Loughcrew monument is "Cairn T," where a beam of light shines into the rear chamber at sunrise on the March and September equinox days. The wonderfully decorated backstone is covered with carved geometric patterns that are illuminated on the spring and autumnal equinoxes. Cairn T, or Hag's Cairn, is of similar design to Newgrange. Traditionally described as a passage tomb, archaeoastronomers demonstrate that Cairn T served as an ancient calendar with an astronomical purpose.

Another solar alignment can be found at Cairn U, with its passage aligned to the cross-quarter days on November 8th and February 4th. These dates are significant because they mark the beginning and end of the shortest daylight quarter of the year. Cross-quarter days fall exactly between the solstices and equinoxes.

Cairn U has a circumference of 160 feet (48.2 m) and a passage oriented to 108 degrees (18 degrees south of east). The highly decorated, but exposed, surface of stone 14 at Cairn U is quite remarkable. It can be found beside Cairn T at the summit of Carnbane East at Loughcrew. The plan of the passage and chamber of Cairn U is similar to that of Cairn L, which is also aligned to the cross-quarter days denoting the winter season. The passage of Cairn L is narrow, opens up to what appears to be six chambers, and is encircled by 42 massive kerbstones. Further attesting to the calendar value of Loughcrew is Cairn S, aligned to the cross-quarter days of May 6th and August 8th — the dates signifying the summer quarter.

The numerous aligned chamber mounds and
spiral carvings at Loughcrew attest to its
mystical value.

There are over 30 chambered cairns on the Loughcrew range of hills. The cairns are probably older than Newgrange, dating to between 3500 and 3300 BCE. The hills, known collectively as *Sliabh na Caillighe* or "Mountain of the Witch," "Hill of the Hag," or "The Storied Hills," are individually called Carnbane West, Carnbane East, and Patrickstown. The word *Carnbane* means the "white cairn," perhaps alluding to the quartzite stones used. All these hills contain legends of giants, witches, heroes, and fairy women. The highest of these peaks is over 900 feet (290 m) above sea level and is also the highest point in Meath, the middle kingdom. The hills form a protective ring overlooking the Boyne Valley, dropping off

▲ Loughcrew features mysterious carvings, intact cairns, dismantled cairns, kerbstones, and solar alignments.

to the southeast, and the lakes and lowlands of County Cavan on the other side. The Boyne Valley and its tributaries feature more megalithic architecture than any other waterway region in Ireland.

Loughcrew is also renowned for the prolific amount of stone carvings within the cairns. Some Loughcrew carved stones contain astronomical symbolism in the form of giant spirals, while other carvings feature geometric and abstract patterns. Most of these glyphs seem completely random, suggesting that they may be engravings of a personal testament. The glyphs have been associated with rituals where an initiate would pass through a vortex, perhaps a passage from the natural to the supernatural realm. There are no less than 27 individually decorated stones inside of Cairn T. The "Hag's Chair" carved boulder, outside of Cairn T, has also been associated with elaborate rituals.

One of the most famous court cairns in Ireland is called *Slieve na Caillighe,* or the "Hill of the Witches." This particular court cairn is still surrounded by an earthen bank. There are seven chambers inside, which take the form of small "alcoves" around the walls. Several of the large upright stones, which divide the chambers, have carved spirals and waveforms upon them, as do the two upright stones flanking the entrance to the cairn.

Getting to Loughcrew

The Loughcrew cairns are located 25 miles (40 km) from Newgrange, situated on three hill summits near the town of Oldcastle, County Meath. Dublin is 53 miles (85 km) southeast of Loughcrew. From Kells, take the R163 to Oldcastle. Along this route look for a sign on the right to the Loughcrew cairns, 10.8 miles (17.4 km) from Kells. Loughcrew is ideal to visit in the spring, when the wildflowers emerge amidst the moss-covered boulders.

megalithic ritual sites

The word *megalith* derives from the Greek word meaning "great stone." Ireland contains a vast number of megalithic monuments that were used in ancient times as ritual areas. There are about 1,200 megalithic structures scattered around the 32 counties of Ireland. Megalithic ritual sites include dolmens (single large chambers), crannogs (artificial islands), barrows (passage tombs), clochans (beehive huts), cairns (mound of stones covering a dolmen), court cairns (gallery with side chambers), aligned standing stones, and stone circles. Most of all Ireland's megalithic ritual sites were created over the last 3,500 to 5,000 years during the Neolithic Era. In popular folklore, the megaliths were either the work of mythical giants, rumored altars of the Druids, or hidden entrances to the Otherworld of the Tuatha Dé Danann.

The purpose of menhirs (standing stones) is as enigmatic as that of the stone circles. Some suggest that they may have marked burials sites, while others explain them as markers along prehistoric trackways. One of the most impressive standing stones in Ireland is called Ballycrovane. This massive stone rises an impressive 17 feet (5.2 m) in height and appears more like a piece of modern sculpture than a megalithic marker. The Ballycrovane standing stone was perhaps erected to mark one of the westernmost points of Ireland.

▲ The Ballybrack dolmen as drawn by Henry O'Neill in 1851.

The Beaghmore Stone Circles in Northern Ireland is a massive site of megalithic cairns, earthworks, and alignment stones. Although relatively unknown, Beaghmore has been called one of the greatest of all ancient ritual sites in Ireland, containing three pairs of stone circles, all varying in size. Each stone circle pair has a cairn between or nearby them. Several rows of standing stones, outside the circles, are described as alignments. Four of the stone rows point to the position of the summer solstice sunrise as it would have been viewed on the horizon 3,000 years ago. Although dating from the early Bronze Age, it appears that Beaghmore was built upon a much older Neolithic ritual site. A seventh stone circle stands alone and is called the "Dragon's

▲ Creevykeel in County Sligo is one of the finest preserved court cairns in Ireland. Three side chambers connect to the main chamber.

Teeth," because it contains 884 small stones bristling across its surface. Legend has it that the stone circles denote the constellations of Ophiuchus and Serpens Caput, which were the special marks of Merlin the Magician (also called Aesculapius), who supposedly mapped out the megalithic system of geodetic astronomy for the world.

Also in Ulster Province in Northern Ireland is the stone circle called Beltany. Located on the leveled summit of Tops Hill, Beltany is associated with the beginning of summer, a time of ritual fires, sacrifices and celebrations of abundance. The name suggests that the pagan festival of Beltane was celebrated at Beltany. The huge circle is 145 feet (44.2 m) in diameter and still contains 64 stones. Originally there were at least 80. The circle at Beltany has all the characteristics of once being an enormous passage cairn. Another belief is that Beltany is a transitional ring between late passage-tombs and early stone circles. The style is similar to the circles at Carrowmore.

Carrowmore is the largest megalithic complex in Ireland and, quite possibly, one of the oldest. It covers an area about 1.5 square miles (2.4 sq. km) and features dozens of dolmens, 30 passage cairns, and three known free-standing stone circles. Similar to Beltany, Carrowmore may be a transitional site where the heavy curbstones of the cairns eventually evolved into true stone circles. Since 1800, at least 24 passage cairns have been destroyed at Carrowmore due to quarrying.

> Although most have been destroyed over the
> ages, almost all of the remaining passage
> cairns have known equinoctial sunrise and
> solstice alignments.

▲ Artist James Moore drew this dolmen in 1849.

The megalithic ritual sites were also the place for court cairns. A court cairn is a prehistoric mound which has several chambers leading off from a central corridor. Similar to a passage cairn, it would at one time have been covered with megalithic stones, rubble, and earth over the large slabs. Almost all court cairns have lost their earth covering, so the elaborate chambers can clearly be seen. In most cases, the entrance arch supported a large stone lintel. In front of the arch was a small courtyard with a floor of rough flagstones and two or more sheltering monoliths. There are over 350 known court cairns in the whole of Ireland, but only five remain in the south.

Creevykeel is among the most impressive court cairns in Ireland, while also one of the few that has been thoroughly restored. Located within a wedge-shaped cairn, this full circular court was originally about 200 feet (61 m) long and had a paved floor. At the eastern end is the main entrance, through a small passage, which leads into an oval forecourt. It is likely Creevykeel was built in more than one phase. Four cremations have been found in shallow pits, leading many to call this particular cairn a court tomb. Some items found in Creevykeel (clay balls for example) hint that court cairns are often slightly older than passage cairns. Other grave goods found include Neolithic pottery, a stone bead, leaf-shaped flint arrowheads, hollow scrapers, and polished stone axe heads. Creevykeel is one of the finest megalith ritual sites in all of Ireland, and also one of the oldest.

Getting to megalithic ritual sites

The Beaghmore complex of stone circles is located 10.8 miles (18 km) northwest of Cookstown on the A505 west towards Omagh in Tyrone County. The Beltany stone circle is located 2 miles (3.6 km) south of the village of Raphoe, one of the few in the northwestern Ireland county of Donegal. Carrowmore is located 2 miles (3.6 km) southwest of Sligo town in Connacht province. Creevykeel can be found just off the Sligo-Bundoran road 1.5 miles (2.4 km) northeast of Cliffony. The richest collection of prehistoric ritual sites can be found in County Cork, particularly in the region around Macroom. The Drombeg Stone Circle is 17 standing stones near Clonakilty, County Cork. About 600 feet (180 m) southeast of the coastguard station at Ballycrovane's harbor, on the Beara Peninsula, lies this impressive Ballycrovane standing stone. About two miles outside of Oldcastle are the "Speaking Stones" — two massive upright slabs that once served as an oracle site in ancient times. Once in the general area of the megalith, it is advisable to ask a local for directions or look for the small signs. The locals will usually be happy to tell you exactly where to find any monument in question.

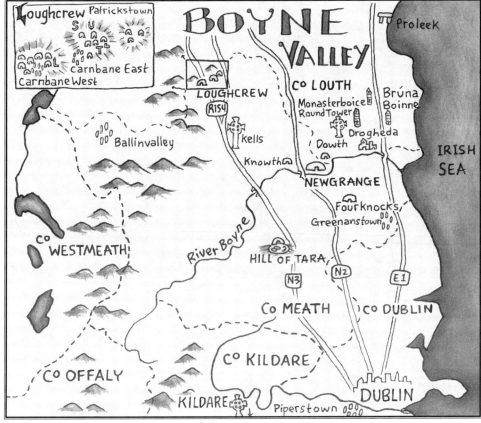

Newgrange

In the verdant green Boyne Valley are three huge earth mounds — the most impressive is called Newgrange. The two other nearby mounds are named Knowth and Dowth. All three are said by dowsers to intersect at key "telluric energy" points, as well as being situated in perfect alignment with seasonal points of solar movements. Newgrange and the other megaliths in the valley were created some 5,000 years ago by little-known kinsmen known as the Beaker People. Based on their distinctive spiral carving motifs it appears as if the Beaker People built in the Boyne Valley, but nowhere else in Ireland. To add further mystery, the Beaker People also constructed monuments hundreds of miles away on the Mediterranean islands of Malta and Gozo. No direct traces of these people have been found anywhere else in the world.

Surrounding the exterior of the Newgrange mound are images of spirals, chevrons, and other symbolic forms carved on the huge stones. There are a total of 97 curbstones lying on their sides around the mound, with the carved patterns also appearing inside the passage. The carvings are believed to be recordings of astronomical and cosmological observations. The internal chamber has a funnel-

▲ The entrance stone at Newgrange features multiple spiral and lozenge carvings.

shaped roof and is externally connected by a long passageway. Whatever rituals or activities the Beaker People may have performed in this internal chamber remain a mystery. The mound covering the internal passage is more than 40 feet (12 m) in height and covers an acre (.4 hectare) of ground. The egg-shaped mound is called a tumulus, rising from the meadow and surrounded by a stone curbing. Over 20,000 cantaloupe-size stones were brought in from 75 miles (120 km) away to create the bulk of the tumulus. The entrance to Newgrange is marked by the elaborately carved Threshold Stone, featuring carved spirals framed by concentric circles and diamond shapes. The outside construction of Newgrange was once surrounded by 38 enormous pillars, but only 12 survive.

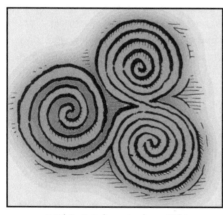

▲ This triple spiral motif is illuminated on the days around the Winter Solstice.

> The site of Newgrange could be the largest and oldest sundial in the world.

Conventional archeologists regard the mounds in Boyne Valley as part of a prehistoric cemetery complex, largely because charred human remains were found deep inside their chambered passageways. The Boyne Valley passage chambers are fine examples of megalithic construction, but Newgrange is more than just a burial tomb. On the days near

76

the winter solstice, December 21st, the entrance passage exactly aligns with the rising sun, illuminating a triple spiral relief sculpture in the farthest recess of the chamber. It was clearly built to mark the final turning point in the sun's cycle, making Newgrange an efficient and accurate sundial.

Getting to Newgrange

Newgrange is located in the Boyne Valley, seven miles (11 km) south of the picturesque Irish seaport town Drogheda, which has a train station and local bus service directly to Newgrange. The site is well-marked along the main N1 Belfast road, if driving by car. The Knowth and Dowth mounds are both found on the nearby road to Slane. All can be visited quite easily on a day trip from Dublin, which is located 28 miles (45 km) due south.

There were nearly 28,000 applications on hand at the Visitor's Center to be inside the chamber of Newgrange for the 2006 Winter Solstice. Only a total of 50 people win the randomly drawn lottery every year to witness the spectacular event. 10 people are allowed inside each of the 5 mornings when the chamber is illuminated around the mid point.

round towers

While over a hundred round towers remain standing, the original number must have been much higher in the early history of Ireland. The ancient *Chronicler Annuals* reports that no less than 75 fell in the great Irish earthquake of 448 CE. Most stand between 66 feet (20 m) and 112 feet (34 m) in height. The doorways are rarely located at ground level, but at a distance off the ground, so ladders or steps would be required for entrance. Windows are mostly featured at the top of the towers and usually face towards the four cardinal compass points. While the func-tion of the round towers remain a topic of heated discussion, it is clear that the builders featured the visibility of the towers into their design. They are prominently featured on the landscape and would have been a beacon to either friend or foe alike.

▲ The round tower at the Rock of Cashel predates all other buildings in the complex.

TIMAHOE,
CLONDALKIN, AND
DEVENISH ROUND
TOWERS

▲ Irish tradition maintains that the round towers were erected by the Tuatha Dé Danann in pre-Christian times.

Throughout Ireland, in all four provinces of Ulster, Leinster, Munster, and Connacht, are the strange round towers that, some believe, come from a pre-Christian origin. Usually the round towers are accompanied by a fully intact, or crumbled, megalithic stone cross. It has generally been assumed that the crosses and towers had been built several hundred years after Christ by the early missionaries. Some think they were built much earlier, while others believe much later. The truth is no one has any proof when the towers were built, why they were built, or by whom.

> The round towers are one of Ireland's greatest mysteries. No one knows for certain who, when, how or why they were constructed.

Irish tradition holds that the towers were built by the Tuatha Dé Danann, a Bronze Age clan that once ruled over Ireland. The Tuatha Dé Danann were Druids with magical powers who introduced four major gifts to Ireland. Those items were: the Stone of Destiny at Tara; the Spear of Lugh, which would always ensure victory; the Sword of Nuadha, from which no one could escape; and the Cauldron of the Daghdha, from which no one would go away unsatisfied. The linking of the Tuatha Dé Danann to the towers is important because the great

▲ Round towers can often be found near old Celtic crosses. Both have been romanticized by artists and writers for many centuries.

battle, in which they won control of Ireland, was fought in a place called the "Field of the Towers."

Establishing a Christian origin is more problematic. Christian emblems, found only in three out of 63 fully intact round towers, have been regarded as modern alterations. The silence about the towers in Irish hagiography (writings of the saints), would seem to indicate a non-Christian origin, as early monk authors were forbidden to reference anything pagan. In almost all cases, the round towers stand alone. It makes little sense to assume they were built for defensive purposes, since they provided little storage space and could have been easily captured by an enemy. It is known that early Irish churches, made of wood and crudely cut stone, were often built adjacent to the round towers. Saint Patrick and his followers almost always selected the sacred sites of paganism to build their early churches. Those earliest churches have long turned to rubble while the expertly built round towers remain.

Round tower researcher Henry O'Brien thinks the towers were "specifically constructed with the twofold purpose of worshipping the sun and moon." Other researchers have variously described them as fire-towers, belfries, watch towers, granaries, sepulchers, forts, hermit dwellings, purgatorial pillars, phallic objects of worship, astronomical marks, depositories of Buddhist relics, Baal fireplaces, observatories, sanctuaries of the sacred fire, Freemason lodges, and many other possible uses. They were pagan and Christian, built long before Christ, or a thousand years after. A new theory demonstrates that the towers were built as a sort of agricultural antennae for helping to energize the soil. The evidence for this theory is in the paramagnetic stones, such as mica schist, used in the round tower construction. The paramagnetic stones are known to help channel natural earth energies into the soil and energize it for greater fertility. Since many contained dirt in the lower portions, each tower became a resonant cavity supposedly tuned by the soil inside.

Getting to the round towers of Ireland

One of the most ornate round towers can be found on Devenish Island in Lower Lough Erne in the Province of Ulster. Ferries cross to the island from a jetty 2 miles (3.2 km) north of Enniskillen on the A32 road. The Kilree Monastic Site features a round tower and high cross. The site is located 1.5 miles (2.3 km) south

80

of Kells in Leinster Province. The famous Rock of Cashel, in the Province of Munster, houses a cluster of ecclesiastical buildings, including a well-preserved round tower standing 92 feet (27 m) tall. Also in Munster is the Ardmore Round Tower located 5 miles (8 km) east of Youghal, well-signed from the N25. In the Province of Connacht is the round tower at Kilmacduagh Cathedral, located about 3 miles (5 km) southwest of Gort on the R460 to Corrofin. At 112 feet (34 m) in height, Kilmacduagh is the tallest round tower in Ireland.

Skellig Michael

In the year 550 CE, a boatload of 50 Christian scholars from France arrived at Cork. They wandered about the country looking for a secure place to settle from the marauding barbarians of mainland Europe. Fearing even the pagans of Ireland, the group chose one of the most inaccessible locations in Europe — a cluster of steep rock outcroppings, barely visible from the southwestern coast of Ireland. The islands feature multiple caverns and fissures caused by geological faults. Here the monks sheltered in the early years before developing a basic monastery on the largest island. Their settlement was dedicated to Saint Michael, the saint of uncompromising truth symbolized by the sword, but also the saint who carries worthy souls to heaven. Little did the monks know that for almost 100 years Western Christianity survived by being isolated in locations like Skellig Michael. The monks, tenaciously clinging to the island devoted to Saint Michael, incubated Christianity while the rest of Europe deteriorated into the Dark Ages.

▲ It is nothing short of remarkable that a band of monks were able to eek out an existence for over 900 years on the barren Skellig Michael. This is neighboring Little Skellig where the monks would go to collect bird eggs.

The sacred hermitage of Skellig Michael was a monastery of early Christian monks with strong Celtic ties.

The very modest living conditions at the monastery illustrate the ascetic lifestyle practiced by the early Irish Christians. The monks lived in stone "beehive" huts, or *clochans*, perched above nearly vertical cliff walls. Centered near the six beehive huts and two small oratories is a tall Celtic cross. The monastery was significantly expanded with a new chapel added around 1000 CE. Three known wells provided drinking water, but not enough to eek out a farming lifestyle. Without support from the mainland, Skellig Michael was doomed. Wind erosion has always made it a challenge to grow food on the western islands of Ireland. Even the extensive mosaic of low walls on the Aran Islands in Galway is barely enough to preserve the topsoil, forcing western Ireland farmers to mix sand and algae with their soil. Over 7,000 miles (12,000 km) of walls extend over the windswept western Irish islands. The monks could only subsist on fish, shellfish, seal meat, along with various birds and their eggs. There is evidence of some herding and farming, but it would have been very difficult due to the rocky conditions.

▲ The Skellig Michael monastery features two small oratories, six "beehive" chambers, and a giant stone cross.

Starting in the 1500s, Skellig Michael became a popular destination for annual pilgrimages, but by then had no permanent residents. As if the monastery is not remote enough, there is a higher spot on the south peak called the "Needle's Eye." This was the terminus to the medieval pilgrims. Today the Needle's Eye is nearly inaccessible unless climbing gear is used.

The monastery on Skellig Michael was sacked by a Viking raid in 823, but basically survived other attacks because it was so remote. The *Annals of Innisfallen* record the event in the year 823: "Skellig was plundered by the heathen and Etgal was carried off and he died of hunger at their hands." In an ironic twist of historic fate a Skellig monk was responsible for baptizing King Olaf Trygvasson, who would later become king of Norway. Both he and his son Olaf II Haraldsson fought against pagan Vikings in converting Scandinavia to Christianity. Both were killed in battle and Olav II would go on to become the patron saint of Norway.

Many centuries later, the monastery went full circle. Rather than hiding from barbarians, it was the Catholic Church that finally sealed the fate of Skellig Michael. The Church suppressed its religious festivals in the 13th century, not long after the small religious colony was abandoned. There was a legend of an underground tunnel rediscovered and then blocked again by the departing monks. For many centuries the island was completely abandoned. In 1826, a lighthouse was built on Skellig Michael. In 1986, some restoration work was done and an official tourist bureau, associated with the island, was established. Restrictions have recently been imposed on tourist access, in the belief that tourist numbers were causing a worrying degree of damage and erosion to the site.

Getting to Skellig Michael

Officially abandoned, the small pinnacle of rock called Skellig Michael lies 18 miles (29 km) off the southwestern coast of Ireland, rising 700 feet (210 m) out of the sea. Since the extreme remoteness of Skellig Michael has until recently discouraged visitors, the site is exceptionally well-preserved. Private boats can be hired from the port towns of Ballinskelligs and Portmagee, but only during periods of clement weather, usually during the summer months.

FRANCE

AND THE LOW COUNTRIES

The real voyage of discovery consists not in seeking new landscapes, but in having new eyes. *—Marcel Proust*

SINCE PREHISTORIC TIMES, France and the Low Countries (Belgium, Luxembourg, and the Netherlands) were located at primary crossroads of trade, migration, and invasion. Over the centuries four basic European ethnic stocks blended into the people of France and the Low Countries. These traditional people were the Celts (Gallic and Breton), Latin (Roman related), Aquitanian (Basque related), and Germanic (Franks, Visigoths, Burgundians, and the Vikings). Besides these "historic" populations, new groupings of people have migrated to France and the Low Countries since the 19th century. The intermixing of people now includes the Poles, Armenians, Jews from Eastern Europe, Arabs from the Middle East, Muslims from North Africa, Black Africans, and the Chinese to name only the most prominent. It is currently estimated that about 40% of the French population is descendent from these latter waves of migrations, making France — and slightly to a lesser degree the Netherlands — among the most ethnically diverse countries of Europe.

The Low Countries, the historical region of *de Nederlanden*, are the countries on low-lying land around the delta of the rivers Rhine, Schelde, and Maas. The Low Countries were host to the first thriving northern towns, built from scratch rather than developed from older Roman cities. All of these emerging cities were characterized by being dependent on trade and manufacturing, and supporting the free flow of goods and craftsmen. Of particular importance for the emerging cities was the manufacture and trade of woolen cloth, Europe's first industry. The emergence of these new commerce centers helped usher in the 12th century reawakening of Europe.

BELGIUM

The tiny country Belgium has direct roots with neighboring France and, to a lesser degree, with the Netherlands and Germany. Belgium is one of the most densely populated countries in the world with 10.5 million inhabitants in an area slightly larger than Maryland. About 6.5 million Belgians are Flemish, 4 million consider themselves Walloons (French speakers), 65,000 speak German primarily, and all the rest are immigrants who speak foreign languages. Nearly every Belgian citizen is fluent in French, spoken primarily in the southern Wallonia region. Flemish is spoken in the Flanders region of northern Belgium, but largely ignored in Wallonia. Flemish is essentially Dutch, but with a slight difference to the way Dutch is spoken in Holland. For the Belgian elite, French was the adopted language of the nobility. The capital, Brussels, is officially bilingual. Much of its modern religious history was influenced by French Catholicism, yet Belgium is the meeting point of the Catholic and Protestant religions, along with the Romantic and Germanic languages. King Charles V of Spain was born in Gent, a wealthy city in Flanders. When he ascended the Spanish throne in 1516, Charles V was regarded as the only emperor to rule the known world, including all of the Americas newly annexed by the conquistadors.

Bruges

The magnificent old section of Bruges is one of Europe's best preserved examples of an intact medieval Gothic city. Sometimes referred to as the "Venice of the North," Bruges has many waterways intersecting the city. As one of the first commercial capitals of Europe, Bruges developed worldwide cultural and economic links and became fabulously wealthy through trade, then went into a prolonged recession when its port accumulated excessive silt. Commerce moved to other cities, craftsmen left, and within a few hundred years of being founded, Bruges became a virtual medieval time capsule.

The first stock exchange was created by Bruges merchants, who used the term *Bourse*. The word is named after Van der Burse, a wealthy merchant who, with others in 1309, institution-alized the "Bruges Bourse." The idea spread quickly around the Flanders region. In less than a decade Bourses opened in Gent and Amsterdam, then around the world.

Bruges was quite renowned in the Middle Ages for hosting an event that began with the returning Belgian crusaders. The procession of the Holy Blood in Bruges is a famous folk festival, based on celebrations of Christ's ascension and collected blood thought to be Christ's

▲ The water canals bisecting Bruges add an ethereal charm, but when the city was founded there were many more, now filled in with dirt.

own. This annual religious event takes place on Ascension Day, always the 40th day after Easter. The parade is made even more important because the Bishop carries a shrine said to hold the Holy Blood brought from the second crusade. Mentioned in 13th century charters, the procession became outlawed following the Reformation (1578 – 1584), and during the French Revolution (1796 – 1819), but was quickly reinstated when time permitted. Today as yesterday, residents dress in elaborate costumes to accompany the shrine through the streets of Bruges.

> The Ascension Day folk festival attracts thousands of devoted pilgrims and townspeople, making the procession the most important event on the Bruges' cultural calendar.

A golden shrine containing the Relic of the Holy Blood is on the first floor of the Chapel of the Holy Blood, built around 1300, but remodeled many times over the centuries. The relic allegedly holds the blood of Christ, yet there is no mention in the Bible that any of Christ's blood was collected after his death. According to recent investigations, the bottle containing the blood was made in the 11th or 12th centuries. It is nearly certain that the bottle was made in the area of Constantinople (now Istanbul, Turkey) and the original design was intended to contain perfume. The relic was brought to Bruges from the Holy Land after the second crusade in the 12th century by the Count of Flanders. It soon became the totem of the city, and oaths of loyalty were sworn before it. The bottle has never been opened since its arrival in Bruges.

The relic is the centerpiece of a larger parade featuring scenes from the Old and New Testaments. The Ascension Day procession can attract up to 100,000 spectators, while more than 3,000 people participate in the spectacle. Many Catholic bishops, priests, and nuns from all over the world come to celebrate this day. When the Holy Blood passes by, everybody stands and becomes silent in reverence. Before the most sacred relic in Belgium passes by the spectators, a parade of scenes from the Bible enlivens the procession. Choirs, actors, trumpeters, dance groups, horse-drawn floats, and animals (ranging from geese to camels) pass by the spectators in a couple of hours. Ascension Day is also known as *Brugges Schoonste Dag*, or "The Most Beautiful Day in Bruges."

Getting to Bruges

The historic old city of Bruges was listed in 2000 as a UNESCO World Heritage Site. Because of its celebrated importance, the city of Bruges is easily accessed from all directions in northern Belgium. The Bruges train station is just a 10 minutes' walk from the city center. A bus leaves for the center every 10 minutes. Some maps also spell the city name as "Brugge."

FRANCE

In medieval times, France was a strategic intersection for early commerce and Christian pilgrimages. Middle Age pilgrims started carving out a network of new roads in France leading to religious destinations. Most were known as the Compostela Routes, so named because they all headed to Santiago de Compostela, Spain, where the body of Saint James (apostle and cousin of Christ) was reputedly buried. Like Hindus venturing to the Ganges River, medieval Christians seeking repentance would travel to either Rome or Santiago. Along these French pilgrimage routes rose newly-constructed cathedrals and bustling cities. The first travel guide for Europe was Aimery Picaud's *Guide du Pelerin,* a book on good and bad places along the various pilgrimage routes.

Avignon

The oldest section of Avignon commands a strategic location in the Rhône Valley, owing its establishment to a natural spur of stone called the Doms Rock (*le Rocher les Doms*). The rocky outcrop at the north end of town would have made any settlement easy to defend because of its fortification value, with strategic sightings overlooking the Rhône River. The town held significant religious status from ancient times. It was almost certainly a Celtic *oppidum*, or "hill fort." During the Roman Empire, the city was a major center of Gallia Narbonensis, but very little of this period remains, except small sections of the Roman forum near Rue Molière. When the early Church began to establish itself in France, Avignon led the way by hosting the seat of a bishop as early as 70 CE. Located strategically for the movement of commerce and culture, the city became fabulously wealthy, but also exposed Avignon to attack by land, river, and sea. It was badly damaged by the barbarian invasions of the 5th century, and ransacked on several other occasions.

The city blossomed architecturally and spiritually with the arrival of the Popes in the 14th century. For this period Avignon became a second Rome. Its university was founded by Pope Boniface VIII in 1303, and became famed as a seat of legal studies. In 1309, at the urging of the French king, the city was chosen by the newly elected French Pope Clement V as his residence. In 1348, the entire city was purchased from the Countess of Provence by Pope Clement VI. Seven Popes in total

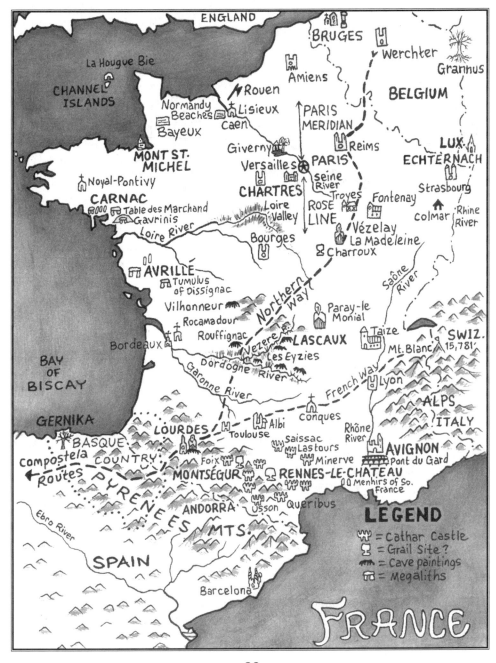

▲ The brooding Palace of the Popes dominates the old city center of Avignon.

ruled while Avignon was the seat of the papacy.

The French Papal Period from 1309 – 1377 was also called the "Babylonian Captivity," in reference to the Israelites' enslavement in the Old Testament. Not only did the Avignon papacy seem to be stolen, but the city became infamously corrupt, similar to the portrayal of Babylon in biblical times. The poet Petrarch condemned the city's corruption, contributing to the papacy's removal to Rome. The return prompted a schism that created twin Popes. The French antipopes Clement VII and Benedict XIII continued to reside at Avignon. Clement VII lived there during his entire pontificate (1378 – 1394), but Benedict XIII was forced to flee to Aragon in 1403, ending any French claim to the papacy. After the embarrassment of moving the Popes back to Rome had faded from memory, Avignon once again flourished in the 17th and 18th centuries with the enrichment of art being produced and collected. The entire city remained papal property until the French Revolution in 1792, when ownership of most religious buildings in France reverted to the state.

> For 68 years Avignon was the "Franco Vaticano," or French Vatican. The Palais des Papes is the largest surviving medieval Gothic palace in Europe.

Construction was planned on a massive scale for the Palace of the Popes, with enough living space to accommodate 500 people in the administrative wing, along with ample quarters for the Pope and his entourage. Almost immediately following the acquisition of Avignon as papal territory, a series of walls was constructed around the city. They were not particularly effective barriers, so instead the Popes relied on the immensely strong fortifications of their palace. This lofty Gothic building, with walls 17-18 feet (6 m) thick, was built from 1335-1364 on the Doms Rock, where many other strategic buildings had once stood. The favorable location made the Palace of the Popes all but impregnable to attack. After being expropriated following the French Revolution, Napoleon ordered the palace to be used as barracks for his troops and their horses. Today, it is one of the most visited museums in France.

Getting to Avignon

Avignon is situated in southeastern France on the left bank of the Rhône River, about 360 miles (580 km) south of Paris, and 55 miles (85 km) northwest of Marseille. There is a train station in downtown Avignon, walking distance to the Palace of the Popes. The train network in France is excellent, and many cities throughout the country connect to Avignon.

Avrillé

In a bygone era there were hundreds of stone monuments around Avrillé, attesting to its prehistoric religious value. Many have been removed, either for superstitious reasons or as a source of readily quarried stones. In most cases, only the very largest dolmens and menhirs have survived the wonton destruction. Sometimes their remote location saved them from being dismantled. In "the Country of the Giants," as Avrillé is called, about half of the monuments are accessible. The other half are on private property and considered off-limits.

> The countryside surrounding the small village of Avrillé is called le Payes des Géants, or "the Country of the Giants." At least 60 megalithic monuments remain standing within a few square miles.

Derived from the Celtic and Breton languages, *men* translates as "stone," *dol* can be either "flat" or "plateau," and *hir* means "long." Thus a *dolmen* is a megalithic monument created by placing a large flat plate on top of several vertical stones, whereas a *menhir* is a large tall stone planted vertically into the ground. These megaliths can be counted in the thousands, located from Ireland to the Near East, with the highest concentration in southern Britain and

▲ Megalithic architecture can be found in all directions around Avrillé.

▲ The city center of Avrillé is built around several menhirs.

northwestern France. Their construction date has been placed around 6,000 years ago. The dolmens we see today are the inner-shell of what had once been a larger structure of un-mortared stones that have long since been removed. Unfortunately, many Neolithic struc-tures in Europe have been dismantled over the centuries as ready made building stone. Most of the dolmens that remain, particularly those in northwestern France and the Basque coast of Spain, have their main axis directed to the south-east to receive maxi-mal sunlight. The menhirs denote compass directions, celestial alignments, and also may be markers of earth energy. Geomancers describe menhirs as captors and transmitters of energy, operating like a sort of earth antennae. The menhirs may have been thought by their ancient builders to enhance fertility of mating couples who were within their perimeter.

The road signs around Avrillé direct drivers to parking areas and trails access-ing the open monuments. Bicycle riders and hikers can also access the megaliths, but a good route map should be acquired from the Avrillé Tourist Office before attempting to explore the area. At least seven of 17 dolmens are open, and at least 16 of over 40 menhirs can be visited. Sometimes closed menhirs can be seen in distant farm fields from dolmens that are open. Just within Avrillé village are five rows of aligned menhirs, somewhat similar to Carnac. Also like Carnac, the megalithic complex is 3 miles (5 km) uphill a gradual slope from the sea.

Getting to Avrillé

The small town of Avrillé is located along the D949 highway in the southwest-ern department of Vendeé, part of the Pays de la Loire region. Avrillé village is located about an equal distance between Les Sables D'Olonne 14 miles (23 km), and Luçon 15.5 miles (26 km), both of which contain the nearest train stations. The best way to visit the Avrillé megaliths is to hire a bicycle or rent a car since the monuments cover a vast area.

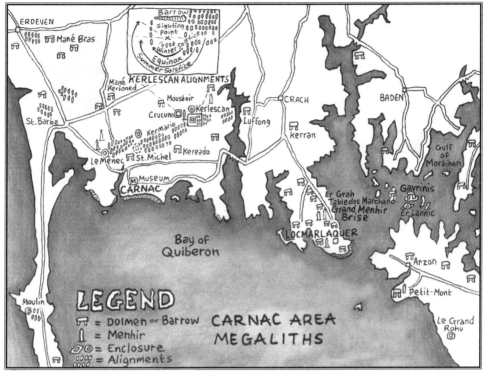

CARNAC AREA MEGALITHS

LEGEND

🏛 = Dolmen or Barrow
𝚰 = Menhir
◎ = Enclosure
ₒₒₒₒ = Alignments

Carnac

The world's largest concentration of megalithic standing stones cluster around a small coastal village named Carnac. Surrounding the region are henges (circular standing stone enclosures), stone alignments in square or arch form, and the famous menhirs (single upright stones) standing in long rows. The long avenues of stones, 2,934 in all, may have been part of an observatory to determine sun and moon alignments. Carnac reached its most complete development around the middle of the 2nd century BCE. In the greater Brittany region, there are several rectilinear or semicircular enclosures bounded by long rows of menhirs. With the exception of Er Lannic near Carnac, none of the stone alignments form a complete circle. It could be that many pieces have been removed over the centuries. Carnac was erected during the Stonehenge era — two impressive megalithic sites divided by the English Channel. The ancient culture in northwestern France had strong cultural ties with religious practices similar to those of megalithic builders on the British Isles.

The age of megalith building in northwestern France lasted from 4500 to 2500 BCE, and since then the stones have fostered much speculation about their origin. Local legend says that a marching Roman legion was cast to stone after a fugitive saint made the sign of the cross and faced down the mighty army. Another story associates the stones to a Celtic cattle cult that lasted into Christian times. In the Middle Ages, the stones were viewed as the work of demons, of wizards, or built by giants who walked the earth before the biblical flood. Many of the megaliths were destroyed or defaced by early Christians, but estimates predict that some 50,000 of them once stood in northern Europe. Currently less than 10,000 remain. Though many have been pillaged as ready-quarried stone, Carnac remains one of the best-preserved Neolithic ritual centers in Europe.

> The elaborate stone rows at Carnac form part of an impressive group of ritual monuments, the largest concentration of megaliths in the world.

The immediate region around Carnac is a diverse landscape of menhirs and monuments. The oldest of these, the famous Grand Menhir Brisé of Locmariaquer, which once stood 66 feet high (20 m) and weighed about 380 tons (344,660 kg), is the king of all menhirs. At one time it likely served as a sighting point in astronomical observations or an incoming ship beacon for the whole Carnac complex. Today, it lies on the ground cracked in four parts. The Kerlescan set of alignments radiate east from a square enclosure, with known alignments to the equinox and the winter and summer solstices. The Gavrinis chambered barrow is one of the most beautiful in the world and is also aligned to the midsummer solstice. The long tumulus features spiral and abstract line carvings. The Gavrinis mound likely predates the creation of the stone rows. The Ménec alignments near Carnac consist of no fewer than 11 nearly parallel

▲ It is still unclear why the long stone rows at Carnac were erected.

lines of menhirs extending more than 3,200 feet (950 m) between two fragmentary enclosures. The Ménec Lines, named for a nearby hamlet, consist of 1,099 individual menhirs. The expansive ritual center had four alignments and also included huge burial mounds. Carnac was likely a large outdoor worship center, but this is speculation because no altar stones have ever been found. The lines of the tallest stones produce astrological information, specifically pertaining to lunar movements.

The small town on the southern coast of Brittany has become a favored destination for New Agers. Dowsers report the stones of Carnac are charged with a discernible magnetic force. Experiments prove the area north of Carnac has a magnetic or electrical force that may have affected people in antiquity as precisely as it does today. Before they were fenced off in 1991, young brides and barren couples would come at night for fertility worship. They would dance around the stones naked, just as their ancestors did thousands of years before. New Agers come for the reported healing powers of the stones. As is common with indigenous religions worldwide, the mere touching of sacred stones is said to have the power to heal a sick person. Such are the ancient memories of festivals enacted to convey the protection of fertility gods — recreated then as now.

Getting to Carnac

Carnac and most of the great megaliths of France lie on the southwest Brittany coast facing the Gulf of Morbihan. The three main sites in this region are Carnac, Locmariaquer, and Gavrinis. Most travelers make their way to the French port cities of Quiberon, Vannes, or Lorient and take the bus or ride bicycles to the ruins from there. In the village of Carnac, there is an excellent Museum of Prehistory. At the alignments outside of town, there is a viewing platform of the fenced-off menhirs. Carnac is also popular with tourists for its mild climate and nice beaches.

Chartres

Most travelers to the Loire Valley, west of Paris, are headed for Chartres, a medieval town graced by a magnificent Gothic cathedral. The Chartres Cathedral ranks with Notre Dame, Amiens, and Reims as the finest examples of Gothic architecture in France. It is particularly noted for its exquisite stained-glass windows. The renowned windows, some 130 in all, are nearly all originals dating from the 12th and 13th centuries when the cathedral was constructed. The windows feature more than 5,000 figures depicting the lives of the saints and various biblical scenes. The radiating symmetries of the stained glass, as well as the light coming through the famous rose windows, are the true marvels of Chartres Cathedral. Also popular with travelers is the climb to the top of the north tower for a spectacular view of the surrounding area.

Chartres Cathedral and its location hold many unique distinctions. The structure spans the development of the Gothic style of architecture in France. The façade and right tower, completed around 1150 CE, shows the difference between the massive and heavy Romanesque style, alongside the lighter Gothic style on the left. The circular rose window, showing over the front door, is a perfect example of a Gothic motif. The builders of the cathedral were master monks who followed laws of sacred geometry, incorporating various ancient "cubits" of measurement. The hill position, where the cathedral stands, corresponds to major ley lines supposedly connecting Glastonbury, Stonehenge, and the Great Pyramids. It was built upon a sacred pagan mound with a grotto, known in antiquity as the "pregnant Virgin," which had first housed a Druid temple, only to be replaced by a Roman one. The geometry of Chartres Cathedral resembles a cross-shaped mandala, and is based upon the nine gates of the human body. The cathedral is unique in being virtually unaltered since its consecration in 1260.

> Chartres Cathedral is one of the finest examples of Gothic architecture in Europe and has more than its fair share of mysteries and wonders.

▲ The two spires of Chartres Cathedral feature two different architectural styles.

Legend speaks of the Knights Templar as recovering the lost language and treasure of King Solomon, and hiding it within Chartres Cathedral. The Templars were keepers of eternal wisdom dating back to Egypt. They were predecessors to the Freemasons. The secret society of Freemasonry is the oldest known existing organization in the world. The legend tells of nine French Knights Templar excavating Solomon's temple in Jerusalem around 1100 CE, returning with its engineering secrets, and placing the treasure under the stones of Chartres Cathedral. To some who believe in a lost language or "key" of Solomon, Chartres Cathedral is the "Rosetta Stone" for decoding the language. With the help of the brilliant French abbot Bernard de Clairvaux, the nine knights, directed by the Count of Champagne, formed the Knights Templar and assisted in the building of Chartres Cathedral upon their return from the Holy Land.

▲ The Orkney Islands contain more prehistoric sites per square mile than any other location in Europe.

▲ An ethereal golden glow blankets the store circle called the Ring of Brodgar in the Orkney Islands, located north of Scotland.

Photo courtesy of the Orkney Tourism Board

Photo courtesy of the Orkney Tourism Board

▲ Loughcrew, Ireland features over 30 chambered cairns across a range of three hills.

▲ Mysterious patterns and geometric designs cover the walls inside the Loughcrew chambered cairns.

▲ The cluster of tiny beehive chambers seemingly cling to the cliffs at Skellig Michael.

Photo courtesy of www.SacredSites.com

▲ Mount Olympus is Greece's highest peak, and the abode of the ancient's mythological gods.

Photo courtesy of www.SacredSites.com

▲ The most famous European Inquisition was against the Cathars of southern France. The crusade culminated in the final siege of Montségur, or "Safe Mountain," in 1244 CE.

Photo by Brad Olsen

▲ The immediate region around Carnac, France is a diverse landscape of menhirs and monuments. The prehistoric religious staging ground was constructed around the same time Avebury and Stonehenge were erected in southwestern England.

▲ The Grand Menhir Brisé of Locmariaquer, which once stood 66 feet high (20 m) and weighed about 380 tons (344,660 kg), is the king of all menhirs. Carnac also features intact dolmens and long rows of standing stones.

Photo by Brad Olsen

▲ "No Digging" for lost treasure is allowed at France's
mysterious Rennes-le-Chateau.

Photo by Brad Olsen

▲ The left tower of Chartres Cathedral in France is of
Gothic design, while the right tower was built in the
Romanesque style.

▲ Stonehenge is an ancient ruined temple on the upland turf of the Salisbury Plain in England.

▲ There are about 100 round towers scattered across Ireland, all expertly built, but of an unknown origin.

Photo by Mercedes Wind schmann, Kincsem Lovaspark Kft.

▲ Could the Attila Domb in Hungary be the most potent earth energy site in Europe?

Photo by Meho Macic, www.BosnianPyramid.com

▲ Could the "Pyramid of the Sun" in Bosnia's Visocica Valley be the first pyramid discovered in Europe?

Photo by Brad Olsen

▲ The Krakow Old City is the heart and soul of Poland.

Photo by Brad Olsen

▲ The view from Saint Peter's dome high above the Vatican City offers a full panorama of Rome.

Photo by Brad Olsen

▲ The ultra-sleek Shrine of Divine Mercy in Poland was built for the growing number of pilgrims who visit the convent of Sister Faustina.

Catholic tradition relates the story of Holy Roman emperor Charles the Bald giving the *Sancta Camisia*, or "Holy Veil" of the Virgin Mary, to the old church on the same site. The old church was replaced by Chartres Cathedral, but the Holy Veil remained and is still on display today. The veil is believed to be the same veil Mary wore when she gave birth to Jesus. The attraction of the veil made Chartres one of the major pilgrimage sites in Europe during medieval times. The veil is in a chapel near the choir.

Getting to Chartres

The small city of Chartres is located about 60 miles (97 km) southwest of Paris, and 20 miles (35 km) from the famous Palace of Versailles. Apart from the Cathedral, Chartres is a small and somewhat undistinguished town. Most travelers who come to Chartres arrive from Paris, which is about an hour away by train or bus. The cathedral dominates the oldest center of town and is easy to find.

caves of the Dordogne region·

The valleys of the Dordogne and Vézère Rivers comprise a picturesque region in central France sprinkled with deep caves and subterranean streams. When human skeletons were unearthed in 1868 from inside some of the caves, what soon followed was a windfall of archaeological evidence from the Paleolithic Era. Most remarkable were the paintings that adorned the caves, not only because of their age, but also for their exquisite coloring and the skill with which they were drawn. A myriad of Stone Age tools, weapons, arrowheads, and bone carvings have also been discovered in the caves.

The most famous of all the Dordogne Valley caves is Lascaux. Painted 17,000 years ago during the last Ice Age in Europe, the paintings of Lascaux are said to be the finest prehistoric works in existence. Included in the famous cave are five or six identifiable styles of rendering, along with abundant images of bison, mammoth, and horse, plus the largest-known prehistoric painting in existence — an 18-foot (5.5-m) bull with an astonishingly expressive face and head. The original Lascaux Cave was completely closed to the public in 1963, due to

▲ This modern sculpture of a prehistoric settler is near the entrance to a Dordogne region cave.

Paleolithic Art

Wooly Rhinos & Mammoth
Rouffignac, France

Huge Horned Bull
Lascaux, France

Mother Horse & Pony
Lascaux, France

Earth Mother
Talisman
Dordogne, France

▲ Paleolithic art is renowned for its realism, scale, and the expertise in which it was rendered.

deterioration from body heat and warm breath of frequent visitors. An exact replica of the cave art panels is open for visitors next to the cave entrance called "Lascaux II."

High in a topographical area of the Dordogne Valley, the Rouffignac Cave is a three level maze of corridors and galleries. Only the upper level, by far the largest of the three, was explored and frequented by prehistoric artists. The Rouffignac Cave was decorated in the Late Magdalenian period of the Paleolithic era, around 13,000 BCE. However, some of the Paleolithic caves and decorated rock shelters in France date back 23,000 years. Rouffignac Cave is best known for its prolific representations of large mammals, particularly woolly mammoths, bison, horses, and woolly rhinoceros. Today, visitors are treated to an efficient tram ride through Rouffignac Cave to view some of the best panels, but, unfortunately, walking the corridors is not allowed.

The earliest artistic renderings in Europe can be found on the walls and ceilings of the caves in the Dordogne region. They represent a concern for hunting, fertility, and regeneration.

Although most cave art is found in the Vèzére and Dordogne River valleys of southwest France, along with the Pyrenees or the Cantabrian Mountain regions of Spain, cave paintings and engravings appear throughout Europe. Apart from animal representations, wall art in Europe also includes abstract images such as lines, dots, and a combination of these elements. Human figures are rarely depicted. There are hand stencils in some caves, made by painting around a spread-out hand, and these are thought to represent male and female symbols used in fertility and initiation rites. Footmarks and fingerprints of young children have been found at certain sites, suggesting rituals for younger members learning about their adult roles. Some images appear to represent people wearing masks, animal skins, or antlers. These animal disguises may be camouflage for hunting or ceremonial dress worn by shaman for hunting rituals.

Getting to the Dordogne region caves

The small town of Les Eyzies has been termed the "Capital of Prehistory," mainly because of the Font de Gaume cave and the excellent prehistory museum, as well as the Le Madeleine site four miles (6.5 km) upstream the Vézère River. The Rouffignac Cave is located 3 miles (5 km) to the south of the village of the same name. Signs will lead the visitor above the Binche Valley to the cave entrance underneath steeply sloping limestone cliffs. The enormous horse depictions of Pech Merle Cave are located in the village of Cabreret in the Lot. Lascaux II Cave is easy to find following the signs from the town of Montignac.

Lourdes

Lourdes was hardly more than a hamlet until 1858, the year a 14-year-old peasant girl named Bernadette Soubirous had the first of 18 visions of the Virgin Mary. This occurred at a location called the *Grotte de Massabielle*, alongside the riverbank of the Gave de Pau. Over a period of several months, the young girl and many townspeople gathered at the grotto and viewed an apparition of the Virgin Mary, or the "Immaculate Conception" as she described herself. Once the girl's visions were recognized by the Catholic Church, Lourdes experienced a building boom and is now one of the most visited destinations in southern France. Bernadette was beatified in 1925 and canonized a saint in 1933.

> Lourdes attracts more than five million
> Christian pilgrims every year, making it
> the most visited pilgrimage destination in
> Europe.

Most visitors who come to Lourdes are hoping for a miraculous cure for their pain and suffering. Some 70,000 visitors are handicapped or have serious physical ailments and are given preferential treatment at the site. Lourdes has been

▲ Lourdes is considered a city where healing miracles occur.

called a "city of miracles," or "capital of prayer," which corresponds with a tangible reality. Well over 5,000 cases of spontaneous healing have been reported, and of those, 65 have been declared miraculous by ecclesiastic authorities following long and precise procedures. Such recognized miracles by the Catholic Church have undoubtedly necessitated the steady increase of pilgrims.

Along the river is the *Cité Réligieuse*, the object of desire for the throngs of faithful flocking to Lourdes. Tucked alongside the riverbank is the moisture-blackened grotto, which predictably houses a statue of the Virgin Mary. Suspended in front of the grotto are rows of rusting crutches offered up by the hopeful. Rising above the grotto is the first church built on the site in 1871. Below the church is a massive subterranean basilica, which can house approximately 20,000 people. On site is a natural spring that was said to have been formed during one of the apparitions. The water from the spring is used for blessings and healing. Because of its famous reputation, many modern Christian pilgrim routes in Europe now lead to Lourdes.

Getting to Lourdes

Lourdes is situated in the foothills of the Pyrenees just north of the Spanish border, and about 75 miles (120 km) southwest of the French city Toulouse. Lourdes is about 20 miles (30 km) southeast of the city Pau, but has its own train station for the multitude of visitors. Pau is one of the best places for setting off into the highest parts of the Pyrenees Mountains. The Lourdes train station is on the northeastern edge of town and the grotto is easily located by following the crowds past the many kitsch religious shops. There are three trains daily from the Gare d'Austerlitz station in Paris, as well as trains from larger cities around France and buses from regional towns.

Mont Saint Michel and the Saint Michael's Line

The most famous sacred site on the Normandy coast, just where it joins the peninsula of Brittany, is the island monastery of Mont Saint Michel, an extraordinary Gothic abbey complex that crowns a steep rock pinnacle. According to Celtic mythology, the sea-surrounded outcropping was a primary ocean tomb where recently deceased souls were conveyed to the afterlife. The first chapel on the mass of granite was built in 708 CE for Saint Michel and quickly became the goal for Christian pilgrims all over Europe. The Gothic abbey was started in 1020, and pilgrims

▲ The causeway leading to Mont Saint Michel is artificial and may be removed in the near future.

continued to arrive during the building phase of Mont Saint Michel. The cathedral was sufficiently completed enough to host Harold the Saxon and William the Conqueror in 1058. It took until 1230 to complete the entire religious complex. Mont Saint Michel is also known as *La Merveille,* meaning the "The Marvel," because of its awe-inspiring qualities and geographical positioning. The seamount is also a fine example of military architecture, having been an impregnable stronghold during the Hundred Years War.

The unusual tide surrounding the island withdraws as far as 10 miles (16 km), leaving Mont Saint Michel rising majestically on a smooth and sandy plain. Thick fog is known to fill the bay and the sea always returns with the rising tide, sometimes racing toward the shore at an astonishing 210 feet (63 m) per minute! With that in mind, it would be wise to know the direction of the tide before embarking on a walk across the vast plain to the outlaying wilderness island. People unaware of the high tide fluctuations have drowned near Mont Saint Michel.

Anyone who sees The Marvel knows that Mont Saint Michel is an extraordinary work of human ingenuity. The abbey's granite was sculpted to match the exact contours of the rocky pinnacle, and even though space has always been a factor, the complex has grown in an inventive geometric fashion. Benedictine monks prayed, studied, and worked on the monastery for many centuries. They were finally evicted in 1874 during the French Revolution when the abbey was turned over to the Historic Monuments Department of the new French government. Nonetheless, Maupassant praised it as "the most wonderful Gothic dwelling ever made for God on this earth." Indeed, Mont Saint Michel looks like a castle out of a fairy-tale book and is one of Christendom's premier pilgrimage sites.

Mont Saint Michel has been described as a compact Gothic version of heaven where land meets the sea. It is positioned on an important energy location along the Saint Michael's Line.

▲ The archangel Saint Michael is a protector of God's heavenly realm.

Modern dowsers describe ley lines as precise locations of potent earth energy, analogous to veins on a leaf or any living entity, including Gaia the living planet. The scientific Gaia hypothesis proposes that the whole earth behaves like one self-regulating organism, wherein all of the geologic, hydrologic, and biologic cycles of the planet mutually self-regulate the conditions on earth to perpetuate life. Along the ley paths, especially at intersection points, humans detected this energy and erected primitive shrines that later became great cathedrals. Great Britain has two central ley lines named after Saint Michael and Saint Mary, which dissect the country and connect major sacred sites. Another noted ley line in Europe is also named after the archangel Saint Michael, the heavenly defender and guardian against Satan. Saint Michael, as head of the heavenly militia, was of great importance to medieval religious sensibility, especially to the French at Mont Saint Michel who held off the mighty English army for a hundred years. Arching across Europe is the Saint Michael's Line, starting at Skellig Michael in Ireland, crossing Michael's Mount in Cornwall to Mont Saint Michel in France, then across the European mainland to the Monte Sant'Angelo grotto in Italy, through the ancient Greek sanctuaries of Delphi and Delos, until it reaches the Holy Land. All across the route are shrines, temples, and statues dedicated to the highly venerated Saint Michael the Archangel.

Getting to Mont Saint Michel

The nearest train station to Mont Saint Michel is 4 miles (6 km) south at Pontorson — a lackluster tourist town. There is an expensive connection bus to the Mont when the train arrives, or bicycles can be rented at the station for an interesting ride to the sea. An alternative train stop is Avranches, where hotel prices are more reasonable. Paris is about 180 miles (290 km) to the west. Travel time is halved on a new high-speed train from Paris to Rennes, along with a complementary one-day sightseeing tour of Mont Saint Michel, which includes a stop in Saint Malo and Dinard. Musical events are held in the abbey during the summer months.

Montségur

The Middle Age crusades were not only directed at Jerusalem, but were issued against enemies of the faith in Europe as well. The most famous European crusade was against the Cathars of southern France, culminating in the final siege of Montségur, or "Safe Mountain," in 1244. The *Cathar* name means "puritan" — a breakaway Christian sect from Eastern Europe that flourished in Italy and France. Their unique view of Christianity so angered the Church that more than 20,000 Cathars were slaughtered in Béziers shortly after they surrendered. Only a complete renunciation of their faith could save them, and very few would. It was on this occasion that Pope Amaury pronounced the terrible words: "Kill them all. God will recognize His own." The Albigensian Crusade, named after the French city Albi, began in 1209 and resulted in the last survivors fleeing to the mountain stronghold of Montségur in 1232, just when the Inquisition tribunals were established. They held off the crusaders for over a decade until capture was imminent. The leader of the Inquisition declared "the dragon's head must be chopped off" as he marched on the stronghold with 8,000 men. The crusaders were so impressed with their resilience that they gave the remaining Cathars two weeks to renounce their faith. Instead of surrendering and walking away, the last 207 Cathars in Montségur spent their last hours praying for salvation from a most certain death. The Inquisition considered Montségur a "synagogue of heresy." When surrender came, all survivors were burned alive near the base of the mountain (called *prat des cramats*) on a huge pyre for their alleged heresies. As such, Montségur became the symbol for Cathar resistance, but the hopes for the entire Languedoc region were dashed. Catharism was soon dead.

> Montségur was the last outpost of a medieval Christian sect called the Cathars. It has since become the focus of Nazis, New Age adherents, vegetarians, and feminists.

The Cathar religion is affiliated with ancient dualistic doctrines that advocate the two fundamental principles of good and evil. As such, the Cathars believed in two opposing gods, they rejected the Resurrection, the Catholic sacraments, and even the death of Christ. For these reasons, they were persecuted severely by the medieval Catholic Church in the 13th century. The Cathars preached the existence of two competing gods — one who was evil and ruled our material world, and another who was good and ruled the spiritual realms. Although they considered themselves Christians and used the significant expression *Bons Hommes* to designate their priests, the Catholics derisively called them *Parfaits*, meaning "Perfects." Living in the physical world was living in hell because the evil god captured the human soul and imprisoned it in the physical realms. Christ was viewed by the Cathars as merely an illusion, sent by the good god to help free humans

▲ Historic and archaeological sites in France are easy to locate by the beautiful roadside signs.

from their miserable condition. Their unique take on Christianity was further distinguished from the Church due to their belief in a matriarchal society. The Cathars were led by a sect called the Perfect, passed on within families under the influence of grandmothers, who were viewed as the guides of the Cathars' consciences. They renounced sex, lived communally, believed in reincarnation, and did not eat meat because it was the product of a sexual union. Their only prayer was the Lord's Prayer, which they recited 40 times a day.

Because of their fierce independence, the Cathars have become a modern symbol of resistance and mysticism. Some historians believed the Cathars chose to die in silence because they hid valuable relics of Christianity. Heinrich Himmler, the Nazi SS leader, commissioned a book on the Cathars and ordered an archaeological dig at Montségur. He was hoping to find the Holy Grail or the Ark of the Covenant, two relics the Nazis thought, if found, would make their armies invincible. None were found and the Nazis of course were defeated. Himmler's exploits only increased the lore of Montségur. Today, about 100,000 visitors come to the remote mountain stronghold every year. Although the crusaders typically destroyed the forts of their enemies, the castle of Montségur remains. It is believed that the inaccessibility of the site saved it because of the difficulty of removing all the stones.

Getting to Montségur

The mountaintop castle of Montségur is located on a 3983-foot (1207-m) tall limestone outcrop in the Pyrenees Mountains of southern France. The nearest large town is Lavelanet on the D117. Lavelanet is 65 miles (108 km) west from Perpignan. The turnoff for Montségur is in the small town of Belesta off the D117. The route to Montségur is uphill from Belesta on the D9. There is a steep hike up a trail to the fort from the parking lot.

Père-Lachaise Cemetery

Easily the largest cemetery in the 20 *arrondissements* that make up the oldest sections of Paris, Père-Lachaise is a must-see for any student of history. Buried here are most of the dignitaries, scholars, musicians, artists, writers, politicians, and celebrities that have shaped French society since 1803, when the cemetery first opened. At first no one wanted to be buried so far away, so Napoleon transferred the remains of prominent people, such as the medieval lovers Abélard and Heloise, to make it more desirable. This was the beginning of pilgrims coming to visit the graves of celebrated people. Hundreds of tourists arrive daily to seek out the final resting place of the famous and infamous: singer Edith Piaf, composer Frédéric Chopin, writer Honoré de Balzac, along with prominent public figures and French military heroes. Also buried there are Modigliani, Delacroix, Sarah Bernhardt, Ingres and Corot, to name but a few. Jean François Champollion, who deciphered the Egyptian hieroglyphic language from the Rosetta Stone, is appropriately buried underneath an obelisk. Gay men make a pilgrimage to writer Oscar Wilde's extravagant tomb featuring a mythical Griffith statue. Lipstick kisses adorn the monument, but the penis of the Griffith was knocked off as a souvenir by a graveyard keeper shortly after it was erected. Similarly, lesbians seek out the gravesites of writer Gertrude Stein and her lover Alice B. Toklas, who rest eternally side by side.

> The Père-Lachaise Cemetery is the most visited graveyard in Europe. Many people come to seek out the graves of important celebrities who have contributed to the enrichment of their lives.

By far the most visited site at Père-Lachaise is the tomb of ex-Doors singer Jim Morrison. So popular is the grave that a full-time guard is posted nearby and a perimeter fence has recently been added. No longer are vigils allowed on the tomb, and no longer does the bust of Morrison's head remain, stolen in 1988. All graffiti has been removed as well. In 1986, two people attempted to dig up the coffin, leading the Morrison estate to install a cube of granite over the tomb. The granite block has an inscription written in Greek, translated as "True to His Own Spirit." An animated crowd is usually on hand, singing Doors songs, snapping

▲ The grave of singer Jim Morrison needs to be cleared of flowers and gifts almost every day. It is the most visited tomb at Père-Lachaise cemetery.

photos, and finding a way to sprinkle marijuana on the tombstone, or position a bouquet of flowers on his grave. Jim Morrison's grave is one of the top five tourist attractions in Paris. The tomb is marked on all cemetery maps and is located in Division Six.

Another popular pilgrimage spot is the grave of author Victor Hugo, who lived most of his life in a mansion (now a museum) around the Place des Vosges near the Bastille in Paris. Victor Hugo penned the oft-adapted play *Les Miserables* and is credited with a large volume of other writings. Certainly fans of his work come to visit the Hugo family plot, but also adherents of the Cao Daism faith in southern Vietnam make the long pilgrimage to Paris to pay their respects to Victor Hugo. The high priests of the Cao Dai faith believe they can communicate with spirits of once-famous people, including Victor Hugo. For a complete description of Cao Daism and their great temple in Tay Ninh, Vietnam, see: *Sacred Places Around the World: 108 Destinations* by Brad Olsen. An interesting photo in the color insert section of this book shows the high priests praying at the altar in Tay Ninh with blue-colored "shadows" next to their bodies. Perhaps the spirit of Victor Hugo and others? These shadows were not visible to the naked eye and only appeared on film.

Getting to the Père-Lachaise Cemetery

The famous cemetery lies in the northeastern district of Paris in the 20th *arrondissement*. The crowded collection of mausoleums and monuments are clustered together in a lovely park-like setting. Open hours are 8 am to 6 pm daily. There is a Metro stop called Père-Lachaise intersecting the #2 and #3 lines. Maps of the graveyard are available in the surrounding flower shops near the cemetery entrances.

Rennes-le-Château

Inhabited since ancient times, Rennes-le-Château has the advantage of occupying a dominant position on a hill that overlooks the surrounding countryside. Early wanderers of the Stone Age left traces of their existence on the hill, but the real history begins with the Romans, who mined gold and silver in the surrounding mountains. And while Roman jewelry and coins continue to be found in the area, the real treasure, perhaps the greatest find of all time, has eluded detection for nearly two thousand years. During the Roman era, the Temple of Jerusalem was looted and destroyed by the troops of Titus in 70 CE. The treasures were taken to Rome and eventually stolen again by the Visigoths in 410 when they sacked Rome. The Visigoths left Rome with the treasures of the Temple and resettled two years later on the shores of southern Gaul, today southern France. What actually happened to the Visigoths' great wealth, possibly including the Ark of the Covenant treasure, only enhances the mystery of Rennes-le-Château.

Rennes-le-Château is rumored to have contained the ultra-sacred Ark of the Covenant and the Holy Grail, among other priceless relics.

Proof of a treasure lies in the puzzling life of the parish priest named Bérenger Sauniére. Sometime in the late 19ᵗʰ century, the poor priest found some mysterious parchments in a narrow pillar in his church altar. A second discovery was made by two workers tilling in front of the new altar with Sauniére overseeing. They discovered a Carolingian flag stone with a sort of "pot full of shining objects" underneath. A third find, the "discovery of a tomb" as Sauniére writes in his journal, revealed new objects and lost secrets. Soon the three discoveries changed his life as the priest acquired sudden and immense wealth. Unfortunately, Sauniére died in 1917 and only told the secret of his finds to his housekeeper, who also died without revealing the source of the priest's enormous riches.

The Church of Mary Magdalene, all adorned in gold and mystery, stands today between the buildings erected by the wealthy and unusual parish priest. The church stands atop an ancient castle, as well as portions of a newer one restored in the 16ᵗʰ century. After his secret discoveries, the projects of the once "poor priest" seem to become endless. Suddenly "enlightened" and "adviced," Sauniére worked tirelessly to restore "all my church" and the immediate surroundings. He builds the garden of the Calvary in the town square, rebuilds the church porch, installs a new confessional, chair, and restores the presbytery. From 1893 to 1897, the people of the little town watched in amazement as

▲ The now-famous church altar where Bérenger Sauniére discovered something that made him fabulously wealthy.

▲ The devil sculpture at Rennes-le-Château now has a replacement head.

masons, carpenters, decorators, and glassmakers transform the church and surrounding area. All the while Sauniére kept quiet, worked on his church, and built himself a fine new home. One of the most unusual additions was a sculpture of the devil at the front doorway to the church. Unfortunately, the original head of the devil was cut off and stolen in 2002 and has yet to be recovered. The legend of Sauniére's wealth has inspired many theories and treasure seekers. As you enter Rennes-le-Château, be forewarned by a sign in French warning visitors: "No Digging!"

Getting to Rennes-le-Château

Perched on the summit of a steep hill in southern France is the mysterious Rennes-le-Château. The nearest town is Couiza and Espéraza. Just outside of Couiza is a sign to Rennes-le-Château, 3 miles (4.5 km) up a winding road. The town is very small, making the chapel, graveyard, garden, and Sauniére's home easy to find.

LUXEMBOURG

The recorded history of the Grand Duchy of Luxembourg begins with the construction of Luxembourg Castle in the year 963. Around this fort, a town gradually developed, which became the center of a small, but important, state of great strategic value. The Grand Duchy of Luxembourg held onto its autonomy to become its own country in the 19th century. Today, Luxembourg is a small landlocked country situated in northwestern continental Europe, bordered by France, Germany, and Belgium. 87 percent of Luxembourg's population are Roman Catholic, and the remaining 13 percent are Protestants, Jews, and Muslims.

Echternach

The small city of Echternach is located on the western bank of the River Sure, and is considered to be the first town established in Luxembourg. It is situated just across the river from the eastern border of Germany, with about 5,100 permanent residents. The town grew around the walls of the Abbey of Echternach, which was founded in 698 CE by Saint Willibrord, the most famous resident of Echternach. Willibrord, an English missionary from Ripon, became the first bishop of Utrecht and was instrumental in Christianizing the pagan Frisians of the Lowlands. He is considered a Christian apostle of both Luxembourg and the Netherlands. As bishop, he directed the Echternach monastery as abbot until his death in 739. Almost immediately upon his death, a stream of pilgrims began making their way to Willibrord's Tomb in the abbey. When notable leaders of the Holy Roman Empire began to visit Echternach — Lothair I, Conrad, and later Maximilian (in 1512) — Willibrord's Tomb soon became a major medieval religious destination, attracting pilgrims from all parts of northern Europe. The abbey has a famous library and illuminated manuscripts preserved from Willibrord's time, but it owes its modern fame to the curious Dancing Procession, which takes place every year on Whit Tuesday, in honor of Saint Willibrord.

▲ The Echternach Dancing Procession concludes at this church that houses the tomb of Saint Willibrord.

From the Middle Ages until now, Echternach's Dancing Procession has attracted thousands of tourists and pilgrims every spring. The procession had taken place annually without interruption from Saint Willibrord's time until 1777. In that year, there was an uneasy relationship with the Church hierarchy, so Archbishop Wenceslas declared the music and procession of the "dancing saints" to be forbidden. Only a pilgrim's walk through the city was allowed, and in 1786 Emperor Joseph II abolished the procession altogether. Attempts were made to revive it ten years later, and though the French Revolution effectually prevented it, but the procession was fully revived in 1802 and has continued ever since. In 1826, officials briefly changed the day to Sunday, but since 1830 it reverted back to Whit Tuesday, the traditional day, which actually has no direct relation to Saint Willibrord himself.

The Echternach Dancing Procession attracts
pilgrims from all over northern Europe.

Participants describe it as both an expression of the Catholic faith and a celebration to
honor Saint Willibrord, whose influence has
spread far beyond the limits of the Grand
Duchy of Luxembourg.

The Dancing Procession of Saint Willibrord traditionally takes place on Whit Tuesday (the first Tuesday after Pentecost), in the week called Whitsuntide, which follows the seventh Sunday after Easter. The event begins at a bridge over the River Sure with a morning sermon by the parish priest. This sermon was formerly performed by the abbot of the monastery, who urged protection against epilepsy, for which Saint Willibrord was invoked. The dance is representative of sick relatives, who are too feeble to attend the procession themselves. After the sermon, the procession begins to move towards the basilica, through the town square, down many picturesque streets, for a distance of about a mile (1.5 km). Holding scarves that link the participants together, while accompanied by a simple polka melody, the pilgrims dance in a curious fashion: three steps forward, then two back, so that five steps are required to advance a single pace. Participants march four or five abreast, holding each other by the hand or arm. Many musical bands accompany the procession, playing a traditional melody which has been handed down for centuries. A large number of priests and religious people also accompany the procession, and sometimes there are several bishops as well. Well after midday the last of the dancers reach the church. On arrival, the dance is continued around the tomb of Saint Willibrord, which is kept in a marble tomb beneath the high altar. In the crypt of the basilica, near the tomb, there is also a holy spring, formerly used for baptisms.

Getting to Echternach

The rolling hills of the Berdorf region, where Echternach is located, is called "The Heart of Luxembourg's Little Switzerland." The closest city is Trier, Germany. Individuals wishing to take part in the procession are advised to check the setup plan (published in Luxembourg newspapers a couple of days beforehand), as the Church issues strict guidelines for pilgrims who wish to participate in the procession.

THE NETHERLANDS

Several rivers converge on the land comprising the Netherlands, making it a sort of river delta country, the most important being the Rhine River. Early medieval maps show most of the northern Netherlands under water, or depicted as swampy marshland. Amsterdam was not even a city until the shallow waters were drained by the industrious Dutch people, who constructed windmills to pump out the water and an elaborate system of dikes to keep the land dry. By doing this, the ingenious Middle Age Dutch people reclaimed vast amounts of land for farming and grazing their animals.

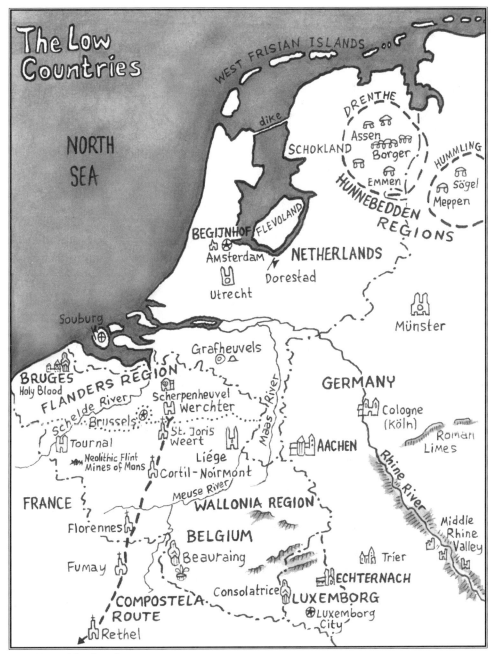

Begijnhof

Amsterdam was founded on 27 October, 1275 when an expanding village at the mouth of the Amstel River was granted a tax charter by the Count of Holland. Gradually, a large number of churches, convents, and monasteries were built in and around the growing city. The Beguines, unmarried ladies who were not nuns

▲ The main Begijnhof church is completely enclosed by other buildings also associated with the Beguines.

but who pledged to help the sick and poor, soon took residence in the medieval city. The center of their activities surrounded a courtyard of houses of the Beguines, or the Begijnhof. The community of single women were devout Catholics, who could pray in their own chapel completely surrounded by the courtyard. The Roman Catholic chapel dates from 1680, replacing others burnt down, and has always been a *schuilkerk*, or "hidden church." In the 16th century, the wars of the Reformation raged throughout Germany and Holland, along with other northern European countries, until 1578 when the city of Amsterdam officially became Protestant. The remaining Catholics went into hiding when civil authorities closed chapels, churches, and convents. The Begijnhof remained open because of its high esteem in the city. Only the chapel was derived of its religious function as Mass was no longer allowed to be read openly. When religious exiles returned to the tolerant city, they were welcomed to stop suppression and help rebuild Amsterdam. Many of these reformers continued their journey to the New World. A plaque on the Begijnhof church, placed by the Reformed Church in America, reads: "The Pilgrim Fathers who settled first in the city of Amsterdam in Holland, the country of their asylum, a shining exemplar of civil and religious liberty, many of whose institutions, transmitted to America through the English Pilgrims and the Dutch who settled in New York, have given the New World a distinctive character."

The congregation has kept English language worship in Amsterdam since 1607 when it was reopened after the Reformation. The Begijnhof has been a symbol for religious tolerance for many centuries.

After the assumption of power by Protestants in 1578, Catholics were forced to hold religious services in hiding. For reasons of safety, Mass was held at a different house each time. When a Mass was planned, usually women from the Begijnhof volunteered to go house to house and tap coded knocks to inform the occupants of the meeting place. Several homes, bordering the inner courtyard of the Begijnhof, served as temporary Catholic chapels. The Protestants of Amsterdam soon turned a blind eye towards Roman Catholic worship services, as long as they were not held in public. One renovated chapel remains in the Begijnhof from this era, featuring a townhouse outer façade, but inside is a large clandestine church. Today, Mass is held openly at the hidden Begijnhof chapel house, and single women still reside in the "woman's island" as they have for the last 700 years.

Another distinction of the Begijnhof is the Miracle of the Blessed Sacrament of 1345, an event that took place before the Reformation. A man living in a nearby home became ill and vomited the sacred host into the fire, but it did not burn. The small wafer was brought to the Old Nicolas Church, but was miraculously returned to the home of the sick man two times. For Catholics in the Middle Ages, this was confirmation enough to recognize the events were at "the hand of God." The tradition of retracing the route of the sacrament in downtown Amsterdam was reason enough for pilgrims to come to the "City of Miracles."

▲ The Begijnhof courtyard is only open to the public for a limited time so that the existing Beguines may lead normal lives.

During the Reformation, Catholics had to go into hiding because pilgrimages were forbidden. In a restricted way, the procession was allowed in middle March, the time of year when the miracle occurred. It remains to this day the modern "Silent Procession," attended by some 8,000 Catholics from Amsterdam, the Netherlands, and other countries. Based on the exact route of the procession from maps of the Middle Ages, Catholics walk the route in silent meditation. Far from the boisterous festival week of the Miracle in the Middle Ages, the modern Silent Procession is a nonviolent demonstration of religious tolerance and a potent reminder of the persecution befallen upon people of an unpopular faith.

Getting to Begijnhof

The Amsterdam Begijnhof and Pillar of the Miracle are separated only by the Amsterdam Historical Museum, all in the heart of the old city. The starting point of the Silent Procession meets in front of the Begijnhof entrance on Spui Square near Rakin. The procession happens all Saturday night into Sunday on the weekend closest to March 15th. The Begijnhof garden and inner courtyard are private, but open to the public in the morning until 1 pm every day of the week.

Opposite the entrance, inside the courtyard at address Begijnhof 30 and 31, is a Catholic chapel whose two adjoining walls have been removed to allow for the galleries of a church.

hunnebeddens

During the megalithic building age — also called the Neolithic Era or New Stone Age — the inhabitants of Drenthe providence, in northeastern Holland, adopted a peculiar building custom from people living in Denmark and northern Germany. They started erecting massive dolmen structures, using the large boulders left behind by Ice Age glaciers. The Neolithic people of Drenthe became known as the "Funnel-beaker culture" because of the characteristic pottery they left behind, usually with burials found in the dolmens. It is not known for certain if the dolmens were exclusively burial locations, ritual sites, homes, or a combination of all these functions. What is known is that most were built 5,400-5,000 years ago by the first farmers of *de Olde Landtschap*, or "the Old Landscape." Hundreds of dolmens, perhaps thousands, once scattered across the Drenthe countryside and the neighboring Hummling area of Germany, but most were destroyed by people who needed stones. Today, there are 52 remaining dolmens in Drenthe and a few dozen left standing in Germany.

Since the boulders used for the dolmens were carried to Drenthe by glaciers, most stones have one relatively smooth side, called glacial polish, as a result of scraping along the ground. The early builders positioned the smooth sides to face inside, including the capstones placed on top of the big stones. Like most megalithic buildings of the Neolithic Era, the structures were orientated with the sun in mind. The builders specifically positioned the dolmens to extend from east to west, with the entrance facing the south to receive maximal sunlight. After the largest stones were in place, the space between the big stones was filled with smaller stones. They were also used for constructing the floor. Finally, a dirt mound was placed on top of the structure with an outer stone circle to hold up the dirt. The southern facing entrance would be the only thing visible under the massive mound. After the practice of building dolmens was abandoned around 2900 BCE, most fell into a state of disrepair. The smaller stones were carted away to be used on other buildings, farmer fences, or to reinforce Dutch dikes. What remains today is the inner-skeleton of a much larger structure. Only the artifacts found and the orientation of the dolmens offer clues into this mysterious early culture.

> The Dutch name hunnebedden means "giants bed." It was thought that mythical barbarian giants were laid to rest in these ancient monuments.

▲ This massive interconnecting dolmen is located adjacent to the National Hunnebedden Museum in Borger.

Some experts believe the hunnebeddens were built as tombs only, but others think they were homes and temples first, while burials were added later when the structures became abandoned and considered graveyards. The largest remaining hunnebedden is in the town of Borger, measuring 74 feet (22.5 m) in length and containing a wide central passage connecting to an entrance corridor. Only the shell remains of most hunnebeddens, including Borger. Other large dolmens in the area include Drouwen, Havelte, Emmen, and the "church without a priest" hunnebedden near Schoonoord. Since the hunnebeddens are the oldest ancient structures in Holland, they have been regarded for a long time by the Dutch as mystical and haunted places. The discovery of buried noblemen, with artifacts for the afterlife, only enhanced the lore. Barbarians, mythical monster men, and tribes of enormous people were described in Dutch folklore as single-handedly hauling the ten-ton (20,000-kg) capstones into place. In reality, the builders were just average-sized people buried with personal items, such as beads, tools, pots, and saucers with food items. In this same region are found the "bog people," a collection of bodies preserved like mummies in peat bogs. Archaeologists believe these people were discarded in the peat bogs as human sacrifices.

Getting to the hunnebeddens

The hunnebeddens, or dolmens, are clustered around the rural village of Rolde, 3 miles (5 km) from Assen. In this area, within a 20-mile (36-km) radius, 53 megalithic monuments can be found. It is best to seek out these 5,500-year-old monuments after visiting the National Hunnebedden Museum in Borger, located next to the D27 roadway. The museum has excellent diagrams and maps showing the position of all the neighboring hunnebeddens. There is the Drents Museum in Assen, which also provides maps and directions to the hunnebeddens.

CENTRAL EUROPE

No man is an island, entire of itself; every man is a piece of the continent, a part of the main; if a clod be washed away by the sea, Europe is the less, as well as if a promontory were. —*John Donne*

THE COLD WAR ESSENTIALLY BEGAN WHEN THE SOVIET Union installed communist regimes in the Central European countries that it helped liberate in World War II, effectively making them puppet states united by the Warsaw Pact. Soviet policy toward religion was based on the ideology of Marxism-Leninism, which promoted atheism as the official doctrine of the Soviet Union. Marxism-Leninism consistently advocated the control, suppression, and, ultimately, the elimination of all religious doctrines. Although religion was tolerated at best during the Soviet domination, Central European citizens stuck to their beliefs, especially in Roman Catholic Poland. Eventually, Mikhail Gorbachev attempted to reform the Soviet Union with the policies of *glasnost* ("freedom of speech") and *perestroika* ("restructuring"). However, the formation of Solidarity in Poland, the fall of the Berlin Wall, and the breaking-off of several Soviet republics starting with Lithuania, eventually led to a coup by Communist Party hard-liners to overthrow Gorbachev. Boris Yeltsin, president of Russia, organized the mass opposition, and the coup failed. In December 1991, the Soviet Union was officially disbanded, ending the Cold War, and allowing the Central European countries to regain their governmental autonomy.

Since the fall of the Soviet bloc and the rise of the European Union, most Central Europeans wish to distance themselves from being considered Eastern European. The idea of a "Central Europe" has come back into fashion since the end of the Cold War, which had sharply divided Europe politically into East and West. The Iron Curtain effectively split Central Europe down the middle, as was the case with Eastern and Western Germany. With the exception of Poland, Slovakia, the Czech Republic, and Hungary, the range of where Central Europe is varies considerably from nation to nation. It is sometimes joked that Central Europe is the part of the continent that is considered Eastern by western Europeans and viewed as Western by eastern Europeans. More than a physical entity, Central Europe is a concept of shared history, in opposition to "the East" as represented by the Ottoman Empire and Imperial Russia.

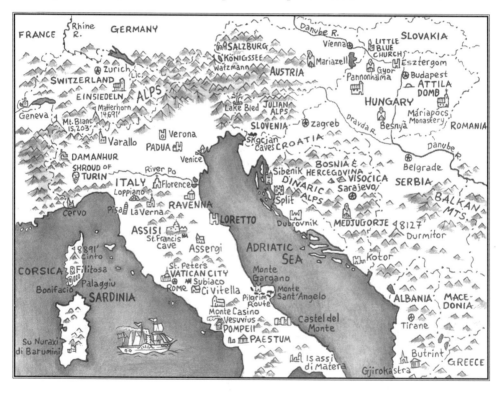

BOSNIA

The event that touched off World War I occurred in Sarajevo on June 28th, 1914, the then capital of the Austro-Hungarian province of Bosnia. There, the Archduke Francis Ferdinand, the Hapsburg heir to the throne of the Austro-Hungarian Empire, was assassinated by a young Serbian nationalist seeking revenge against Austria for the annexation of Bosnia. The cause and effect was the Great War, or the War to End All Wars, one of the bloodiest conflicts in modern history. Such a fiercely independent spirit led to the resistance of the Nazis in

World War II, and the disintegration of Yugoslavia at the end of the 20th century, which also ended in bloodshed. It may be, with the breakup of Yugoslavia into seven different countries, that a peaceful balance may finally be restored to the region after 100 years of turbulence.

Bosnia is not without its share of archaeological mysteries. Massive pyramids have been recently discovered near the town of Visoko, along with huge stone balls uncovered in various places across the country. The ancient stone spheres have been found at several locations in central and northern Bosnia. More than 40 such spheres, the biggest reaching a circumference of 17.5 feet (5.3 m), were located exclusively in the region surrounding the northern town of Zavidovici, while several dozens of the stone balls were found scattered across the wider region of northern Bosnia. Interestingly, the only other place where stone spheres of this dimension have been found is in Central America, whose pyramids are remarkably similar to the kind of pyramids located in the Visočica Valley. One researcher thinks the strange, perfectly-shaped balls were utilized as some kind of "energetic spot" by prehistoric Europeans.

Medjugorje

The otherwise nondescript small town Medjugorje came onto the Catholic radar in 1981 when the Virgin Mary appeared on a hill in front of six Croatian children. At the time of their visions, the kids ranged in age from 10 to 17. Also at that time, Bosnia-Herzegovina was a part of communist Yugoslavia, a country where organized religion was frowned upon at best. Within days of the Virgin Mary's appearance, she called herself *Gospa*, meaning the "Mother of God." Word spread quickly to the neighboring villages and soon other witnesses began to see the apparitions along with the children. The communist authorities became weary of such claims and sent in doctors to examine the visionary children and ordered them to keep away from the hill.

A Franciscan friar in a Medjugorje church was among those to witness the apparitions with the children. When he learned that the authorities were coming to arrest the children, the pastor hid the children in his parish church. Eventually the pastor was caught, sent to prison, tortured for over a year, and forbidden to ever return to Medjugorje. Yet more and more people flocked to the small town to catch a glimpse of the vision site. Many people, along with the children, began to see the Virgin Mary on a daily basis, in a number of locations. In one case, hundreds of witnesses claimed to have seen the sun spin on its axis and the word "peace" spelled in Croatian across the sky. Around this time, Mary gave herself another name: "the Queen of Peace." Despite the authoritarian grip, the apparitions continued and the legend grew by leaps and bounds.

Medjugorje is the fourth most famous Marion
shrine in the world. It is preceded only by
Guadalupe in Mexico, Lourdes in France, and
Fátima in Portugal.

▲ Approximately one million communion wafers
are distributed to the faithful at Medjugorje
every year.

Pilgrims continued to flock to Medjugorje during the dark years of civil war in Yugoslavia. After the war, Croatians identified the site with a growing surge of nationalism. Yet, despite hundreds of witnesses, the bishop of Mostar, who has jurisdiction in the matter, has called the apparitions of Medjugorje a "collective hallucination." Both he and the Pope have forbidden organized pilgrimages, a fact routinely ignored by bishops of the United States and Europe. Several commissions of psychologists, scientists, and theologians have all repudiated the visions. But this hardly seems to discourage the many thousands of faithful who arrive every year. Organized tour groups from several countries descend upon the small hamlet to meet the visionaries who still live in town, share lengthy and fervent prayer, and confess their sins. Vigils and fasting also occur at Medjugorje. It has been recorded that over one million communion wafers are given out each year at Medjugorje's masses.

Getting to Medjugorje

Most pilgrims arrive by plane at the Split/Dubrovnik Airport in Croatia, transferring by private coach to the village of Medjugorje. Sarajevo is 84 miles (140 km) northeast, Split is 96 miles (160 km) west, and Dubrovnik is 90 miles (150 km) south from Medjugorje. The ride from any of the 3 cities takes about 3 or 4 hours. The once small and quiet Herzegovina village has been transformed into a booming shrine town replete with gift shops, religious-themed restaurants, and dozens of tourist motels. In order to climb the 1,400-foot (425-m) Mount Krizevac (Cross Mountain), a minimum of an hour is needed. Due to the rocky terrain, it is recommended to pack a pair of sturdy shoes for a trip to Medjugorje.

Visočica Valley Pyramids

This newly discovered pyramid complex in central Bosnia is the most recently added sacred site in Europe, and quite possibly one of the oldest on the continent. The Bosnian Pyramid, or Visočica Hill, is the first confirmed pyramid to be discovered in Europe. The hill incorporates all of the classical elements of a true pyramid. The Bosnian Pyramid features a flat top, four perfectly shaped 45-degree slopes, four corners precisely oriented to the four cardinal compass points, and an entrance complex complete with underground passages. Because there are parallel similarities to the Pyramid of the Sun in Teotihuacán, Mexico, it has been named the "Bosnian Pyramid of the Sun" or *Bosanska Piramida Sunca*. Similar to major pyramid sites around the world, there are smaller, ancillary pyramids located nearby. These smaller Visočica Valley pyramids have been named the "Pyramid of the Moon" or *Piramida Mjeseca* in Bosnian, the "Pyramid of the Dragon" (*Piramida Zmaja*), the "Pyramid of Love" (*Piramida Ljubavi*), and the "Temple of the Earth" (*Hram Zemlje*). The three main pyramids appear to have been designed and positioned to form a perfect triangle.

For thousands of years, a stone-faced quadrilateral pyramid of monumental size remained hidden beneath the vegetation outside the town of Visoko, according to the Bosnian archeologist Semir Osmanagić, who started excavations in 2005 and has produced some startling discoveries. His initial assessment of the Bosnian Pyramid of the Sun depicts a central staircase ascending a step pyramid

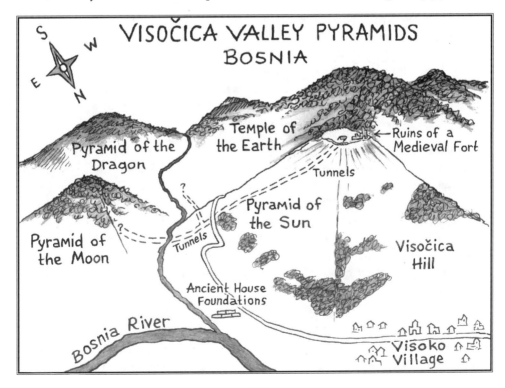

▲ This postcard of the Visočica Valley clearly depicts the "Pyramid of the Sun" decades before it was discovered.

to a flat top that once supported a temple — dated to be about 12,000 years old. He assigns the builders of the Visočica Valley Pyramids to be pre-Illyrians, people who lived 27,000 years ago in the Balkan region. It is known that hunters and farmers have continually inhabited the Visočica Valley for at least 7,000 years. Osmanagić, who intensively researched pyramids in the Americas, Asia, and Africa for the past 15 years, says he's positive that he found the first pyramid in Europe, which is quite similar in design to the ones located in Central America and Mexico. Scientists and reporters alike have confirmed the Pyramid of the Sun to contain distinctive rooms and a monumental causeway. The estimated size of the pyramid is 722 feet (217 m), or one-third taller than the Great Pyramid in Egypt. Geologists confirm that Visočica Hill could not be a natural formation, because the colossal, right-angled stone blocks uncovered do not occur in nature, unless fitted by the human hand. The stones are laid in four rows, characteristic of a major construction project. The paved entrance plateau features fitted stone blocks, clearly indicating a highly developed civilization with advanced building skills.

> The Visocica Valley Pyramids appear to be a unique type of construction, where fitted stones were placed around an existing hill to form the shape of a pyramid.

Preliminary tests using sonar sounding devices, ground scans, and satellite imagery of the terrain offer evidence that at least one pyramid, if not possibly several, really do exist in the Visočica Valley. Several different techniques, such as remote sensing by satellite, thermal imaging, artificial illumination, and radar topography have experts mapping geometric features in the valley. The three biggest pyramids seem to be positioned in a triangular form, perfectly matching with the four major directions in the world. What's more, the northern face of the Pyramid of the Sun deviates not more than a half inch (12 mm) from the position of the polar star.

Perhaps the most intriguing aspect of the Pyramid of the Sun is an extensive tunnel complex discovered beneath the formation. An international team of experts confirmed the finding of two passages intersecting with distinctive 90-degree angles, an in-built ventilation system, along with steps leading down into what appears to be a tomb. The three largest pyramids may all interconnect by underground passageways. In one of the tunnels, a large polished monolith has been found with unknown carved inscriptions, including arrows and a shape similar to the letter "E." Another large sandstone block, clearly carved by human hands, also revealed additional symbols, giving researchers a glimpse of early European writing.

Another excavation at nearby Pljesevica Hill (the Pyramid of the Moon) uncovered fitted sandstone plates, vertical walls, and right-angled fitted stones. The sandstone plates were used for the terrace foundations of the step pyramid. Stone tiles with a distinctive pattern, arranged like a mosaic, were also found at the Pyramid of the Moon. In both pyramids, a white cement-like substance was used to hold the blocks together. A scientific analysis of the connective material used to bind the blocks showed that calcium hydroxide was present in the construction of both pyramids. The binding materials had a 97% chemical similarity on each site proving the builders knew how to utilize oxidized connective materials. The picture that emerges is that the ancient builders were very sophisticated stone working masons.

Getting to the Visočica Valley Pyramids

The Visočica Valley Pyramids are located near the town of Visoko, about 19 miles (30 km) northwest of Sarajevo, the capital of Bosnia-Herzegovina. Although little infrastructure currently exists for heavy tourism, the pyramids in central Bosnia may soon transform the tiny Balkan countryside into a world archaeological marvel. It is advisable to rent a car in Sarajevo and travel to the site by road.

BULGARIA

Roughly the size of Ohio, Bulgaria attracts prospective travelers with its old European charm, alongside an emerging *haute couture* perspective with its new generation of post-Cold War hipsters. From remarkably well-preserved frescoes in medieval churches to fantastic Roman ruins, Bulgaria is a treasure-trove of sacred sites awaiting the throngs of tourists who have yet to discover this Balkan gem. Outside the city of Plovdiv is the remarkably intact amphitheater of ancient Trimontium, meaning "three hills," confirmed by researchers to have been founded before Athens and Rome occupied this remote corner of southeastern Europe. Some of the rural villages appear as they have for a thousand years, replete with horse-drawn carts trundling down cobbled alleyways and elderly people still performing laborious tasks, such as carrying buckets of well water and collecting firewood.

Rila Monastery

The founding of the Rila Monastery begins in 927 CE when a hermit named Ivan Rilski ventured deep into the Bulgarian wilderness and located a suitable cave to settle. Ivan Rilski later becomes known as Saint John of Rila, whose name is given to the monastery he would eventually establish. The hermit-saint lived in a cave not far from the monastery's location, welcoming spiritual seekers into his humble dwelling. The monastery complex was built by his students, who came to the mountains to receive a Christian education. Saint John of Rila was canonized by the Eastern Orthodox Church, making both his cave and burial place near the monastery highly-revered pilgrimage destinations. His ascetic cave dwelling and tomb were incorporated into the monastic complex, which subsequently played an important role in the spiritual and social life of medieval Bulgaria. After a devastating fire, the monastery was completely rebuilt in the 19th century. It is the largest Renaissance building in Bulgaria.

A recognized holy location for all Bulgarians, the Rila Monastery is the largest and most famous Eastern Orthodox religious complex in the country.

▲ The Rila Monastery is surrounded by intricate fortifications, now used mainly as guest rooms. The defensive tower was built in 1335 by a local ruler.

The Rila Monastery is a recognized holy place for all Bulgarians, as well as for others in the Eastern Orthodox faith. It is one of the most significant cultural locations in Bulgaria, where over the course of many centuries intensive spiritual, educational, and creative activities flourished. To the average Bulgarian citizen it represents independence, religious culture, a proud national identity, and an awareness of their Slavic heritage. Ever since its creation, the Rila Monastery has been respected and financially supported by the Bulgarian rulers. Large donations were made by almost every tsar of the Second Bulgarian Empire up until the Ottoman Conquest, making the monastery a cultural and spiritual center of Bulgarian national consciousness. The monastery reached its apogee from the 12th to the 14th century. The defensive tower of Khrelio, built in the 14th century, can be found in the courtyard. The church was painted by the most famous artists of the Bulgarian Renaissance. It is an architectural and artistic composition of enormous dimensions, representing the cultural zenith of Renaissance craftsmen, icon-painters, woodcarvers, and artisans of all trades. The Rila monks remained in close contact with other Eastern spiritual centers abroad, including the Zografou Monastery at Mount Athós, Greece.

By 1400, Rila was a feudal powerhouse in Bulgaria, controlling scores of villages, serfs, and various properties. The Ottoman invaders from Turkey damaged the monastery, but it survived and came to symbolize national survival. The monastery regained its wealth and prestige after the Turks left, only to be re-taken by the communists in 1946. After the fall of communism in 1991, the monastery returned to the Eastern Church, where it has staged yet another comeback. Once as low as eight, the number of monks in the monastery is on the increase. The Rila Monastery continues to function — today playing host to hundreds of pilgrims and tourists who arrive every day, making it the most visited attraction in Bulgaria. There is a splendid library, guest accommodations, and a historical museum with exhibits featuring various monastery-related subjects. The Rila Monastery was included in the World Register of Historical Sites in 1983, and is also listed in the directory of UNESCO World Heritage Sites.

Getting to the Rila Monastery

The Rila Monastery can be found perched high on the craggy slopes of the northwestern Rila Mountains, the highest mountain range on the Balkan Peninsula, snuggled tightly in the deep Rilska River valley. It is situated 75 miles (122 km) south of Bulgaria's capital Sofia, or just 17 miles (29 km) east from the Sofia-Thessaloniki Highway turnoff. The monastery is at an elevation of 3,785 feet (1,147 m) above sea level. Any tour or hotel operator in Sophia can arrange group or private day trips to the Rila Monastery.

CZECH REPUBLIC

After the Allies were victorious in World War I, Czechoslovakia developed as one of the successor states to be carved out of the failed Austria-Hungarian Empire. It retained its independence until the Nazi's annexed it as an "independent" state in March, 1939 under the patronage of Germany. Prague, the capital, was liberated by the Red Army on May 5th, 1945 to enthusiastic cheers. Soviet dictator Joseph Stalin wasted no time in establishing a uniform bloc of satellite states into which Czechoslovakia was annexed in September, 1947. The communists did not trust spiritual values and quickly suppressed all religious activities. Houses of worship went vacant while church representatives and Catholic writers were interrogated by the Secret Police, who answered only to Moscow. No Catholic mass services were held until the Velvet Revolution freed the country from the bonds of communist oppression in 1989. Slovakia became an independent country in 1993.

Infant Jesus of Prague

In 1611 CE, a new church was started in the Malá Strana, or "Lesser Town," situated near the foothills of the Prague Castle. The Church of Our Lady Victorious was originally built for German Lutherans and was dedicated to the Holy Trinity. It was one of the few late Renaissance churches constructed in Prague, inspired by Roman classicism. After the victory of the Counter-Reformation in Czech lands, the emperor turned the re-consecrated church over to the order of the Descalced Carmelites, an order of nuns growing quickly in Spain. The Carmelites, led by Saint Teresa of Avila (see: Avila, Spain page 280), also powerful in the Counter-Reformation, wished to see the Carmelite order succeed in Prague. Saint Teresa had the reputation of donating a statuette of the Infant Jesus while founding new convents. The new reverence for the incarnation emphasized the human side of Jesus Christ as a small child: innocent, unassuming, and pure. The Teresian Carmelites parted with their prized relic as a wedding gift to promote goodwill, and to further the veneration of the infant cult farther to the east. The statue of the Infant Jesus was brought to the Malá Strana in 1628 where it has remained to this day. It reportedly has performed many miracles to the countless faithful who have come to worship at the altar where it is enshrined.

> The Infant Jesus Shrine in the Church of Our
> Lady of Victory is the most important place of
> pilgrimage in Prague.

During the Thirty-Year War, the Saxons invaded Prague and pillaged both the Malá Strana church and the monastery. The soldiers broke off the infant's hands and threw the broken relic behind the altar in a pile of debris, where it remained forgotten for many years. The statue was recovered, restored, rebuilt, and redisplayed. Soon the "little Prague Baby" became the object of worshippers once again. Many subsequent miracles were attributed to the Infant, including the protection of Prague during the Swedish siege. In 1655, the Bishop of Prague put a crown on the Infant's head, symbolizing the royal divinity of God. Commoners brought votive gifts out of love and gratitude. The upper class and religious authorities donated a variety of ornately-decorated dresses for the small relic. In all, the Infant Jesus has over 300 different dresses, with the oldest in silk velvet having been created in 1700.

After the fall of communism, the Carmelites returned to the church, where they now aid the large groups of tourists and pilgrims who visit the church every year. The Infant Jesus of Prague is worshipped by believers throughout Europe, India, the Philippines, Australia, and especially Latin American countries. Replicas and devotional sanctuaries to the Infant Jesus of Prague can be found worldwide. Missionaries spread devotion of the Infant Jesus to Kerala in South India, founded a Carmelite monastery near Genoa, Italy, and established a mission in the Central African Republic. Dozens of different prayers are recited at the various Infant Jesus shrines around the world.

Prague has been nicknamed the "City of Palaces and Gardens," and the "City of 100 Spires." Few cities in Europe can match the architectural splendor of Prague. This capital city retains 600 years of a rich heritage, barely touched by war or natural disaster. So valuable is the historical core of Prague that UNESCO declared 2,165 acres (866 ha) of the city as a World Heritage Site, including the Infant Jesus Shrine. The city preserves artistic movements and styles from the Middle Ages to the present. The historical core of the city is situated on both banks of the Vitaua River and consists of six sections, all formerly independent urban units before being unified in the 18th century. Dominated by the Prague Castle, it has been developing uninterrupted ever since the 9th century. It contains ornately designed government buildings, fortifications, and several Gothic cathedrals, including Saint Vitus, long regarded as the spiritual symbol of the Czech state. The Old Royal Palace, inside the Prague Castle complex, is also worth a look. The royal environs of the western part of Prague are connected to the eastern side by several bridges, none more famous than the Charles Bridge, started in 1357 and still in excellent condition today. Other buildings exceptionally preserved

▲ Images of the Infant Jesus can be found all around Prague.

include: the 15th century Powder Tower, originally part of the city-wide castle fortifications; the Loreta Church, containing a copy of the Italian Santa Casa, which inspired pilgrimages; the Saint Nicholas Cathedral, perhaps the finest Baroque building in Prague; and the enigmatic Astronomical Clock in the Old Town Square. Prague is a city with many faces and infinite charm.

Getting to the Infant Jesus of Prague

The Church of Our Lady of Victory (Kostel Panny Marie Vítézné) containing the Infant Jesus relic is located at Karmelitská #9 in the Malá Strana quarter. It is a five-minute walk from the western portal of the Charles Bridge. Prague has an international airport, a busy train station, and many bus routes serving the capital city. A good way to become acquainted with Prague is to register for a walking tour, most originating and ending in the Old Town Square.

HUNGARY

The Hungarian language is supposedly one of the hardest to learn, along with being one of the most unique languages spoken in Europe. Hungarian is a Finno-Ugric language, unrelated to any neighboring spoken tongue. The language is most closely related to Finnish and Estonian, yet Hungary is physically located hundreds of miles away from both of these countries. For about 95% of the population, Hungarian is their preferred first language.

Hungary's landscape consists mostly of the rolling plains of the Carpathian Basin, sliced down the middle by the mighty Danube River. The Hungarian Great Plain was a prized possession to a multitude of invading forces, but miraculously the Hungarian people retained their religion, culture, language and autonomy through the turmoil of many centuries. Similar to Poland, most of the religious population is Catholic. Unlike Poland, Hungarians are not particularly religious people, with no more than 25% actively practicing Catholicism today.

Attila Domb

The territory that is now Hungary has been specializing in the healing arts since Roman times. The Héviz Spa is a large, hot spring lake, regarded as a natural healing location, where local and tourist alike come year round to cure themselves. Long before "wellness" and "fitness" entered the Hungarian consciousness, local people recognized the curative powers of certain locations. For their many aches and pains, Hungarians are known to take a large amount of prescribed pills and medications. Conversely, there is also a strong emphasis on regional thermal baths as an "alternative" to modern medicine. Other Hungarians turn to shamans and traditional Hungarian healing methods to relieve physical suffering. Visiting mineral baths, hot springs, and energetically charged sites are among the new alternative therapy options. One of these locations is the popular *Attila Domb*, or "Attila Mound."

The Attila Domb is now part of the commercialized Kincsem Lovaspark, a tribute to the legendary "wonder mare" horse named *Kincsem*, or "My Treasure," which was born in 1874 on this land near Tápiószentmárton. Count Ernô Blaskovich raised the mare that went undefeated in all the races she ran. Along with raising a world famous race horse, Count Blaskovich believed that Attila the Hun, known as "the Scourge of God" when his barbarian hordes overran Europe in the 5th century CE, built his wooden palace at the mound site. According to the documentations of a Byzantine envoy named Priskos Rhetor, it is quite likely that the fortified wooden palace of Attila was located somewhere near Attila Domb. The Count's claim would be partly substantiated by the archaeologists who excavated Attila Domb in the 19th century. Instead of relics from the legendary Hun, the team found a solid gold statue called *Csodaszarvas*, or the "golden deer." The statue was confirmed to be a Scythian relic, cotemporaneous with Attila, and now housed in Budapest's *Nemzeti Múzeum* (National Museum).

The Scythian mound hinted at signs of a potent energy within, observed more than a century ago by herdsmen who noted that their horses were somehow attracted to the site. The horses spent unusually long hours here, and sick horses were seen frequently lying down on the mound for many hours. The veterinarian of the estate concluded that there were markedly less illnesses among the horses at this farm, and that the foaling rate was greatly above average, in fact more frequent than anywhere else in the country. Rumors about the special energy source of Attila Domb soon spread, attracting people by the hundreds, who sought relief from their aches and pains. The "healing mound" gained popularity, mainly because of the testimony of many sick people who reported a distinct improvement in their condition. Some spoke of healing right after visiting the mound, while others reported increased wellness after visiting the mound on several occasions. Human vitality research commenced in the 20th century to determine the therapeutic qualities of Attila Domb.

▲ Travelers come from near and far to benefit from the energy of Attila Domb.

The Attila Domb became famous for its mysterious magnetic energy and the power it worked on horses. Thousands of tourists from all parts of the world arrive annually to experiment with the curative impact of the energy field on the human organism.

The scientists' measurements revealed a beneficial energy-radiation emanating from the mound, which can facilitate a healing process in the human body. The center of this energy flow is on the Attila mound, but its curative effects can be felt around the general area surrounding Kincsem Lovaspark. Some earth energy researchers, or geomancers, report a strong ley line crossing through the mound. This also corresponds to the Saint George Line that supposedly extends across Hungary. The scientists have not yet reached an exact conclusion as to where this energy comes from, whether these energies are part of the planet's regenerative system, or if there might be an underlying force behind the observed peculiarities and manifestations. Others correctly point out that Hungary is a location where the crust of the earth is thinnest, thus the magma is closer to the surface and produces many of the country's natural hot springs.

To those who believe in the regenerative power of earth energy, it is well known that most illnesses result from a state of vitality imbalance. The barren hill has a noted "special area" which emits an intense pulsation of magnetism. The subtle radiation of a ley line helps people to recover their deficiency, which not only affects the organs, but helps harmonize the energy-flow throughout the entire body. Visitors to Attila Domb are told to watch out for signs of dizziness, shortness of breath, tingling in the palms, the feet, and an overall surge in energy. Some visitors have experienced an intensification of their pains, headaches, and listlessness immediately following a visit, but after several visits these symptoms abated and feelings of exhilaration, good health, and high energy ensued.

On any typical day there can be over 200 people on the benches and tree stumps scattered around Attila Domb. One night in the spring of 2001, a stranger placed a statue of the Virgin Mary and a bunch of flowers on the mound. Offerings continue to appear near the statue. The grounds of Kincsem Lovaspark include such attractions as a bust of Attila the Hun designed by a modern sculptor, the Kincsem museum, equestrian training and riding, carriage rides, and a small zoo. The nature area contains raczka sheep with their distinctive dreadlocks and curling horns, Mangalica hog's with curly short hair, ponies, donkeys, horses, and even an ostrich. Using all historical data available, construction began in 2007 at Kincsem Lovaspark to recreate an exact likeness of Attila the Hun's timbered mansion fort, featuring a wine cellar, restaurant, exhibition area, and an open air stage. The 25,200 square-foot (7,000 sq.-m) facility can also host conferences and exclusive parties.

Getting to Attila Domb

The Attila Domb is situated on 37.5 acres (15 ha) of somewhat drab scenery near an undistinguished town called Tápiószentmárton, some 30 miles (50 km) southeast of Budapest on Route 31. Thousands of Hungarians drive there by car every year, or take one of the many organized bus tours out of Budapest. A

four-star hotel, a restaurant, simple apartments, and fast food stands are available on site, so people can stay and visit Attila Domb more than one day, which is the recommended treatment for those seeking results from such illnesses as high blood pressure, aching joints, listlessness, and other ailments.

POLAND

Poland as a sovereign nation was founded at the end of the 9th century, but lost its independence in 1795 when it was partitioned off to the then superpowers Russia, Prussia, and Austria. For over 100 years, Poland was not identified on any new European maps. It only regained its national identity after World War I, mostly at the insistence of US President Woodrow Wilson, a close friend of Polish composer Ignacy Paderewski, who later became Poland's first Prime Minister.

Poland is a deeply religious country, with approximately 95% of the population being Roman Catholic. Poland is also considered part of "Slavic Europe," the region in eastern and central Europe where the Slavic languages are spoken. The main religion for most Slavic people is Eastern Orthodox, but another large grouping includes Catholicism and Islam. The Slavic speaking countries consist of Russia, Belarus, Ukraine, Poland, Czech Republic, Slovakia, Slovenia, Croatia, Serbia, and Bulgaria.

Krakow Old City

Few places in the world host so many venerated buildings as the old city center of Krakow. There is also no other place in Central Europe where one can find so many tombs of persons recognized by the Catholic Church as saints or blessed. So impressive is this old city that a papal legate declared in 1596: "If there wasn't a Rome, Krakow would be Rome." At present, seven saints, eight blessed persons, and a similar number of people believed to have been saints are buried in the churches of Krakow. Studded with religious buildings seemingly poking around every corner, over 200 churches exist in the old city and outer confines of Krakow. Of these, 16 beautiful churches make up the "Krakow Route of Saints," almost all containing a tomb of a saint or a blessed person. Even the Wieliczka Salt Mine, just outside the city, is filled with numerous chapels located deep underground. But no son of Krakow in modern times could be as esteemed as Pope John Paul II. As a young man, Karol Wojtyla became a priest, preached at his own parish church, and was elevated to Archbishop of Krakow before being elected to the Holy See on October 16th, 1978. Pope John Paul II undertook many pilgrimages to Krakow since taking the Seat of Saint Peter in Rome. On his first visit to Krakow after being elected Pope, John Paul II reminisced: "Let me look once more at Krakow where every stone and every brick is dear to me.

Therefore I request you to accept the whole spiritual heritage named 'Poland,' with the power of your faith, hope, and love." Weaving its way throughout the old city of Krakow and beyond is the "Route of John Paul II," commemorating the places and events from his celebrated life.

> The Krakow Old City is the oldest metropolitan area in Poland. The Cathedral of Krakow on Wawel Hill is Poland's spiritual capital and symbol of the nation's identity.

By far, the single most important site in Krakow is Wawel Hill. The magnificent complex of Gothic and Renaissance buildings — primarily consisting of the Cathedral and Royal Palace — overlooks the old city from a high rocky hill along the Vistula River. For over 500 years, this was the Polish royal residence, until the beginning of the 17th century when the capital was moved to Warsaw. During the reign of the Krakow kings, the city was endeared as *totius Poloniae urbs celeberrima*, "the most celebrated Polish city." Dominating the square atop Wawel Hill is the famous cathedral, called the "Sanctuary of the Nation." The first king of Poland, named Ladislas, was crowned here with his wife, Jadwiga, in 1320. This first coronation in Krakow was to be followed by over 30 Polish kings and queens until the 18th century. The present cathedral was rebuilt in 1364

▲ The cathedral inside the Krakow Castle is where kings and queens were crowned to rule Poland and buried upon their passing. It is a national treasure of Poland.

133

when it was consecrated and began to serve as a necropolis for the beloved royalty and saints of Krakow. Archaeologists have recently determined that Wawel Hill was occupied long before the Middle Ages. The earliest traces of habitation on the hill date to the Paleolithic Era. Subsequent Neolithic and Bronze Age people settled here as artisans and tradesmen. The hill also figures prominently in legendary stories of princes slaying dragons and a princess who killed herself instead of marrying a foreigner and betraying Poland. But most of the Wawel monuments, particularly the stately Royal Castle and the Cathedral, enshrine the highest values of Polish culture, inspiring a feeling of national pride.

Jutting away from the castle and river is the rectangular-shaped old city center of Krakow. A green ring of parks indicate where the former city walls stood, which today are almost all gone. At the core of the old city is Rynek Glowny, Europe's largest medieval market square. Flanking it are several churches, including the famous Saint Mary's, one of the most magnificent Gothic cathedrals in Europe. Founded by Krakow burghers in the 13th century, it is more famous as the place of the bell tower's trumpeter, who took an arrow in the throat while frantically playing to warn the city of an impending Tartar invasion. To this day, a modern trumpeter sounds off every hour with a simple broken-off solo to reenact the fate of this 13th century hero. A historical route called the "Royal Way" starts at the only remaining city gate and commemorates the route followed by returning royalty and heads of state. From the Florianska Gate, dignitaries usually bowed in the presence of Saint Mary's before passing across the Market Square on the way to Wawel Hill. The "Jewish Heritage Route" takes visitors just outside the old city to the eastern part of Krakow that used to be populated by a sizeable Jewish community. The route passes several synagogues and features Szeroka Street, the center of the Jewish ghetto before World War II. During the war, all the Jews in the ghetto were removed. So important are the buildings of Krakow that the old town, Wawel Hill, and the Jewish section called Kazimierz were collectively grouped as one of the original UNESCO World Heritage Sites, the same list of 12 sites that also featured China's Great Wall and Egypt's Great Pyramids. Today, the list contains over 700 locations.

Getting to Krakow Old City

Convenient lines of transportation make any visit to the old city easy. Krakow has an international airport and features a busy railway station with connections to every large city in the region. The train station is one block away from the old city. Many streets leading to the Market Square are pedestrian-only zones. From Krakow it is easy to do day trips to Auschwitz / Birkenau World War II concentration camps, the Shrine of Divine Mercy, or the famous salt mines at Wieliczka. Located in south central Poland, Krakow is also the gateway to the High Tatra Mountains on the Slovakian border.

Czetochowa

The industrial city of Czetochowa (Chenstokhova) is known around the world as a place of miracles, thanks to the sacred relic of one single image. The painting of Our Lady of Czetochowa, or the icon of the Black Madonna, is kept in the Pauline Monastery of Jasna Góra. Every year, the shrine is visited by four to five million pilgrims from 80 countries worldwide. From June through September, over 200,000 pilgrims walk to Jasna Góra in a solemn oath of faith. The longest pilgrimage route spans 380 miles (600 km) across Poland and takes about 20 days to cover the distance. On the Assumption Day of August 15th, the Warsaw Pilgrimage comes to Czetochowa every year as part of the oldest pilgrimage in Poland, initiated in 1711. Other festival and feast days attract thousands of reverent pilgrims, some making the final portion of the journey on their knees. The Black Madonna picture has inspired thanks, pleas, prayers, and healings in both difficult and joyous times. Thankful pilgrims, whose prayers have been answered, leave behind canes, crutches, braces, and votive offerings in the Chapel of Our Lady.

> Czetochowa is the biggest pilgrimage center for Marian devotion in the world. Jasna Góra translates as the "Mount of Light."

The Black Madonna picture is surrounded with ritual and legend. Everyday Mass is given just before noon, followed by monks from the monastery playing the trumpet. After noon Mass, the portrait is covered for several hours. The sacred icon is embellished with a dress that changes periodically, so only the face and the hands of the mother and child can be seen. The legend says that Saint Luke the Evangelist created the portrait, painted on a table built by Jesus himself, but carbon dating determines it was rendered in the 5th century by an unknown artist. It is painted in the Byzantine style, which further verifies the 5th century dating. The painting itself is credited with all the spontaneous healings that have taken place in the chapel. Only a strong faith is required.

Many people write notes with their prayers to be deposited in small boxes near the Black Madonna. Another legend tells of how the picture was stolen by robbers in 1430, but could not be taken because the horses refused to move. No beatings or coaxing would make the animals budge, so the would-be robbers decided to deface the picture instead and leave

▲ Thousands of crutches and votive offerings are found in a side chapel of Jasna Góra.

it behind. Later, a soldier slashed the cheek of Mary on the painting two times. Mary is now painted on the canvas copy over the wooden original. It hangs above the altar to this day, the object of devotion to millions of pilgrims.

The Jasna Góra monastery was built in 1382 upon the highest hill in the region. Supposedly, the Madonna icon in spirit chose the location because, once again, the horses refused to travel farther. The Duke of Opole took this as a sign and chose Czetochowa, a small and unremarkable village at the time, as the site for the chapel and monastery. The Black Madonna was taken from a town in Russia as booty by the Duke's army. Thus began the Jasna Góra Monastery with 16 monks from Hungary. The monastery grew in size over the years, with the impregnable walls added in 1620. The Baroque basilica was added in the 17th century, along with many other adornments. The fortifications surrounding Jasna Góra were strong enough to repel a two-month siege by the Swedes in 1655, followed by attacks from the Austrians, Russians, Napoleon's army, and finally the Nazis. Although the occupiers of Poland could have destroyed or looted the monastery, they left it alone, mainly because it was already a recognized sacred site by the Vatican. Even the valuable Treasury was left untouched. The fact that all the invaders could have destroyed Jasna Góra but did not only contributed to the icon's reputation as the guarantee of Poland's very existence. The monks of Jasna Góra, who never numbered over 100, closely guarded the relics over the centuries. The monks are of the Pauline Order, followers of Saint Paul the Hermit, the desert mystic. Today, some 60 Pauline monks continue to live and work at the Jasna Góra monastery.

Getting to Czetochowa

Located in south-central Poland, Czetochowa is 90 miles (135 km) northwest of Krakow and 120 miles (200 km) southwest of the capital Warsaw. The Jasna Góra Monastery is easily located in the northwestern part of Czetochowa. Pilgrims can ride the train or special buses to the religious complex. From the train station, turn right on the wide al WMP Boulevard and walk the 1.8 miles (3 km) wide roadway straight to the monastery.

Shrine of Divine Mercy

In the realm of Catholic saints, sometimes it is the most humble and unnoticed servants who receive recognition after their selfless lives come to an end. Such is the case of Sister Faustina, who lived a life of hardship to become a favored visionary of the revelations. Born in 1905, the third of ten children to a very poor Polish family, Faustina Kowalska joined the Congregation of Sisters of Our Lady of Mercy at the age of 20. Known as a hard worker and volunteer of the humblest tasks, Sister Faustina cooked for others, gardened, and kept watch over the convent door without complaint. Since childhood, she distinguished herself by a love of prayer, obedience, hard work, and strong feelings to help alleviate human suffering.

Practically uneducated, simple, yet very pious, Jesus chose Faustina to be his Apostle of Mercy through a series of visions. Throughout her religious life, she was endowed with numerous miracle graces, such as apparitions, visions, stigmata, prophecy, and the ability to read human souls. Few people outside her convent in Krakow-Lagiewniki knew much about her. She died in 1938 of tuberculosis at the age of 33, the same age Jesus Christ died on the cross.

When alive, Sister Faustina dutifully recorded her revelations in a diary. During her first revelation of a Merciful Jesus, he instructed her to seek out an artist to paint an image of what she saw. Three years later, the famous image of Jesus radiating a clear and red ray of light from his heart was painted under the supervision of Sister Faustina in the Vilnius convent. The cult of the Divine Mercy first began in Vilnius and spread to

▲ The image of Jesus Christ as visioned by Sister Faustina has become the lasting legacy at the Shrine of Divine Mercy.

the various places where Sister Faustina lived and ultimately died. Her numerous visions and teachings relating to the Divine Mercy started a small apostolic movement in 1935, which grew quickly after her death. During World War II, and during the communist control by the Soviet Union, many Poles were taken away to Siberia and Kazakhstan. These refugees would spread their devotion to the Divine Mercy all across central Asia. In 1993, Sister Faustina became beautified, and in 2000 she was canonized a saint by Pope John Paul II. Devotion to the Divine Mercy is mainly centered at Lagiewniki near Krakow. The Holy Father John Paul II appointed the convent where she died as the capital of the cult, and added: "For it was here that there originated the message of the Divine Mercy, which Christ Himself wished to pass on to our generation, through the meditation of the Blessed Sister Faustina."

The Shrine of Divine Mercy is one of the fastest growing places of pilgrimage in the world. Over one million people arrive at the Shrine annually.

▲ The modern Shrine of Divine Mercy was built next to the older church and convent to accommodate the huge influx of visitors in the last decade.

The crux of Saint Faustina's message is threefold: to remind the world of God's merciful love for every human being; to convey new forms of devotion to the Divine Mercy; and to renew Christian life according to the spirit of trust and mercy. Jesus was clear in his instructions to Faustina, emphasizing the prayer: "Jesus, I trust in You." For with this trust and charity, Jesus promised great progress on the road to perfection, the grace of eternal salvation, and many other blessings. Jesus also requested the first Sunday after Easter to be remembered as the Feast of Mercy in all Catholic Churches. The Catholic Church permitted the devotion in 1959 when the feast day and all of Faustina's revelations became recognized. Today, the Shrine of Divine Mercy in Poland receives pilgrims from all around the world, including the Philippines, Australia, and the United States. After Czetochowa, it remains the most popular Catholic shrine in Central Europe.

Getting to the Shrine of Divine Mercy

Pilgrims soon outpaced the capacity of the small chapel and convent of Saint Faustina, so a much larger modern basilica and scenic tower were added and consecrated by the Pope in 2002. It is now called the Lagiewniki Sanctuary and World Centre of God's Mercy. It is located 5 miles (8 km) from the old city of Krakow in the suburb Lagiewniki. Take the #19 tram from Krakow and get off at "Sanktuarium Bozego Milosierdzia" stop. The religious complex is a short walk up the hill past many souvenir vendors. Taxis can also be hired from Krakow.

SLOVAKIA

Czechoslovakia split up peacefully, but the framework for that split came first from the breakup of the Soviet satellite countries. The first major cracks appeared by early 1989 in Poland when the Poles attempted to hold free elections. Shortly after, Russian President Mikhail Gorbachev started *glasnost*, or "freedom of speech," and vowed not to use violence. The end of state terror meant the eventual end of communist regimes in the former Soviet bloc. An apt saying is that the disintegration of communist power in Central Europe lasted for 10 years in Poland, 10 months in Hungary, 10 weeks in East Germany, and 10 days in Czechoslovakia. In one of the friendliest exchanges of power in modern times, Slovakia was granted independence in 1993 with no bloodshed.

Little Blue Church

The tiny republic of Slovakia, or *Slovensko* to natives, is a small, narrow country landlocked in Central Europe. The boundary is defined by the Danube River to the west and the High Tatra Mountains extending along the northern border with southern Poland. The country's other mountain ranges have long defined the country and its distinctive ethnicity. Although now independent, Slovakia has a long history of annexation, military domination, and cultural repression from its much stronger neighbors in all four directions. Yet, somehow, a strong national identity remained, likely due to the Slovakians' view towards religion. Catholicism is much stronger here than in the Czech Republic or Hungary. Overflowing churches on Sunday is a common sight throughout Slovakia. In the far eastern part of Slovakia are the famous wooden churches, long an endearing image of the pious country. But few religious sites evoke the sentimentalism as the Little Blue Church near the heart of Bratislava, the new capital.

Splitting the city of Bratislava is the Danube River, just beyond the meeting of the Moravia River. The confluence of these two waterways is considered one of the most strategic in Europe, accessing the Czech heartland and southern Germany. The critical overlook of the two rivers is dominated by the Castle of Devin, a very important archaeological dig in Slovakia. The Celts had a densely populated settlement on the hill in the first century BCE. After the Roman conquest, it was a military action station. The Great Moravian Empire and the later Hungarian Empire both established vital fortifications on this strategic cliff. Napoleon's army was so intimidated by the Castle of Devin that they nearly annihilated all traces of it during a siege. In 1809, the French reduced the fort to rubble with their constant barrage of cannon shots. Fortunately, Napoleon spared the old city of Bratislava, containing many buildings from the Habsburg Baroque period when the city reached its architectural pinnacle. The city has always been an important trading center with its strategic river access points, but it is also renowned for its overland trade routes. The exact city center of Bratislava was founded on the crossroads of the Amber Route extending from the Adriatic Sea to the Baltic Sea, and the eastern land routes connecting Vienna to the Far East. Thus, Bratislava has always been an important intersection for commerce, ideas, culture and religion. The city exemplifies a certain Central European cosmopolitanism, at the junction of three nations and three languages (German, Hungarian, and Slovakian). All the influences have left their mark, especially the Hungarian contribution of the Baroque glory days. The Art Nouveau-designed Little Blue Church was built by Hungarian architect Edmund Lechner with all the character-

▲ The charming Little Blue Church in an icon of downtown Bratislava.

istic richness of a Central European cream cake. Inside and out, it is decorated in light blue pastel colors that resembles a fairy tale gingerbread house.

The Little Blue Church is dedicated to Saint Elizabeth, the city's one and only saint, born in the Bratislava Castle.

Saint Elizabeth was the daughter of Andreas II, a Hungarian king who ruled Bratislava. She was a descendent of the Arpad dynasty and could have easily lived the rest of her life in the lap of luxury. Instead, she felt untold compassion for the underprivileged and devoted the rest of her life to caring for the poor. Even marriage would not hamper her devotion when, at the age of 14, Elizabeth married Louis IV, the future landgrave of Thuringen in Germany. Throughout the marriage, her husband would support her numerous charitable works, enabling her to continue helping others. However, tragedy struck six years later when Louis IV died suddenly in 1227 while on a crusade. A widow at 20, Elizabeth fully devoted her life in helping the poor while entirely turning away from a world of wealth and privilege. Saint Elizabeth of Hungary lived only to be 24 years old. Four years after her death, she was canonized by Pope Gregory IX in 1235 and has become known as the patron saint of the poor. Her short life (1207 – 1231) was devoted to the sick and suffering and thus she has also become the patron saint of charity, widows, and the pursued. She was buried in Vienna, Austria, but her remains were exhumed in 1911 when they were brought back to

Bratislava. A new church was built for her remains inside the main altar of the Little Blue Church. Depicted nearly everywhere inside and out are resplendent mosaics of the life of Saint Elizabeth. The most popular image is the saint with a bouquet of roses, representative of the food she distributed to the poor. Another version of the story tells that she could miraculously change the roses into food and beverages. Saint Elizabeth's Church, or unofficially the Little Blue Church, owes its striking blue walls, façade, and the glazed roof shingles to the extraordinary woman who had riches, but felt compelled to devote her life to helping others.

Getting to the Little Blue Church

Just east of the old city of Bratislava, three blocks north of the Danube River and hidden away behind Safárikovo námestie, is the Little Blue Church on Bezruaova and Gajova streets. It is easy to find by following the river sidewalk east to the *Stary Most* (Stary Bridge), crossing the street, and turning left on Bezruaora. The locals call the church *Modry Kostolik*, meaning "Blue Church." Bratislava has an international airport, a bustling train station, and many bus routes connecting the city to many others in Central Europe.

EASTERN EUROPE

Everyone is really responsible to all men for all men and for everything. —*Fyodor Dostoevsky*, The Brothers Karamazov

THE COUNTRIES COMPRISING EASTERN EUROPE have a long history of being subjected to brutal invasions from the east, but had never been extinguished culturally. With a mixture of the last pagans and Eastern Orthodox, Protestant, and Roman Catholic religions, the sacred places in this chapter offer a unique view of European culture straddling the near east delineation with Asia. In European Russia, such major divisions of culture include the Dnieper River, the Volga River (also called *Volga-Matushka* or "Mother Volga"), and the Old Siberian Road (in Russian, the *Staryi Sibirskiy* Tract). It is undeniable that these early trade routes, especially the Volga, made significant contributions to early Russian development. The territorial expansion of Eastern Europe extends to the Ural Mountains, which contain no less than 30 monuments symbolizing the civilization divide between Europe and Asia. From the Greeks to the Vikings, ancient cultures have long coveted the territories of Eastern Europe.

The sound of Viking oars slicing through the rivers of Eastern Europe was heard frequently in the 9th century until the 11th century. The Scandinavians, feeling the tensions of too many people in too little space, launched an invasion that would take them to all points on the European continent. Dragon-headed ships made their way southward through the many waterways of eastern and central

Europe. Their ruthless acts of piracy and daring voyages overshadow their contribution to commerce and trade. The Vikings, after all, were out for profit. In the early part of the 9th century, the eastern Vikings, who were called the *Varangians*, established their base southeast of the present-day city St. Petersburg, which they named Novgorod. From this city, they followed the mighty Volga to the Caspian Sea, and the Dnieper and Don Rivers to the Black Sea. Once in the Black Sea the Vikings made incursions onto Constantinople and other targets around the Mediterranean Sea.

BELARUS

When considering the enormous size of European Russia extending east to the Ural Mountains, Belarus can be pinpointed as the geographic center of Europe. The country is renowned for the warm-spirited character of its people along with its rich cultural and spiritual heritage. Belarus, the land of a thousand lakes and rivers, is abundant in historic monuments. The earliest record of what is now known as Belarus started in the 6th century when the region was settled by Slavic people, the same genetic stock of people who dominate the country today. The early Slavs gradually came into contact with the Varangians and became organized under the state of Rus'. The 13th century unfurled the terrible Mongol invasions that devastated most of Eastern Europe. Rus' was divided up and Belarus became stable again after annexation by the Grand Duchy of Lithuania.

During the Soviet era, the country was annexed as Byelorussia, or the White Russian Soviet Socialist Republic. Nazi Germany launched Operation Barbarossa in 1941, invading the Soviet Union via Belarus. Byelorussia offered little resistance and remained under Nazi control until 1944. Once again the country was laid to ruin and much of its population perished during the German occupation. It took 30 years for the population to recover its pre-World War II levels. The Holocaust devastated all Jewish communities throughout Belarus, none of which would recover. After the war ended in 1945 and desperate for a lasting peace, Byelorussia was among the 51 original signatories establishing the United Nations in San Francisco, California.

Zhirovitchy

Despite a troubled history, the monastery complex of Zhirovitchy remains one of the most venerated religious centers in Belarus. Its prize possession is a holy icon called the "Mother of God," dating from the 15th century. The sacred image began attracting pilgrims and soon the monastery became the richest in all of Belarus, then part of Lithuania. Such notoriety attracted the attention of opposing religious factions in neighboring countries. The Orthodox monks were forced to defend their monastery against the advances of the Uniate Church and

▲ The "Icon of Zhirovitchy's God's Mother" is housed permanently in this Eastern Orthodox church.

Roman Catholicism. In 1609, the Uniates captured the monastery and retained control until the 19th century. The Mother of God icon was venerated by the Uniates and the Roman Catholics alike. In 1730, the icon was crowned according to the manner of the Western Church. When the Eastern Orthodox Church recovered the monastery in 1839, it became the first location in western Russia where Orthodox worship was restored. The Zhirovitchy monastery is famous for its architecture and is currently the primary center of Orthodox education.

> Zhirovitchy is a recognized place where miracles occur, famous for an icon known as the Mother of God.

The Zhirovitchy convent and monastery hold one of the most revered icons of Maria in all of Christendom. Called the "Icon of Zhirovitchy's God's Mother" or simply the "Mother of God," the tiny icon was responsible for the founding of this northwestern Belarusian religious community. The story begins in a forest owned by an Orthodox nobleman named Alexander Soltan, which was then part of the Lithuanian Grand Duchy. In 1470, several shepherds were startled by an unusually bright light shining through the branches of a pear tree. When they approached the tree, they saw a small oval icon of the Mother of God inside a pear. The relief image is carved in a piece of stone 2.25 inches (56 mm) tall and 1.72 inches (43 mm) wide. The herdsmen paid homage to the icon, and then collected it for their lord. Soltan was not impressed by the herdsmen's story and locked the icon in a casket. On the following day, he told his guests about the icon and opened the casket, but was surprised to see it was missing. After a few days, the herdsmen found the icon in the same tree and once again presented it to Soltan. This time he treated the icon with great reverence, vowing to build a church dedicated to the Most Holy Theotokos near the pear tree where it was found. A wooden church was built, a congregation formed, and then a monastery was founded. Soon a village appeared alongside the monastery. In the mid-16th century, the church burned down, but the holy image miraculously survived and was once again found intact, this time standing on a large rock in the woods. Everyone agreed this phenomenon was a sign of God to rebuild Zhirovitchy bigger than ever before. Again the Mother of God was the focus of their desire. Today, the icon is kept in the Cathedral of the Dormition inside the Most Holy Theotokos Monastery, and remains deeply venerated by the faithful.

The main complex of buildings comprising the Zhirovitchy convent and monastery were built in the early part of the 17th century. These buildings have great architectural and historical importance to the people of Belarus. The most famous buildings include the Dormition Cathedral and the Cathedral of Basilian Monastery. These two cathedrals are built in the Baroque and Classicism styles. The 18th century Holy Crossday Church and the 17th century Theological Seminary of Zhirovitchy are both designed in the Baroque style. The Yavlenskaya Church, completed in 1672, and the Cross-Erecting Church of 1768 also contribute to the architectural composition of the monastery. The Theological Seminary was re-established as the Minsk Priesthood Seminary at the close of World War II. Zhirovitchy is the only operating seminary in Belarus today. Also of interest in the Grodno region is Slonim town, only 6 miles (10 km) away from Zhirovitchy. The Slonim district features several religious influences, situated at the confluence of the Shchara and Isa rivers. There is a Catholic Church dating from the 16th century, a Bernardinian Convent, and a Jewish synagogue from the 17th century.

Getting to Zhirovitchy

Zhirovitchy (also spelled Zhirovitsy) is 90 miles (150 km) due west of Minsk, the capital of Belarus. The famous monastery complex, under jurisdiction of the Minsk Diocese, is located next to the village of Zhirovitchy in the environs of Grodno City, near the corner of Belarus bordering Poland and Lithuania. The feast days are May 7th until the 20th.

LITHUANIA

The Republic of Lithuania is located on the northeastern shore of the Baltic Sea alongside its neighbors Latvia and Estonia. Lithuania is the largest in size and most populous of the three Baltic states. Estonia and Latvia have strong ties with Scandinavia and both remain mostly Protestant, while Lithuania is firmly Roman Catholic, similar to its southern neighbor Poland. The Grand Duchy of Lithuania rose to prominence in the 14th century by the muscle of a highly effective army. The duchy won famous victories against Mongols in the east, Turks in the south, and Teutonic Knights in the west. By the 15th century, the Grand Duchy of Lithuania controlled territory across much of Eastern Europe, extending from the Baltic Sea to the Black Sea.

Lithuania was the only majority-Catholic country during the Soviet era. Nearly 50 years of communist rule in the Baltic countries ended with the advent of Polish-inspired *perestroika* and *glasnost*. The anti-communist movement that grew in Lithuania, called Sąjūdis, declared its independence from the Soviet Union on March 11th, 1990. Lithuania was the first Soviet republic to assert its independence, even though the Soviet authorities attempted to suppress their secession on many occasions. The Soviet attack on a Vilnius television station on January 13th, 1991 resulted in the death of 13 Lithuanian civilians and drew international condemnation. The last Russian troops left Lithuania on August 31st, 1993 — even earlier than their departure from East Germany. Roman Catholicism has been the predominant religion of Lithuania since its Christianization in the 14th century. Nearly 80% of Lithuanians are Roman Catholic. Catholic priests were influential in leading the resistance against the communist regime. Because of the decades of Soviet occupation, most Lithuanians also speak Russian.

Hill of Crosses

The origin of the Hill of Crosses is concurrent with the interesting history of Lithuania. The hill can be found near the town of Siauliai, founded in 1230 CE when Lithuania was a mostly pagan confederation. In fact, the province of Siauliai was the last region of mainland Europe to convert to Christianity, finally doing so in 1413 through its union with Poland. The Teutonic Order occupied Siauliai during the 14th century, and it is speculated that the custom of planting crosses on the hill began as a protest to Teutonic subjugation. Lithuanian Catholics have embraced the site since medieval times, when the nostalgic duchy was a powerhouse in Europe. The hill remained after Russia invaded the country in 1610. The hill remained after the Partitions of Poland of 1772 and 1796 made Lithuania disappear as a country altogether. The hill remained during the late 1800s when the act of erecting Latin crosses was forbidden by Czarist Russian Orthodox authorities. The hill remained when the political structure of Eastern Europe fell apart in 1918, and Lithuania once again needed to assert its identity. Throughout Lithuanian history, the Hill of Crosses was used as a sacred place by its citizens to pray for peace, for national pride, and remembrance for a long list of loved ones who died fighting for their freedom and independence.

▲ The Hill of Crosses is a profound sight to behold. When considering its turbulent history, the "power of place" becomes readily apparent.

The Hill of Crosses took on a new importance during the Soviet era when the country was officially annexed as the Lithuanian Soviet Socialist Republic. Although Soviet authorities forbade explicit religious symbols, thousands of new Latin rite crosses were erected illegally in this final chapter of Lithuanian oppression. It has been estimated that 36,000 national leaders were executed or deported during the Soviet occupation of Lithuania. In 1961, all crosses were removed and tractors leveled the hill. The Soviets bulldozed the site on a total of three occasions. Soviet authorities even went so far as to cover the hill with sewage and waste. Despite Soviet prohibitions, Lithuanians defied authority by continually erecting crucifixes on the hill until it became a nationally recognized anti-communist resistance shrine. Lithuanians used the hill to passively demonstrate an allegiance to their national identity and proud heritage. Even though the Soviets worked hard to remove new crosses almost as soon as they arrived, by 1985 they had given up and the Hill of Crosses flourished once again.

> The Hill of Crosses is a Catholic site, but it also symbolizes the cruel history of Lithuanian uprisings, wars, revolutions, occupations, and a continuous struggle for independence.

Devoted pilgrims from all over the world have contributed not only crosses, but giant carvings of Lithuanian patriots, statues of the Virgin Mary, and thousands of tiny effigies and rosaries. The Hill of Crosses is filled with visiting pilgrims' heartfelt tributes, prayer messages, and works of art. The crosses are varied and sometimes unusual. Most are carved of wood, but others are made from metal or sculpted plaster. Some of the most dramatic crucifixes can rise several meters in

149

height. Portraits of loved ones, saints, and national heroes sprinkle throughout the forest of crosses. On windy days, the sound of rosaries, bells, and other hanging tributes chiming together create a musical element that has been described as mystical. On September 7, 1993, Pope John Paul II visited the Hill of Crosses during a visit to Lithuania, declaring it "a place for hope, peace, love and sacrifice." He also recognized the Roman Catholic hill for its role in the nonviolent resistance that helped end communist rule in Eastern Europe.

Getting to the Hill of Crosses

The Hill of Crosses is located just outside the small industrial city of Siauliai (pronounced shoe-lay), near the border with Latvia. The Lithuanian name for the site is *Kryžiu Kalnas*. Tour group buses leave regularly from the capital Vilnius to the national pilgrimage center. Vilnius is located about 100 miles (160 km) to the southeast. Visitors to the site are expected to be respectful and quiet when they enter the labyrinth of paths and stairways on the twin-ridged hill. Devotional donations are allowed, but nothing is to be removed.

MOLDOVA

The Republic of Moldova is a small country in southeastern Europe, with few exports to speak of besides agriculture. Moldova remains the poorest country in Europe (GDP per capita is less than $1,000). This former Soviet republic is landlocked between Romania to the west and Ukraine to the east. Historically a part of the Kingdom of Romania for centuries, Moldova was annexed forcefully by the Soviet Union during World War II, becoming the Moldavian Soviet Socialist Republic. This somewhat unknown country boasts a rich history, but similar to other countries in the former Soviet Union it has been conquered on many occasions and has struggled to preserve its identity. Moldova declared its independence on August 27th, 1991, and currently aspires to join the European Union.

Tipova

Most Moldavians would recognize Tipova as the real power place in the country. Tipova is the largest and oldest Orthodox cave monastery in Eastern Europe. Long before the feudal state of Moldova was formed, a community of monks established the original settlement around the 10th century CE. The earliest cells were dug inside the steep cliffs situated 330 feet (100 m) directly above the Nistru River. The calcareous stone is relatively soft and easy to carve, allowing the monks to create a unique settlement partly dug into the cliffs. The hermitage monastery features an amazing panorama of the Nistru gorge and the countryside across the river. In ancient times, a Geto-Dacian fortress occupied the same area. Traces of the 4th century BCE fortress are still visible. The oldest section of the monastery consists of 19 enlarged caves built on the same level and connected by a narrow path. The greatly admired Moldovan ruler Stephen the Saint and his wife Maria Voichita were supposedly married in Tipova. Another legend tells how the mythological poet Orpheus spent his last years on these hills and was buried in a nearby nook by a scenic waterfall. The last part of the monastery was built in 1756 when a new section was added, divided into large parts, and separated by massive columns. The most popular attraction of Tipova is the "Sleeping of the God's Mother" church, a spacious underground sanctuary featuring a hemispherical arch roof, imitating the sky.

> The Tipova and Saharna cave monasteries are
> equally sacred in Moldova, attracting many
> pilgrims throughout the years.

The nearby Saharna cave monastery is a close cousin to Tipova, as both are considered the most popular religious pilgrimage destinations in Moldova. Both reside above picturesque river valleys, surrounded by country gardens, rolling vineyards, woodlands, and pastures. A special pilgrimage route connects the two monasteries. From "Grimidon" rock, the highest place along the route, the road turns off to the Saharna monastery complex, featuring the "Saint Trinity" church. Saharna includes the unique relics of Saint Cuvios Macarie, along with a supposed footprint of Saint Maria. The legend says that a monk from the monastery observed the shining figure of Saint Maria standing upon a tall boulder. The monk discovered a footstep in the rock when he reached the apparition site. His vision was considered to be a divine announcement and evidence of the holy purity of Saharna. The Trinity church was founded in 1777 near the footprint. The original wooden chapel was replaced by a brick church built in the old Moldavian style, decorated with a rich display of frescos. Meanwhile, both communities of Orthodox monks continued to expand over the next two centuries. After World War II, both the Tipova and Saharna monasteries were systematically closed and destroyed by Soviet authorities. In 1975, both monasteries were finally protected as museums, and in 1994 religious services resumed. Both locations are open to tourism daily. Both Tipova and Saharna are now recognized as having an indisputable value for the people of Moldova.

▲ The Tipova monastery erupts from a series of caves bordering the Nistru River.

Getting to Tipova

The Tipova cave monastery is located just outside of Tipova Village. The ancient sanctuary of Tipova (also spelled Tsypova) can be found on the high cliffs facing the Nistru River (also called the Dniester River). The site is located about 60 miles (100 km) north of the capital Kishinev (also spelled Chisinau). Tourists can explore the splendid pathways through the Tipova nature reserve surrounding the archaeological site. The Saharna cave monastery is located near Saharna Village, fronting the gorge where the small Saharna River empties into the Nistru River. Saharna is about 50 miles (85 km) north of Tipova, and 67 miles (110 km) north of Kishinev.

RUSSIA

After the Russian Revolution and atheist-inspired communism took hold, Soviet authorities sought to control the Russian Orthodox Church and, in times of national crisis, to exploit it for the regime's own purposes. Their ultimate goal was to eliminate it altogether, but they never quite succeeded. During the first five years of Soviet power, the Bolsheviks executed 28 Russian Orthodox bishops and over 1,200 Russian Orthodox priests. Many others were imprisoned or exiled. Believers were harassed and persecuted. Most seminaries were closed, and publication of most religious material was prohibited. By 1941, only 500 churches remained open from a high of about 54,000 prior to the Russian Revolution.

The eastern boundaries for Europe are drawn within Russia, the largest country in the world. The Caucasus Mountains, extending between the Black Sea and the Caspian Sea, define European Russia to the south. The former Soviet republic Kazakhstan is considered a central Asian country. But the most distinct boundary is the north-south running Ural Mountain range, bisecting European Russia from Asian Russia. Many sacred places exist within Asian Russia, but those will be included in the Far East book. Within European Russia, the Valdai Hills act as a natural divide between the two national competing capitals Moscow and St. Petersburg.

Mount El'brus

The mythical Mount El'brus is an extinct volcano located in the western Caucasus mountain range. The massive mountain rises near the southernmost extremity of European Russia, close to the border with Georgia. Other spellings include "Alburz," "Elburg," or "Elbruz." For those in northern Iran, it is described as either *Haraiti* or *Hara Barazaiti,* translated as the "Cosmic Mountain." The ancient Iranians gave it the name "El'brus" around the 2nd century BCE, naming it for a mythical chain of sacred mountains. Locals named it *Mangitau*, meaning "the mount of thousand mount heights." From time immemorial, the majestic El'brus attracted a steady flow of spiritual seekers. The mountain is sacred to all people in the region, no matter in which country they reside.

Being of a volcanic origin, Mount El'brus features the sometimes strange rock formations known to geologists as granits, gneisses, tuffs, and dia-

▲ Mount El'brus can be seen for hundreds of miles in all directions on a clear day.

bases. Certainly these bizarrely shaped arrangements would have given a supernatural impression to those with no knowledge of volcanism. The ancients called the mountain "Strobilus," the Latin word for pine cone (derived from the Greek word *strobilos*), a long established botanical term that describes the contour of the volcano's summit. El'brus is a stratovolcano that has lain dormant for about 2,000 years, but there is always the possibility it might erupt again. Although it has long been extinct, it still retains its gently sloping, conical shape. It is part of the Central Caucasus, but is located several miles north of the main crest of the range. It is the highest mountain in the Caucasus Range, which defines the southeastern most region of Europe. The Kura and Qvirila rivers flowing south of Mount El'brus delineate the border with the Asian continent. The west summit of Mount El'brus rises 18,510 feet (5,644 m), making it the highest mountain in Europe. Of the twin cones rising on its summit, the eastern peak is slightly lower at 18,442 feet (5,621 m). Either summit can provide incredible views of the entire Caucasus region.

> Mount El'brus is the highest peak in Europe, defining the border between Europe and Asia. To the ancient Greeks, it was the mythological peak where the hero Prometheus was chained.

References to Mount El'brus appear several times in Greek mythology. Most popular is the story of Zeus chaining Prometheus at the summit of Mount El'brus as punishment for supporting the Titans in their war against the Olympians. He was tortured for 30 years by "an eagle with outstretched wings, sent by Zeus, to feed upon his immortal liver." In spite of being tortured, the Titan persisted in his attitude of defying the lord of the Olympians. Finally, with the permission of

Zeus, Prometheus was rescued by the divine Hercules, who slew the eagle and broke the prisoner's chains. Prometheus was the god of fire, a clear reference to the volcano's historical activity.

Traditionally it was forbidden to ascend El'brus, yet some brave souls always tried. Those who risked the mountain's chilling slopes often returned to the valley with stories of hallucinations, strong headaches, or other symptoms now recognized as altitude sickness. Sulphuric gases emanating from the mountain's active fumaroles could have played a role. But to superstitious locals, it seemed to confirm the wrath of the gods. Not to be daunted, the lower of the two summits was first ascended in 1868, and the higher in 1874 by a British expedition. Even today the locals will tell mountaineers that one must approach El'brus slowly, modestly, and with sincere respect. She is a haughty queen they say, never to be taken lightly. Beautiful and placid on the surface, wearing her upper slopes of icy glaciers like ermine robes, she has been known to turn on mortals in a moment's notice. When angry, she fumes foul gases and stirs up fierce storms, which are notorious for causing climbers to become dizzy or lose their way. To avoid the wrath of El'brus, the locals will recommend a pre-climb supplicant, a prayer, or any humble offering.

Climbing Mount El'brus

Mount El'brus rises about 12 miles (20 km) north of the main range of the Greater Caucasus, and 40 miles (65 km) southwest of the Russian town of Kislovodsk, the main portal for climbers. El'brus is part of Russia's Kabardino-Balkar Republic. The summit is capped in ice year round, feeding 22 glaciers from its slopes, which in turn gives rise to the Baksan, Kuban, and Malka Rivers. All told, the mountain and its vast complex of glaciers cover some 56 square miles (146 sq. km) of terrain.

There are a wide variety of climbing routes to the summit, but the most popular route, the route with no dangerous crevasses, continues more or less straight up the slope from the end of the mid-mountain cable car station. During the summer, it is not uncommon for 100 people to be attempting the summit via this route every day. The climb is not technically difficult, considered only a basic snow-ice climb. However, most climbers find it physically arduous because of the high elevations and the frequent windstorms. The best months for climbing are June, July, August, and September. Most climbers collect their gear in Mineral'nye Vody, Russia. The nearest major airport would be Kiev, Ukraine, or Tbilisi, Georgia.

Saint Basil's Cathedral

The famous Saint Basil's Cathedral is an icon of central Moscow, the capital city of Russia. It was commissioned by Ivan the Terrible and built on the edge of Red Square between 1555 and 1561. Saint Basil's is located at the southeastern end of Red Square, just across the street from the Kremlin's Spasskaya Tower. Not particularly large, it consists of nine chapels built on a single foundation. The cathedral's design follows that of contemporary tented churches common throughout Russia. The Russian people have traditionally perceived Saint Basil's Cathedral to be a symbolic connection between Europe and Asia.

Ivan the Terrible commissioned the cathedral to celebrate his capture of the Tartar stronghold of Kazan in 1552. The name given by Ivan was the "Cathedral of Intercession of the Virgin on the Mound" or simply "Pokrovskiy Cathedral." The initial concept was to build a cluster of chapels, one dedicated to each of the saints on whose feast day the tsar had won a strategic battle.

▲ Saint Basil's Cathedral is the most recognizable building in Moscow.

Although seemingly haphazard, the construction of a single central tower unifies these spaces into a single cathedral. After Ivan the Terrible's reign, it became better known as the "Cathedral of Saint Basil the Blessed," or simply "Saint Basil's Cathedral." The name change occurred because Tsar Fyodor Ivanovich had a new chapel added in 1588 above the grave of the renowned "holy fool." Saint Basil the Blessed became a Russian Orthodox saint after he foretold of a fire in 1547 that would sweep through Moscow. Saint Basil was originally buried in the Trinity Cathedral that stood on the site before Ivan had it torn down for his church, but Basil's tomb was so revered that it remained interred. Legend has it that Ivan the Terrible was so impressed by the beauty of Saint Basil's Cathedral that he ordered the architect's eyes removed. Postnik Yakovlev was supposedly blinded to prevent him from ever designing a more magnificent building.

> Saint Basil's Cathedral has miraculously survived many threats of destruction over the years, only enhancing its divine status.

The original design featured eight individual chapels, each topped with a brightly colored onion dome commemorating a victorious battle. The ninth chapel was erected 30 years later to house the tomb of the cathedral's namesake, Basil the Blessed. Despite its apparent disorder, there is an underlying symmetry to the iconic cathedral. The original design of eight chapels is based upon deep Christian symbolism. The number eight is an architectural representation of the "New Jerusalem" — the Heavenly Kingdom as described by Saint John the Divine in the Book of Revelation. Saint Basil's star-like ground plan denotes a deeper religious meaning — the eight-pointed star consists of two superimposed squares, which represent the four corners of the earth, the stability of faith, the four Evangelists, and the four equal-sided walls of Jerusalem. The eight-pointed star itself symbolizes the Christian Church as a guiding light to humankind, indicating the way to the Heavenly City. The kingdom of the 8th century — the promised Heavenly Jerusalem — will begin after the second coming of Christ. The number eight also denotes the day of Christ's Resurrection according to the ancient Jewish calendar. The number eight also represents the Virgin Mary, frequently depicted in Eastern Orthodox iconography wearing a veil decorated with three eight-pointed stars.

With such revered qualities, it is hard to believe that the cathedral narrowly escaped destruction on several occasions. Napoleon was so impressed with Saint Basil's Cathedral that he reportedly wanted to take it back to Paris with him. After learning that removal was not possible, he ordered it destroyed. The French placed several kegs of gunpowder inside the cathedral and even lit the fuses. A sudden — some say miraculous — rain shower appeared at exactly the right moment to prevent the explosion. A century later, the cathedral was again threatened with destruction, this time by the atheist principles of the Bolshevik regime. In 1918, communist authorities assassinated the church's senior priest, closed the cathedral, confiscated all its property, and melted down the church bells. Joseph Stalin considered the removal of Saint Basil's in the 1930s because the cathedral prevented his soldiers from leaving Red Square en masse. In another of his twisted decisions, Stalin ordered a prominent devotee of Russian culture, architect P. Baranovsky, to prepare the cathedral for demolition. The architect refused by sending a bluntly worded telegram to Stalin stating he would rather cut his own throat on the steps of the church before he would oversee its destruction. For some reason, Stalin cancelled his decision to remove Saint Basil's Cathedral, however Baranovsky was sent to the gulag for five years.

Getting to Saint Basil's Cathedral

Saint Basil's erupts in a delightful profusion of swirling onion domes supported by redbrick towers at the far end of Red Square in Moscow's innermost old city. Bus, tram, and subway routes all access the Kremlin section of Moscow, the capital city of Russia. Saint Basil's should never be confused with being part of the Moscow Kremlin, which is situated right next to it on Red Square in the nucleus of the city. It has no relation to the Kremlin other than proximity, but that makes it easy to locate.

Sergiev Posad

Sergius of Radonezh, the founder of the Holy Trinity Lavra at Sergiev Posad, was born in 1314 to a wealthy family. His childhood was reportedly filled with solitude, prayer, fasting, and hard work. At the age of 23, after his parents' death in 1337, he decided to leave for the desert along with his elder brother, Stephen. The brothers didn't make it much farther than the hinterland outside of Moscow, where they decided to establish their hilltop hermitage in a meadow surrounded by a dense forest. The first thing they built was a monk's cell

▲ The Sergiev Posad religious complex is an inspiration to the people of Russia.

and a small church, which they devoted to the Trinity. That was the birth of Sergiev Posad, which would attract fellow monks, the Russian Orthodoxy, and ultimately would become a source of inspiration and pride to the Russian people. "In the land of Moscow and all over the world there is no other monastery equal to this one," said the Archdeacon Paul of Aleppa.

> Sergiev Posad is the spiritual home to the Russian Orthodoxy, similar in importance to the Vatican. Trinity Cathedral is the focal point for prayers and pilgrimage, just as Saint Peter's Basilica is the object of worship for Catholics.

Many Russians regard Sergiev Posad as the most beautiful religious complex in Eastern Europe. Its Byzantine influence was imported from the Mediterranean region (via the Ukraine) after the first location of Russian Orthodoxy, Pechersk Lavra in Kiev, was destroyed in the 13th century by invading Mongols. Shortly after Pechersk Lavra was laid to ruins, the patriarchy established a safer residence in Moscow, then a small provincial town. Greek control of the Orthodox Church was shattered in 1453 when the Turks conquered Constantinople, significantly reducing the influence of the Greek patriarchy. Kiev and Moscow became rivals for Orthodox supremacy in Russia. The monk Sergius of Radonezh couldn't have timed the founding of his monastery any better, because in 1337 the new Russian Orthodoxy was ready to develop its administrative center away from the more volatile south. Saint Sergius inadvertently became a national symbol of Russian and Orthodox unity, inspiring resistance to the new Tartar threat. The humble wooden monastery was sacked in 1422 by invading Tartars, only to be rebuilt with the centerpiece Trinity Cathedral housing the hallowed remains of Saint Sergius in a silver reliquary. When Ivan the Terrible smashed the Tartar capital of Kazan in 1552, he commissioned the Uspensky (Assumption) Cathedral at Sergiev Posad.

The monastery took on a mythical potency and became the most important pilgrimage destination in Russia. Over the following centuries, the monastery grew very powerful and wealthy.

Shortly after its founding, Sergiev Posad became the Russian Orthodox Church's administrative center, headed by a patriarch who is elected by bishops and serves for life. It also attracted a large amount of pilgrims from its founding date until today. The object of the pilgrims' devotion is the tomb of Saint Sergius in the Holy Trinity Lavra, the Sergius Well, and the Assumption Cathedral with its five blue domes capped with gold stars and crosses. The town surrounding the monastery became incorporated in 1742, largely because of the religious city's growing demand for workers. Because its name carried a strong religious connotation, Soviet authorities renamed the city "Zagorsk" in 1930, translated as "a town beyond the hills." The name *Sergiev Posad*, meaning "the settlement of Sergius," came back into official use in 1991.

Sergiev Posad is one of the cities included in Russia's famous Golden Ring. The dozen or so locations in the Golden Ring are among the most picturesque, oldest, and best preserved historic cities in Russia. All of these cities prominently feature Russia's famous onion domes. The Golden Ring includes the locations where some of the main events of Russian history played out, including the formation of the Russian Orthodox Church. These ancient towns have been called "open air museums" and feature unique monuments of Russian architecture, including kremlins, monasteries, cathedrals, and churches. The Golden Ring cities formerly comprised the region known as Zalesye. Tourism associated with the Golden Ring plays a major role in the regional economy. Just outside the Golden Ring is Svetloyar Lake, where the legendary city Grad Kitezh sank in the 13th century. A fringe element believes the city is alive underwater, and possibly even underground. Svetloyar Lake, a place of Russian legend, has gained the title "Russian Atlantis." The invisible Grad Kitezh underneath Svetloyar Lake is now a biospheric reserve supported by UNESCO, with some USA grants involved in the clean-up of this unique site.

Getting to Sergiev Posad

Sergiev Posad is a city about 45 miles (72 km) outside of Russia's capital Moscow. The city is the administrative center of the Sergiyevo-Posadsky District of Moscow Oblast. Sergiev Posad has a population around 140,000. The Moscow–Yaroslavl railway and highway pass directly through the city, making it very accessible for those wishing to make a day trip from Moscow. Many of Golden Ring cities are located along the M8 highway northeast of Moscow, or can be reached from Yaroslavl Railway Station in Moscow. Svetloyar Lake is in the Volga region, opposite the city Nizhniy Novgorod.

Valaam

Many sacred sites worldwide share a common aspect called the "power of place," loosely defined as a location's perceptible spiritual value that transcends religious priorities, cultural importance, and the long test of time. According to accepted tradition, blood sacrificing pagans lived on Valaam Island in pre-Christian times and worshipped the deity Baal, also called Beles. Originally an ancient Semitic god, Baal was a fertility deity commonly worshipped in natural settings. The cult of Baal spread with the sea-faring Phoenician people from the Mediterranean region to the far reaches of northern Europe, and quite possibly on trading missions to North America (see: *Sacred Places North America: 108 Destinations* by Brad Olsen). Since Valaam is the largest island in Lake Ladoga, itself being the largest lake in Europe, the sheer power of this place would be apparent. Thousands of years later, when the first missionaries of Christ came to these northern reaches, they met fierce resistance from the heathen populations. Scandinavia and Lithuania were among the last places in Europe to resist Christianity, but eventually they capitulated. The holy apostle Andrew traveled from Novgorod to the Valaam Islands with a vengeance. He succeeded in converting the Scythian and Slavic people, all the while destroying pagan temples wherever he went. In Valaam, he did the same and raised a stone cross in commemoration.

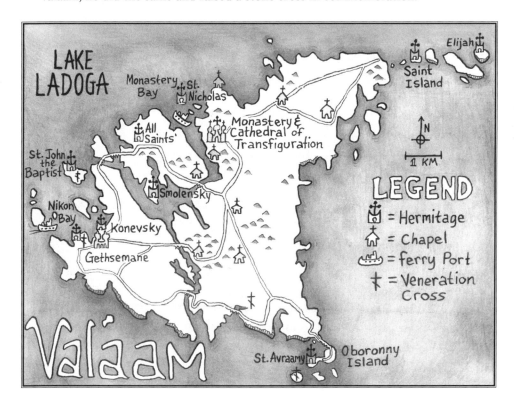

▲ The Cathedral of Transfiguration is the largest religious building on Valaam Island.

The isolation of the Valaam monastery would have inspired the resident monks to feel closer with God by living deep in a northern Russian forest and far from any hint of civilization. The organized monastic presence on Valaam dates back over 1,000 years, prior to the Baptism of Rus' in 988 CE, and the subsequent Christian propagation of Russia in the 10th and 11th centuries. It is not exactly clear when the monastery was founded, as the Valaam cloister is not mentioned in any documents before the 16th century. Whatever the actual founding date may be, it is known that the Valaam monastery was among the first western outposts of Eastern Orthodoxy. The monk's original enemies were the pagan tribes, later to be provoked by the 12th century Catholics of Tavastia, and finally the 17th century Lutherans of Sweden. Monastic life was interrupted for long decades after the devastation left by several invasions. Many memorials, historical records, and monastery relics were destroyed or plundered in the invasions. The monastery libraries and manuscript depositories were burned or stolen, including the priceless hagiography of Saint Sergius and Saint Herman.

The Valaam Monastery is called "Mount Athós of the North" because of its long Eastern Orthodox tradition, far away from the temptations of the outside world.

For many centuries, Valaam was the most important isolated monastic center for the Russian Orthodoxy, in a similar way that Mount Athós inspired the Mediterranean Orthodoxy. The saints Sergius and Herman followed in later centuries to continue the mission of converting non-believers. The deeds of these first saints strengthened Orthodoxy in northern Russia, especially the foundation of a monastic cloister at Valaam which became a stronghold of Orthodoxy in the early centuries of Christian proliferation. Saint Herman traveled to Russian Alaska, becoming the first "American" saint because he was the original missionary to bring Orthodoxy to North America. He came to America as a young monk in 1794 as part of the Russian expansion into Alaska. Saint Herman eventually returned to Valaam where he died. The remains of saints Sergius and Herman were transferred during the Swedish invasion, but when the danger was past, the monks brought the holy relics back to Valaam and hid them somewhere on the island. To commemorate the sacred relics return to Valaam, a Church celebration is conducted annually from September 11th to the 24th. For many centuries, Valaam was an important religious and cultural center, supported by Russian Tzars and the Russian Church. The island attracted monks because it was a haven for those seeking a life of solitude and prayer. The Russian Revolution and rise of communism closed Valaam as a religious sanctuary. Finally, after almost 50 years, in December 1989, monastic life was restored to Valaam, and since 1991 Valaam has been directed by the Patriarch of Moscow, who appoints the Abbot. At present, there are over 100 monks and novices living at the monastery. They follow a very strict monastic rule. The sound of the hauntingly beautiful ancient Znammeny chant, that had long been a part of Valaam tradition, is being heard once again. Many pilgrims come to the island, especially for the feast days of saints Sergius and Herman in July and September, and for the Transfiguration feast in August.

Getting to Valaam

"Valaam" refers to the large main island, the monastery, as well as an archipelago of about 50 islands of various sizes located in the northern part of Lake Ladoga. Ladoga also holds the distinction of being the largest lake in Europe. The Valaam Archipelago is one of the most interesting cultural, historical, and natural attractions in northern Russia. Valaam is about 135 miles (215 km) northeast of St. Petersburg in Karelia. This area of Russia is near the Finnish border, and in previous centuries had been occupied by Sweden. Ferry boats traverse Lake Ladoga every day from the Karelian port towns of Sortavala, Lahdenpohja, and Pitkyaranta. Each trip from the lake towns will take about an hour. There are also river cruise trips available from St. Petersburg and Moscow. The large overnight cruise boats make the trip between St. Petersburg and Valaam in 11 hours. Those individuals who would like to visit the monastery for more than a day are required to contact the pilgrimage department of the Monastery Podvoria in St. Petersburg and at Valaam.

UKRAINE

In antiquity, most of the southeastern region of modern Ukraine was populated by pagan nomads from Iran called the Scythians. The Scythian Kingdom lasted from 700 BCE to 200 BCE, and served as a land bridge for the Arian people to migrate into Europe. In the 3rd century CE, the Goths arrived, calling their country Oium, and establishing the Chernyakhov culture before leaving the region to defeat the Roman Empire. In the 7th century, the territory of the modern Ukraine was the core of the state of the Bulgars (often referred to as Great Bulgaria), who had their capital in the city of Phanagoria. During the 10th and 11th centuries, the territory of Ukraine became the center of a powerful and prestigious state in Europe called the Kievan Rus' which established the national identity of Ukrainians, as well as other eastern Slavic nations. The 13th century

Mongol invasion dealt the Rus' empire a devastating blow. The resilient Ukrainian people eventually emerged from the destruction, largely due to their unwavering faith. The dominant religion in Ukraine remains Eastern Orthodox Christianity.

Pechersk Lavra

The origin of the Pechersk Monastery in Kiev corresponds with the introduction of Christianity throughout the Kievan Rus' in the 10th century. At that time, the first Christians were usually hermits living in secluded caves. In the Slavic languages, Pechersk means *pechera*, or "caves," which are found in abundance along the cliffs of the Dnieper River valley. Some of the caves are naturally formed, but most were painstakingly carved by the hermits and monks. There is an entire network of caves that extends beneath the monastic settlement of Pechersk Lavra. The caves provided shelter, security, storage, and locations for hand-carved chapels, monastic cells, and burial caves. To keep the new religion alive in its formative years, the ruling class commissioned the building of impressive churches. They also supported the activity of the early monks, encouraging them to come out of seclusion and travel the countryside to preach the Christian faith. These early monks can claim responsibility for establishing the original monasteries of Orthodox worship throughout the Ukraine. Such are the humble origins of Pechersk Lavra, the most important location of the Ukrainian Orthodox religion. It eventually earned the term "Lavra," an honorific title given to a monastery of extra-size and religious importance.

Kiev Pechersk Lavra, also known as the "Kiev Monastery of the Caves," is the first monastery founded in the Ukraine or Russia. It was officially established in 1051 by the monks Anthony and Theodosius, and soon became the most important center of Orthodox Christianity. According to the early 11th century Primary Chronicle, Anthony, a Greek Orthodox monk from the Esfigmenou

▲ Many fantastic religious buildings make up the Pechersk Lavra complex ...

Monastery on Mount Athós, returned to his homeland and settled in Kiev as a missionary. He chose a cave within the Berestov Mount overlooking the Dnieper River. Within a few years, his group of disciples grew into a sizeable community. Prince Iziaslav of Kiev ceded the whole mount region of 75 acres (30 ha) to the Antonite monks, who eagerly founded a new monastery above ground. The prince hired the finest architects from the Orthodox capital of Constantinople to build Pechersk Lavra.

Designed at the time to rival the magnificent Hagia Sophia in Constantinople, Kiev's Saint Sophia Cathedral at Pechersk Lavra serves as the headquarters for the Ukrainian Orthodox Church.

During the next ten centuries, Pechersk Lavra played a significant role in the cultural and religious life of Eastern Europe. Indeed, the whole religious city was designed to become a "new Constantinople" of the Ukraine. The history of the religious complex is full of important events, both negative and positive. It was plundered in 1240 by the Tartars, and for the next two centuries it barely survived. During this dark period, many of the monks fled north to Sergiev Posad, establishing a rival monastery near Moscow in 1337. A century later, the Russian and Ukrainian Orthodox churches split, each becoming the cultural heart of their respective countries. The spiritual and intellectual influence of Pechersk Lavra contributed directly to the spread of Orthodoxy throughout the Russian world. In its heyday, the monastery owned 80,000 serfs, several villages, and other monasteries in the Ukraine. Decline came quickly once again with the rise of communism and the destruction of Kiev from aerial bombing in World War II. Many of the damaged buildings have been restored and the Ukrainian government is in the process of returning the property to the Orthodox Church.

The 86 buildings and churches of Pechersk Lavra make up a splendid collection of different Byzantine architectural styles from the past. Some of the most notable buildings are the Uspenskiy Cathedral, Bell Tower, Troitskaya Church, Hospital Church, All-Saints Church, Refectory, and the Dormition Cathedral, which was used as a model for many other cathedrals in the Ukraine. Situated on a hillside, the monastery grounds are split into two parts called "Upper Lavra" and "Lower Lavra." The below ground catacombs are similarly divided into two groups, the Near Caves and the Far Caves. Along the serpentine passageways can be seen small chapels and the monastic cells where the early hermits lived. Numerous exhibitions and museums educate visitors into the history, national traditions, and folk art of Pechersk Lavra. Most religious pilgrims are attracted to the walking circuit of monastic churches. Today, the architectural complex of Pechersk Lavra is both a collection of unique museums, grandiose religious buildings, and a functioning monastery. The Kiev Pechersk Lavra also serves as the residence for the head of the Ukrainian Orthodox Church.

▲ ... but the Saint Sophia Cathedral is undoubtedly the crowning achievement of Pechersk Lavra.

Getting to Pechersk Lavra

The ancient cave monastery is located very close to downtown Kiev. The physical address of Pechersk Lavra is 21 Sichnevogo Povstannya. Take the Kiev subway to Arsenalna or the Pechers'ka Metro Station, then catch the trolley bus to the monastery. Signs mark the way from all directions. According to its promotional literature, Pechersk Lavra is Kiev's main tourist attraction, having hosted nearly 50 million visitors in the past few decades. For a different kind of tour, visitors can explore the caves by candlelight, peering into the open coffins of deceased monks.

SCANDINAVIA

In the beginning of time there was nothing:
No sand, nor sea, nor cooling surf;
There was no earth, nor upper heaven;
No blade of grass—only the Great Void.

—*Völuspá*, Viking creation mythology from
The Sibyl's Prophecy

THE MOST FAMOUS SCANDINAVIANS IN HISTORY were the valiant, wrathful, and purely pagan people known as the Vikings. Unlike the earlier marauders of mainland Europe, the Vikings had a splendid mythology with gods possessing hero-like attributes and a deep reverence for the afterlife. Their runic stones give the impression of magical power. They were among the last people of Europe to resist Christianity, well into the 12th century. Almost all Vikings were illiterate, and the written evidence of their history was recorded by the first Scandinavian Christian monks. Although brutal and rapacious in their conquests, they were master seamen, able to travel as far east as Persia (via the Volga River and the Caspian Sea) or to the northeastern shores of North America. They set out from their bases in Scandinavia to plunder all that was valuable — Christian relics from churches and monasteries, slaves from Europe, coins from Samarkand, and even a 5th century bronze Buddha statue from northern India. They inscribed their runic letters inside the Hagia

Sophia in Istanbul and on the lion statues at Delos, Greece. The sheer technical cunning of their voyages makes the Norsemen among the greatest explorers from European history. Their exploits are best remembered and romanticized in the operas of Wagner.

DENMARK

The Kingdom of Denmark is a small country, about 200 miles (375 km) long from Skagen in the north to the river Eider in the south. Unlike the other Scandinavian countries it is very flat, with the highest point a mere 591 feet (173 m) above sea level. The Jutland Peninsula shares a common border with Germany, but the rest of Denmark consists of islands of all sizes. Although small, Denmark holds the strategic position of controlling ocean-going traffic with the Baltic Sea on one side and the North Sea on the other. As the "southern gateway" to Scandinavia, Denmark has traditionally had far more economic, political and cultural contact with the rest of Europe. Thus, most European influences reached it first, including Christianity, despite the resistance of the pagan population.

Jelling

The transition from a pagan faith to a Christian one, along with the birth of a nation called "Denmark," began at Jelling. In the center of the small town are two imposing mounds, with a small church in between, flanked by large runestones and modern graves. King Gorm the Old was buried as a heathen in the Northern Mound about 958 CE. King Gorm's wife, Queen Thyra, is traditionally thought to be buried in the Southern Mound. Both mounds were built of stacked grass sod, not dirt. The remains of what is believed to be King Gorm were later re-buried inside the church.

Gorm's chieftain status was passed down to his son, Harald Bluetooth. Even though Harald was born a pagan, he accepted Christianity on behalf of his subjects after being crowned king. To mark the occasion, Harald erected a runestone at Jelling that became known as the "Baptism Stone" or the "Birth Certificate of Denmark," commemorating his conversion, and the nation, to Christianity. Before his death, King Gorm erected a runestone at Jelling with the name "Denmark" written in runic writing for the first known time. This second stone at Jelling has suitably been termed the "Name Certificate of Denmark."

▲ The famous Jelling church is sandwiched between two massive burial mounds.

167

▲ The "White Christ" image on the Baptism Stone can be found on all Danish passports.

Jelling was the center of the Kingdom of Denmark in the Viking Age and remains the cultural identity of the country.

King Harald Bluetooth is famous throughout Denmark. It was he who ordered the construction of several large circular fortresses manned by elite troops all over Denmark, including Aggersborg; the largest Viking fortress ever built, which once contained 48 longhouses. About six miles (10 km) south of Jelling, Harald ordered the building of a monumental bridge across the Ravning Enge, or "water meadow." The half-mile long (800-m) bridge was so large and well-built that it wouldn't be until 1935, almost a millennium later, that another bridge in Denmark would surpass it in size. But Harald's greatest achievement would be the words he carved on the Baptism Stone at Jelling. It reads: "King Harald commanded the erection of this stone in memory of Gorm his father and Thyra his mother. It was he who conquered Denmark and Norway and converted the Danes to Christianity." The location of the stone is placed exactly between the two mounds.

Also between the mounds is the Jelling Church, the fourth to be built on the exact same location. All three of the previous churches burned down, but the fourth was made of travertine stone, quarried from a nearby spring in 1100, and still remains. Excavations of the church in the 1970s revealed a male skeleton, believed to be King Gorm. When his son started to convert the Danes to Christianity, he ordered the first wooden church built, completing the construction by reburying his father in the new church. Although Gorm is regarded as the founder of the so-called Jelling Dynasty, it was Harald who consolidated power and became the first real king of Denmark.

Harald's son, Sven, also had lofty aspirations. With his coming of age, Sven began to amass his own army to challenge Harald for the throne. When that fateful day arrived, Harald Bluetooth was fatally struck with a poison arrow from one of Sven's archers. He was laid to rest in Roskilde on the island of Zealand. The descendents of Gorm and Harald still occupy the throne of Denmark today. More than 150,000 tourists visit Jelling every year.

Getting to Jelling

The small town of Jelling has its own train station on the green line from Copenhagen to Struer. The church and mound site is one block away from the station. Many tour companies of Denmark make a stop at Jelling. In 1994, Jelling was added to the UNESCO list of World Heritage Sites, the first location in Denmark added to the prestigious list. A museum and bookstore are located across the street from the Jelling Church and mounds.

Lindholm Høje

Perched on a hill with a commanding view, the Lindholm Høje burial ground was in consistent use during the Germanic Iron Age and the Viking Period, or from the 4th to the 10th century. Almost 700 people were buried here, with the oldest graves situated on the highest part of the hill. Lindholm Høje is the tallest rise in the surrounding area, a location considered both strategic and sacred to the Vikings. There are only a few inhumation graves — also the oldest — as the practice soon changed to cremation. More than 600 of those interred were cremated and, of these, more than half are surrounded by a standing stone enclosure. Interestingly, several longhouses were also erected on different parts of the hill, further attesting to its importance. Also on the hill is one of the few farm fields preserved from Viking times. The long ridges that can be seen were created by a Viking farmer, who used a plough with a mound-board to turn the earth. Around 1000 CE, a storm covered the road, field, and gravesites with drifting sand. The road was blocked and the pagan graveyard soon became abandoned. In the mid-1950s archaeologists uncovered the site and found the wheel tracks of the farmer's cart still intact.

▲ Many of the Lindholm Høje burials are within an oblong ring of stones, symbolizing a ship.

Lindholm Høje is one of the best preserved
and most famous ancient monuments in
Denmark.

The oldest cremation graves are surrounded by a triangular, oblong or circular stone arrangement. The setting of upright stones in a round fashion was to recreate the form of a ship. Sometimes, the stones from an older grave were removed to create a new grave. When the rocks were removed, like the longhouse post holes, the empty spaces filled in with soil of a darker color. Archaeologists used the soil colors to determine the position of every object that once stood at Lindholm Høje. It was common for the dead to be cremated in their clothes within the newly created stone enclosure. Buckles and jewelry remained after the fire, along with personal items, such as spindles, knives, whetstones, as well as bones from food offerings. Many graves also included the bones of the deceased person's dog.

Only two inhumation graves contained a stone marking, or headstone. One of these two special burials contained a sword, a so-called "scramasax" blade from the Germanic Iron Age, alongside the body. Therefore, this grave can be positively dated from the beginning of the 6th century. This distinguished warrior, like so many others, was buried with his dog. Today, Lindholm Høje is the most famous ancient graveyard in Denmark.

Getting to Lindholm Høje

Lindholm is the name of a suburb across the Limfjorden from Denmark's 4th largest city, Aalborg. The ancient burial site and modern museum are located 1.2 miles (2 km) from the Lindholm train station. It is at the north end of the street *Vikingevej* ("Viking's Way") on the south facing hill. There are various Viking-related events held at the site all year round.

FINLAND

With a quarter of its land located above the Arctic Circle, Finland occupies the extreme northern latitudes of Europe. At this northern position, agriculture becomes a challenge, since full days of darkness extend for several months a year. Even in the far south of Finland, the daylight hours never reach more than six hours during winter. The Finns have thus become proficient greenhouse farmers, using the lumber from their ample timber output to supplement energy consumption.

Lapland

In the extreme northern latitudes of Europe live a group of small, sturdy people known as the Lapps. Long before the Viking Age in Finland, there were semi-permanent inhabitants living above the Arctic Circle. The original inhabitants of northern Scandinavia were the Lapp people, closely related to the prehistoric Saami of Norway. When the Vikings migrated to Finland in the first millennium BCE, the Lapps were forced to move farther northward into the Arctic regions of Finland and Russia. The Khibiny Mountain region in Russian Lapland features a multitude of lakes, labyrinths, and rock carvings that remain sacred to Finnish Saami people. There is much evidence that the Laplanders had contact with the Vikings, in spite of undoubted language differences. The Lapps traded with the Norse, mostly furs, whale bones, walrus tusks, and ropes they manufactured specifically for Viking ships.

Lapland is not a separate country — it belongs to Norway, Sweden, Finland, and Russia. It is very cold in this region of the world and winter lasts for nine months. For two months the sun never rises above the horizon. Modern Lapps live mostly in the interior of Finland, moving with the changing hunting and fishing seasons. Reindeer are the sacred animals of these semi-nomadic people, as the animals provide food, shelter, clothing, and other necessities. However, it was not until fairly recent times that the Lapps began to keep large herds of reindeer. The Mountain Lapps remain mostly nomadic people who move constantly in search of food for their herds of reindeer. They pitch their tents wherever there is enough vegetation to feed the herds. The Lapps live on reindeer meat, fish, milk and cheese. They dress in clothes made of wool and reindeer skins. The hide from the reindeer, along with birch, were used to make a *lavo,* or a teepee-like dwelling. The lavo's central smokehole doubled as an entrance into the spiritual realms.

> The Laplanders, among others, formed a
> belief called the "World Tree" to explain the
> complexities of their universe.

The Lapps of modern-day Finland, and the Koyak tribes of the central Russian steppes, constructed a cosmology formulated around the concept of a World Tree. In this ancient mythology, the World Tree was seen as a kind of cosmic axis, onto which the planes of the universe are fixed. The roots of the World Tree reach deep into the underworld, its trunk is the "middle earth" of everyday existence, and its branches extend upwards into the heavenly realm. The North Star was also considered sacred, since all other stars in the sky revolved around its fixed point. They associated this "pole star" with the World Tree, as the central axis of the universe. The top of the World Tree touched the North Star, and the spirit of the shaman would climb the metaphorical tree, thereby passing into the realm of the gods.

Almost all Scandinavians have seen the evening phenomenon called the northern lights, or aurora borealis. In the winter months, it is common to view a greenish glow near the northern horizon. If watched closely, the lights will slowly fade and pulsate. People have long created myths about the lights, believing they were reflections from the world's edge or the glow of a powerful deity. Quantum physics now explain the

▲ Saami family members pose in front of their tents from this 1900 photograph.

lights as emanating 50-80 miles (80-120 km) above the earth's surface, a result of high energy gas particles colliding in the sun's atmosphere, breaking down atoms. Electrical particles are slung out into space, forming a solar wind, the plasma composed of protons and free electrons. The earth's magnetic field bends these particles in the upper atmosphere, where they excite atoms that in turn give off the play of light — light that has long fascinated viewers in the northern latitudes.

Getting to Lapland

Perhaps the ideal way of reaching the northern latitudes of Scandinavia is by train. The area covered by Lapland lies mostly north of the Arctic Circle, including parts of Sweden, Norway, and Russia. In Finland, the Lapp terrain is like a low plateau, containing many marshes and lakes — the most important of which is Lake Inari in Finnish Lapland. The Khibiny Mountains in Russian Lapland can be found in Murmansk Region on the Kola Peninsula. Most of Lapland lies within the tundra region. The best time to visit is in the summer months.

GREENLAND

Greenland is the largest island in the world, consisting of a surface area of 840,000 square miles (2,184,000 sq km), a length of 1,650 miles (2,640 km), and a breadth of 760 miles (1,216 km). Nearly all of it lies above the Arctic Circle, and about five-sixths of it is permanently under ice. From Viking times onwards, European settlers have been confined mainly to the southwest coastal region of the island. It is only here where grass, bushes, and a few small trees grow. Today, Greenland is administered by the government of Denmark.

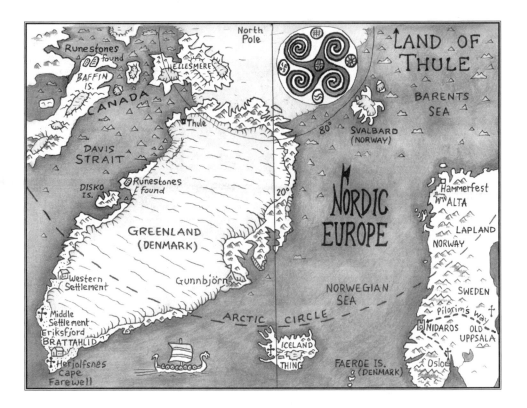

Brattahild

Around the year 960 CE, a boy named Erik the Red and his father, Thorval, were involved in a murder. Both were forced to leave their home in southern Norway and, like so many Scandinavians before them, found a new home in Iceland. Erik inherited his father's temper and he committed two murders in Iceland around the year 985. The Iceland parliament banished him from the island for three years. With nowhere else to live, Erik went in search of a western land, which had been reported by a wayward sailor a few years earlier. When Erik rounded Cape Farewell, on Greenland's southern tip, he discovered his own promised land. He named the land "Greenland" after the green grass valleys on the southwest side. Erik was excited that this new land was suitable for grazing animals, making it habitable for his people.

When he returned, he was not interested in living in Iceland again, but in starting his own colony at the new location he discovered. Since farmland was in short supply in Iceland, it was easy for Erik to recruit people to move with him. In the following summer, Erik led a fleet of 25 ships, each fully loaded with cargo and emigrants. Unfortunately, only 14 ships made it to Greenland after a fierce storm sent some ships back to Iceland, and sank a few others. In its prime, Greenland's Eastern Settlement contained about 200 homesteads, and the

Western Settlement, about 300 miles (480 km) to the north, included another 100 homesteads. In all, the Viking population of Greenland totaled some 3,000 people. Erik the Red and his family settled on the finest piece of land, a homestead in a village he named Brattahild at the end of Erik's Fjord.

Christianity reached Greenland via Erik's eldest son, Leif, after he was christened by King Olav Trygvasson of Norway in 999 while on a trading mission. Leif returned with priests to undertake the missionary work of converting the Greenland settlers. This would prove to be an uphill battle as many Vikings, including Erik the Red, refused to give up their pagan gods. The Greenland colonies would become the last remnant of pagan worship after it had been all but extinguished in Europe. Many refused to convert, including most of the settlers in the Western Settlement, while others (like Leif's mother) embraced Christianity. The famous Scandinavian stave-churches were likely the answer to the old heathen temples, of which none were preserved. A typical stave-church was very large, made of timber, and often found atop existing foundations, likely old pagan temples.

The very next year, Leif set off on a voyage of discovery to a land reported even farther to the west. He took along his crew from the Norway trading mission, most of them baptized Christians, in search of much needed timber resources. Leif found ample wood supplies along the northern Atlantic coast of North America. He also discovered wild grapes growing in a land he named *Vinland*, or "Wineland." When Leif returned to Brattahild, with a cargo of choice lumber materials and several caskets full of wine, the settlers renamed him "Leif the Lucky."

> Brattahild is renowned for being the final vestige of European paganism and the set-off point for the first recorded explorations of North America.

Situated at the "crossroads" of the Arctic region, Iceland is located closer to Greenland than to mainland Europe. The Vikings were prolific sea and river boat travelers. They left cairns with runic inscriptions 900 miles (1,440 km) north of Cape Farewell. From Brattahild, the Vikings made their crossings to North America via Cape Farewell. It is possible to

▲ This frozen tundra would be unsuitable for colonization. Only select areas in the far southwest of Greenland could support the grazing livestock the Vikings imported via their trading vessels.

▲ This small Brattahild stave-church over-looks Erik's Fjord in southern Greenland.

pinpoint the location of Leif's Vinland on the eastern seaboard of the United States. The area of New England, from southern Maine to Connecticut, is the only place where grapes grow wild. Several other known Viking missions left Brattahild to explore and colonize around Vinland (see: *Sacred Places North America: 108 Destinations* by Brad Olsen for other Viking locations).

What makes Brattahild especially intriguing is the lack of any mass burials found in the various excavations of the settlements. Literally thousands of Greenland Vikings vanished without a trace. It is very likely that the eastern and western colonies migrated once again, this time to the temperate climates of North America where they intermingled with the numerically dominant native population. Such tantalizing clues, such as Indian arrowheads and corn, have been found at Brattahild. These items could have gotten there by an interaction between the Vikings and the Native Americans.

Getting to Brattahild

The ruins of Brattahild have been excavated, together with those of other village farmhouses, monasteries, and churches fronting Erik's Fjord. There is a youth hostel there, and a small store. More extensive facilities are available at Narsarsuaq across the fjord. The only way to reach Greenland is by chartered flights or hired boats from Labrador, Canada, or Iceland.

ICELAND

The Scandinavian country of Iceland is aptly named because one-eighth of the island's surface area is covered by glaciers. It is also the land of fire, as Iceland has dozens of active volcanoes and more than 200 steam vents. In 1963, off the coast of Iceland, submarine volcanism gave birth to the new island called Surtsey.

Iceland continues to grow as new magma is emplaced underground and lava erupts on the surface. Sometimes the active volcano surrounds an ice cap, as is the case with Myrdalsjokull Glacier in southern Iceland, where volcanism and glaciation work in close proximity. At different intervals, the searing lava melts the ice and can cause devastating floods. Eruptions occur in Iceland every five years or so; yet, the Icelandic people love their northern country and could not imagine living anywhere else. The heat of the volcanoes provides the Icelandic people with virtually free energy and relaxing therapeutic hot springs.

Viking Parliament (althing)

The first Viking colonizers landed at the southwestern tip of Iceland called Vestmannaeyjar, or "the isles of men of the west," an archipelago of 13 small islands. When the first colonizers landed in 874 CE, Iceland was one of the world's last large uninhabited islands. In one of the greatest migrations ever recorded, 70,000 Vikings relocated to Iceland in less than 60 years. In the year 930 CE, the Norse had established one of the first parliaments in the world — the *althing* or "assembly place," where chiefs and free men met to settle disputes. The free men of Viking times were the backbone of society. They were the essential middle class: the farmers, traders, hunters, craftsmen, and servants to the wealthy. The free had a right to fully express themselves at the althing, where public issues were discussed and decisions taken. Although social standing and wealth were important in influencing public decisions at the parliament, any free man could make a case and even overturn the opinion of a king. The powerful King Olaf of Sweden was recorded as saying: "for it is the custom of that country that every public concern depends more on the people's uniform will than on the power of the king." As such, all major social decisions had to be accepted by free men to gain formal validity.

▲ Thingvellir was located in the canyon pictured above. The cliffs are at the junction of two tectonic plates on the mid Atlantic range.

The Icelandic Vikings are regarded as the first people to formulate a truly democratic society. They invented the concept of a parliament, or a legislative body of voters.

During the last two weeks of June, the Viking Parliament would convene at a place called *Thingvellir* (literally "parliament plains"), an open field facing a long and narrow cleft of lava rock that offers ideal acoustics for public speaking. Chieftains and their followers would come from all over Iceland, set up camp, and prepare for the issues to be addressed. Each day, the Icelandic parliamentary sessions were held at the base of a cliff face called Almannagjá. Voices would reverberate from the perpendicular wall behind the speaker and project out to the assembled crowd. The place where the speaker would stand was called Law Rock. The "lawspeaker," or *lögsögumaör*, presided over the legislature (*logrétta*) and this man acted as the parliamentary president. He was responsible for knowing all the laws and being able to recite them at the althing during his three-year term. With the lawspeaker presiding, free men would debate the merits of community issues, pass sentences on the accused, and issue new laws by a truly democratic process.

Although settled and organized, the Vikings of Iceland were nonetheless some of the most brutal warriors who ever lived. A slighted Norseman was not known to turn the other cheek. The resulting blood feuds stretched far beyond the shores of Iceland. Some men were forced to migrate to Iceland after being expelled from Norway or Denmark. Others found themselves being judged by the althing of Iceland and themselves being sent away from the island. Such was the case of Erik the Red, who went on to establish the Greenland colonies after his three-year banishment from Iceland.

Besides settling blood duels and land disputes, the Viking Parliament helped stabilize a new nation from the more or less unorganized groups of people, who continued to migrate to Iceland during the end of the 9th century. It established a new set of laws that ruled over free men and chieftains alike. The free republic of Iceland survived in its original form, with the althing as its central legislative system, until 1262 when the king of Norway succeeded in bringing the island nation into his dominion. Despite annexation, the memory of the Thingvellir lived on in the hearts and minds of the people. This site represents the golden age of Icelandic

▲ The trail approaching the old Viking Parliament gives the visitor a sense of anticipation. Both Icelandic history and unusual geological formations are found in abundance.

freedom. From the dawning of their nation, Thingvellir is an inheritance that dates back more than a thousand years. Even today, modern Icelanders speak a language which is only slightly different from that spoken by their Viking ancestors.

Getting to the Viking Parliament

The site of the first Viking Parliament at Thingvellir is located 31 miles (50 km) to the east of Iceland's capital Reykjavík. Many tour companies offer day trips to the foremost historical site of Iceland, or it is possible to rent a car and drive independently to the location. The lava plain of Thingvellir is not only a national shrine of Scandinavian history, but it is also famous for its strange and brightly colored geological formations.

NORWAY

Of all the Scandinavian countries, Norway is the most mountainous, with large tracts of untamed wilderness, and the most amount of coastline. The highest mountain in northern Europe is Norway's Mount Galdhøpiggen, rising 8,148 feet (2,469 m) above sea level. Many mountains in Norway are permanently covered with ice and snow. The coastline is characteristic of the deep fjord inlets, many featuring spectacular glaciers or waterfalls cascading into the sea. In spite of the northerly latitude, the warm waters of the Gulf Stream allow most boat harbors to stay open all winter. Norway still has wild roaming herds of reindeer, elk, wolf, bear, wolverine, fox, and marten. These animals used to be an important source of food and fur to the Norwegian people.

Alta

The rock carvings outside the small fishing village of Alta, in the far northern reaches of Norway, represent one of the most prolific collections of Stone Age petroglyphs to be found in all of Europe. At least 3,000 individual carvings can be found at the rock art site called Jiepmaluokta, just outside of Alta. Also nearby the town are other rock art sites: Bossekop, Amtmannsnes, and Kåfjord. In addition, there is a rock painting (pictographs) site in nearby Transfarlv. It is estimated that the oldest rock carvings are 5,600 years old and the site remained in continuous usage until about 500 BCE. Building foundations from the Late Stone Age are located nearby. Whatever kind of rituals or activities took place at these five sites remains a mystery, but the rock carvings offer tantalizing clues.

The rock carvings in Alta represent the largest known collection of petroglyphs in northern Europe.

The large majority of carvings at Alta depict wild animals. Reindeer are the most common, followed by elks, bears, geese, ducks, swans, fish, and in a rare instance, whales or porpoises. The humans are mostly seen hunting or herding the land animals, or fishing for the sea animals. The prolific amount of animal motifs may suggest the carvings were created to invoke some sort of hunting magic. It could be that the carvings were made to attract the animals to the hunting grounds. Another theory is that the animal was documented as an official "kill" after being taken down. No two animals are exactly alike. Indeed, several reindeer have unique

Alta Rock Art

Fertility Ritual Dance

Floating Shaman over Boat & Crew

Bear, Elk, Duck, and Whales

Shaman with Drum   Skier   Hunter

180

body patterns with vertical and horizontal dots, or partially filled areas of color. In the pre-Christian culture of the Saami — closely related to the Laplanders — the people believed that the gods were able to create a new animal from the skeleton of a sacrificed animal.

Some of the human representations at Alta are far more puzzling than the animal drawings. Magic drums, confiscated by Christian missionaries, depict Saami shaman mythology from the underworld and the realm of the dead, to everyday life of Saami people and their relation to nature. It is known that the Lapp and Saami shamans used drums to induce ecstatic dancing, which would put the dancer into a trance-like state and allow the person to predict the future of the clan or look back into the past. Some figures have lines or dots around them, possibly representing the shaman of the group. Other people are seen involved in shamanic activities. Situated among the animals of the Alta carvings are people in long boats, sometimes with a person "floating" over the crew — perhaps depicting a shaman traveling in the spirit world. Less mysterious are the hunters and fishermen in the boats. In some carvings, people are seen with skis on their feet in pursuit of animals. These depictions are an important historical documentation of the use of skis over 3,000 years ago.

The "Arctic rock carvings" were designed to present some kind of control over the natural world, especially the animal kingdom. In the transition from the Old to the Late Stone Age, humans began to put a higher priority in living permanently at one place. Such a pattern of habitation would have created a greater desire to leave a mark, a record in stone, to demark a ritual site filled with imagery contributing to the tribe's sustainability. With the huge amount of petroglyphs found at Alta, this must have been a very important ritual location for a very long time. Today, the rock carvings are listed in the UNESCO directory of World Heritage Sites.

Getting to Alta

The name Jiepmaluokta, or Hjemmeluft to use the Norwegian name, describes "seal bay" next to the town of Alta. On both sides of the bay, footpaths access the rock carving sites from the centrally located Alta Museum. Alta is in the far northern part of Norway, known as Finnmark. Alta is accessible by bus or train from Hammerfest, or flights on Widerøe Air.

Nidaros

Since prehistoric times, the confluence of the River Nid and the massive Trondheims Fjorden inland sea has been an important meeting place and seat of power in central Norway. At the confluence of river and fjord, the Vikings held the althing, or "assembly place," to decide on matters of the community. One of the largest pagan Viking temples ever known was situated on the headland. As

▲ The Flateyjarbok, the most magnificent of the medieval Icelandic manuscripts, shows the Viking and missionary King Olaf II Haraldsson being killed in the famous Battle of Stiklestad in 1030 CE.

was common throughout Europe, pagan temples were not destroyed but reconsecrated into Christian places of worship. Nidaros was converted over in this way, including the coronation crowning pagan and Christian kings. In the early Middle Ages, all of Norway's kings were acclaimed at Øretinget, which is at the mouth of the River Nid. Beginning with the pagan Harald Fairhair (865-933 CE), all the Norwegian kings right up to the modern time have been crowned or blessed in the city Trondheim. But nothing would make Trondheim, or Nidaros as it was known 1,000 years ago, as famous as the burial place of Saint Olaf and the enormous cathedral his legend would inspire.

The Nidaros Domkirke is Scandinavia's largest building of the Middle Ages and Europe's northernmost medieval cathedral. It was built to honor Saint Olaf, the patron saint of Norway.

Olaf was Christianized in Rouen, France while serving as an officer for noblemen in Normandy. When he returned to Norway to reclaim his throne in 1015, he took with him English bishops to baptize his heathen countrymen. He became the first national king to unite the entire country and establish a legal system for both church and state. His power intimidated his enemies, culminating in a fierce battle for control of Norway. In an attempt to consolidate his power, Olaf II Haraldsson was killed by pagans in 1039 at the Battle of Stiklestad. After the battle, his body was laid to rest in the original Nidaros church. Within weeks of his sudden death, several miracles supposedly occurred: a solar eclipse; spontaneous healings; and large numbers of pagans wanting to be baptized. Olaf was sanctified a martyr and apostle. The death of no other man has had such an impact on the history of Norway.

Olaf became a deeply loved saint in a short period of time. He was the defender of the monarchy and protector of the needy, the champion of peasants and sailors, and the patron saint of traveling merchants and city dwellers. He became larger than life and soon the king-saint legend would inspire pilgrimages from all the Scandinavian countries to visit his tomb. In order to accommodate the pilgrims, the Nidaros church became greatly enlarged and altered over the years. He was honored just as much in neighboring countries as he was in Norway. In all, some

▲ Nidaros was the grandfather of all Olaf churches throughout Scandinavia. It was a popular pilgrimage destination until the Reformation.

340 "Olaf churches" were established in northern Europe, with both Sweden and Iceland hosting more than even Norway.

Shortly after his death, Norway had at least 52 Olaf churches. Today, only 17 remain. As the Olaf tradition flourished, so did the desire for his faithful to make a pilgrimage to his tomb. The original church grew by leaps and bounds to accommodate the bands of pilgrims, ultimately achieving cathedral status in 1152. After Olaf was buried, the cathedral became the traditional resting place of all Norwegian royalty. Even if subsequent kings died in other parts of the country or abroad, Trondheim was their desired final resting place. For 200 years the city became the seat of the archbishop, the royal family, and became the first capital of Norway. Catholic pilgrims continued to pay their respects to Saint Olaf, that is, until the Reformation of 1537, when the practice was banned.

The silver used for Olaf's shrine was taken to Copenhagen and melted down to mint coins. The archbishop feared for his life and had to flee the country. Although the Reformation and several fires badly damaged the Nidaros Domkirke, the cathedral has been gloriously restored. Again, pilgrims are making the long journey to Trondheim to visit the famous cathedral. The "Pilgrim's Way" is now a specially marked route for modern travelers, extending from Oslo to Nidaros. Another route is signposted eastward into Sweden.

Getting to Nidaros

The colossal Nidaros Domkirke dominates the skyline in the old section of downtown Trondheim. Although Trondheim is Norway's third largest city, it is still small by modern city standards. The cathedral and associated complex of buildings are ten city blocks south of the central train station and ferry port. The nearby city of Stiklestad recreates the famous battle where Olaf was killed. Stiklestad also features a Middle Age market at the end of July to commemorate the event.

SWEDEN

The southeastern provinces of Skåne and Halland were a part of Denmark in the Viking Age, only to be ceded to Sweden in 1658. The south of Sweden was prized because of its accessibility by boat and the warm coastal climate, which is ideal for growing crops. Apart from burying the dead with their personal possessions, archaeologists discovered the hull of an old ship buried on high ground at the site of Ale Stenar, located in the Skåne region. The rich grave discoveries at Birka reveal Viking clothing, featuring silk borders, embroideries with gold thread, and other exotic ornaments, all of which have a distinct Oriental appearance. The Vikings of Sweden looked eastward, but remained in contact with the other countries of Scandinavia. It was primarily from Sweden that the Vikings departed on their epic river journeys into Russia, the Near East, and southern Europe.

Gamla Uppsala

Early in the 6th century CE, three pagan kings were buried in enormous earthen mounds at Gamla Uppsala. Their names, as legend would have it, were Aun, Egil, and Adils, each commissioning a mound to demonstrate the power of their divine kingdom. The royal burial mounds have been looted over the years, but excavations in the 19th century revealed additional human cremations on the outer flanks — likely added for the prestige of being buried at Gamla Uppsala. Also found deep within the mounds were a fine array of artifacts and barrows, or passage tombs. Perhaps the richest find was at nearby Valsgärde, where several boat graves of various ranking chieftains were discovered, buried alongside specific prized possessions for their final journey into the afterlife.

The mounds were important symbols of latter-day Vikings, reminding them of an era when the Ynglinga dynasty was the leading royal family in Scandinavia and all worshipped the god Frey. Today, 250 mounds remain in the general area, although there were likely many more. None of the hundreds of mounds would hold the significance of the first three mounds at Gamla Uppsala, a sacred burial and ritual center for nearly 1,000 years. This remarkable area is one of the largest funeral areas in Scandinavia and a monument to Sweden's colorful prehistory.

The three mounds also have affiliated names with the three Aesir gods: Odin, Thor, and Frey. Living Viking kings and battle heroes elevated themselves to divine status alongside the gods. For example, the King of Svear, a very powerful person, had his residence and court built at Gamla Uppsala for the prestige value. The remains of several large halls have been uncovered next to the mounds, including two royal terraces and a pagan shrine. Parts of a palisade and a boat launch have also been discovered. The name *uppsala* derives from the term "open halls," referring to the porticos of the pagan kings.

It is believed that the largest pagan temple in Sweden stood at the site, only to be rededicated or demolished to make way for the Christian cathedral in the 12th century. Some historians believe the old brick pagan temple was extant and incorporated into the first cathedral. The traveling Christian Adam of Bremen describes the pagan temple: "A gold chain surrounds the temple. It hangs over the roof of the building and its gleam can be seen by persons approaching from a great distance, because the actual temple precincts, situated on level ground, have hills placed round about them like a theatre."

The temple was also the center of grisly pagan activities at Gamla Uppsala. Adam of Bremen describes a blood-thirsty sacrificial rite: "Nine (males) are sacrificed (every nine years) and their blood is offered as propitiation to the gods. The bodies are strung up in a grove near the temple. So revered is this grove by the heathen, that every tree is credited with divine power as a result of the death

▲ The mounds of Gamla Uppsala were centered around a sacrificial grove of trees and what was likely the largest pagan temple in Sweden.

and decay of the sacrificed bodies. There are dogs and horses strung together with human beings, and one of the Christians has told me that he saw 72 bodies hanging there altogether. They also sing, as is common at such sacrificial festivals, many different songs."

> Gamla Uppsala, or Old Uppsala, is the most
> ancient temple city in Sweden, the residence
> of pagan kings, later to be the See of the
> Catholic Archbishop.

When Christianity overcame paganism, the Church could not accept any less exalted location for their cathedral than that of the great Uppsala pagan temple. No doubt the old sacrificial site was of strategic importance to the early development of Christianity. Heathen temples, according to the Pope, were not to be destroyed but to be converted into churches. Festivals were to be held on the accustomed days, and the oxen that used to be sacrificed to the gods were now to be slaughtered for a church feast. The merrymaking at pagan festivals was to continue under the patronage of a Christian saint, and pilgrims to Christian shrines still took the traditional routes, which had been used since prehistoric times.

A small timber chapel was replaced by a large central-towered building. The new church was the first cathedral in Uppsala, as well as the residence of Sweden's first archbishop. At the time of changing beliefs, Adam of Bremen believed that when the pagan temple was finally destroyed, the result would be the conversion of the entire Swedish population. This finally happened, but it took over 100 years. Eventually, a much larger house of worship was built in new Uppsala to become Scandinavia's largest cathedral. It includes the tomb of Saint Erik, Sweden's patron saint. Saint Erik led a crusade to Finland, forcing the Finns to accept Christianity. Erik was beheaded by his enemy and supposedly a small spring gushed from the site of his execution. His bones were transferred to a reliquary in the new Uppsala cathedral. On Saint Erik's Day, in the springtime, his relics would be carried to old Gamla Uppsala, the church he helped complete. The pilgrimage of Saint Erik was discontinued in the 16th century during the Reformation. The "Path of Saint Erik" still connects 3.7 miles (6 km) of well-marked trail from the Uppsala cathedral to Gamla Uppsala.

Getting to Gamla Uppsala

The archaeological pagan site and church of Old Uppsala are located 3 miles (5 km) north of the modern city Uppsala. Buses run every half hour from the Uppsala train station to the archaeological site. Valsgärde is located a mile (1.7 km) north of Gamla Uppsala. There is an interpretive walk, a restaurant, and museum at Gamla Uppsala.

Gotland

During the entire duration of the Iron Age, before and during the Viking Era, the central Baltic Sea island of Gotland was a major hub of trade. To the north lay the Swedish trading center, Birka, and the fur trapping regions of Finland; to the east were the river routes to the Slav countries and Arabia; to the west was southern Sweden and Norway; and to the south, Denmark and Germany. Gotland continued as an active trading center during Roman times, but was never occupied by the Romans. Many objects from the height of the Roman Empire have been found there, attesting to the long reach of the Gotland merchants. In the Viking Age, lavish burials containing rich artifacts were prepared for deceased merchants. Some of the best preserved metal-worked artifacts come from Gotland tombs.

For an island with no decent natural harbors and a rugged terrain, it is amazing that the island of Gotland achieved such a high level of prominence. The island is ringed by imposing granite cliffs, which may have been advantageous for deterring the deep-draught war ships of neighboring countries. Lacking natural harbors, it does have shelving beaches, which were ideal landing places for the shallow-draught Viking vessels. As a result, Gotland became one of the richest of the Scandinavian trading cities. Out of the 200,000 silver coins found in Scandinavia from the Viking Age, no less than half were found on the little island of Gotland alone. 40,000 silver coins originated from Arabia, 38,000 were German, and 21,000 were of Anglo-Saxon origin. These coins, largely recovered from merchant graves, can only represent a fraction of the huge amount of coins that must have passed through the merchants of the island.

Gotland is not only known for its large number of silver coins, but also for its graphic "picture stones."

▲ This picture stone from Gotland comes from the parish of Lärbro in the north of the island. In the semicircular section on top, it depicts a battle scene, below which are two scenes likely depicting a burial and the entry of that warrior into Valhalla.

Gotland features a number of famous Viking monuments called "picture stones," dating from the 6th to the 11th centuries CE. They

▲ The first major thrust of the Viking Era involved trading rather than raiding. In the 8th century, the Swedes established trading posts in southern Finland and in present-day Latvia, Lithuania, Estonia and Russia. Gotland was the hub for the Viking's river network of Asian-European trade and travel.

are generally large upright slabs of stones set into the ground. Almost all are single-sided relief carvings, containing various symbols and graphic scenes. Most are difficult to decipher, for they refer to episodes in Scandinavian history and literature, which are now lost. Among the common themes depicted are men and women, mythical subjects, and Viking ships filled with armored men. The picture stones are most frequently found in the vicinity of cemeteries and churchyards. Many of them date from pagan times before Christianity came to Gotland. Their origin and purpose is not always clear, but many were probably tombstones, while others appear to have been memorials along popular roads, or located on the site of ancient farmsteads. Most remarkable are the sheer size — some are taller than two standing men.

Getting to Gotland

The island of Gotland is off the east coast of southern Sweden. Gotland is accessed by ferry, airplane, or across the Baltic Sea by chartered boat. Visby airport has more than 25 flight connections to Stockholm — every day, all year round. Flight time from Stockholm to Visby is only 35 minutes. In the summertime, there are flights to Gotland from Malmö, Gothenburg, and Oslo, Norway. The ferry company Destination Gotland has 16 departures per day during the summer and at least one going to each of the mainland ports every day of the year.

GERMANY

AND THE ALPS

Whatever your heart clings to and confides in, that is really your God. —*Martin Luther*

ONCE A LOOSELY-AFFILIATED BAND OF BARBARIAN TRIBES, what is today Austria, Switzerland, and all of Germany were first unified as territories under the Holy Roman Empire in the 7th century. Pope Leo III envisioned the Holy Roman Empire in hopes of implementing stability after centuries of being sacked by the barbarian hordes from the north. He also wished to resurrect the Western Roman Empire, but he needed the help of Rome's old enemies — Germany, France, and the countries of the Alps region. In 800 CE, Pope Leo III crowned the Frankish king Charlemagne as the first Holy Roman Emperor, even though the empire and the imperial office did not become formalized in Germany until decades later. Charlemagne went on to adopt the title "Augustus" from earlier Roman times. The Pope's crowning of Charlemagne as Augustus formed a model that successive kings would continue to emulate. Charlemagne and future kings were sworn to defend the Pope, which prompted the notion of the *Reich* being the protector of the Western Church. The Vatican continues to employ the well-trained Swiss Guards who serve as the Pope's personal body guards.

In 1517 Martin Luther initiated the Reformation, dividing Catholics and the newly-organized Protestants. The empire became partitioned along religious lines, with the north and eastern parts of Germany becoming Protestant, and the southern and western regions of Germany and Austria largely remaining Catholic. The Empire was formally dissolved in 1806 when the last Holy Roman Emperor abdicated, following a military defeat by the French Army under Napoleon. For the German territories, Napoleon reorganized much of the empire into the Confederation of the Rhine. This ended the so-called First Reich.

AUSTRIA

The horizontally-shaped Austria is a rugged mountain country where it meets Germany, Switzerland, and Italy, but juts into Central Europe as a rolling plain. The Alps dominate the western and central part of Austria, which flatten into the Danube River plains in the northeast and east. It is an extremely beautiful country — both the mountain vistas and baroque cities are among the finest to be found on the continent. The territory of Austria was originally known as the Celtic kingdom of *Noricum*. Largely due to its northern proximity to Italy, Austria was occupied rather than conquered by the Romans during the reign of Emperor Augustus Caesar. Since the Celts of this region were longtime allies with Rome, Augustus created the province Noricum in 16 BCE, which is approximate to the borders of present-day eastern Austria.

After the Roman Empire collapsed, it was occupied by several Germanic tribes, the last being Charlemagne in 800 CE. The official language, German, is spoken by almost all residents of the country, but Austria's mountainous terrain led to the development of several distinct German dialects. In the early 21st century, about 73% of Austria's population remains Roman Catholic, and 5% Protestant. An influx of immigrants from the Balkans and the Middle East has introduced the ever-growing Islamic religion to Austria. All Christian denominations in Europe have been on the decline for decades, especially Roman Catholicism, which has suffered continent-wide decreases in the last few decades. Over 12% of Austrians do not belong to any religious denomination.

Salzburg

For some people, especially those who reject organized religion, music is their true faith. Music has a way of making people cheerful, inspired, optimistic, and tranquil. It elevates the spirit and frees the mind. Few musical categories excite people the way classical music can, and no city in Europe embodies classical music quite like the northern Austrian city of Salzburg. The city itself is like a harmony, tucked between verdant green hills and the Salzach River, the classic baroque architecture sings a song of traditional beauty.

Salzburg is famous for music festivals year round, often with multiple events happening in a single month. Each season features different festival themes, all accompanied with musical stages. Perhaps the liveliest is the Saint Rupert's Festival at the end of September. The patron saint of Salzburg is toasted with schnapps, fun fairs, and a large dose of traditional church

▲ Salzburg is divided by the Salzach River. The oldest part of the city — the Salzburg castle and the city just below it — features narrow streets and baroque architecture around every corner.

music. In the compact old city of Salzburg, there are no less than eight concert halls and live music theatres. Undoubtedly, Salzburg hosts more musical events and classical concerts than any other place in Austria or neighboring southern Germany. While Vienna has larger venues for events, Salzburg has more frequent events in smaller halls.

One person is synonymous with the city of Salzburg and classical music. Wolfgang Amadeus Mozart was born in the old city of Salzburg on 27 January, 1756. The classical music child prodigy began writing his first symphonies at the age of eight while living at number 9 Getreidegasse, the Mozart *Geburtshaus*, or birthplace. Now a museum and rather crowded place of pilgrimage, the third floor flat features period decorations and musical instruments, including a baby-sized violin used by the composer as a child. When Amadeus was 17, the Mozart family moved to a more spacious apartment across the river. This house is also a museum commemorating the place where he lived until 1780. In those seven years, he composed the majority of his Salzburg works. Tourists coming to see the two residences of Mozart can take an audio tour through Salzburg, which is devoted to the other regional attractions that influenced Mozart's life. Everyone who visits the old city of Salzburg eventually comes to the Mozartplatz, home to a statue of the composer. The statue overlooks the Glockenspiel, a charming 17th century musical clock, whose vibrant chimes attract crowds at 7 am, 11 am, and 6 pm.

> Salzburg is undeniably a city of music, but it is also one of the finest baroque cities in Europe. It has also shaped history, especially when it was the home to the powerful archbishops, who kept the city Catholic during the Reformation.

▲ The statue of Mozart at the Mozartplatz is the site of numerous outdoor music festivals.

In the compact old city center of Salzburg, one can see many towers, spires, or domes decorated with the shining symbols of Christendom. Dominating the skyline above the city is the *Höhensalzburg*, or the Castle of Salzburg. Begun around 1070 to provide the archbishops with a refuge from threatening German princes, the fortress was gradually transformed into a regal courtly seat. As southern Germany ebbed and flowed during the Reformation, Salzburg acted as an anchor for the region. Salzburg can be largely credited for Austria and Bavaria remaining mostly Catholic today. In the Middle Ages, the city served as a See, which extended over much of southern Germany, growing extremely prosperous on the revenues derived from the lucrative salt trade (for which the city is named). The city's High Baroque appearance was created by the ambitious Prince-Archbishops in the 16th and 17th centuries. Wolf Dietrich and Paris Lodron are credited for hiring artists and craftsmen from the Southern Alps to recast Salzburg on the model of Rome. Salzburg acted as the Roman Iuvavum and spiritual principality until 1801. The Dom, or Salzburg Cathedral, was built between 1614 and 1668 in the Vatican style. From the marble walls to the sculptures and paintings, the Dom is the largest church in Salzburg and also the most prominent. Horse drawn carriages can be hired in the Dom platz. Elsewhere, Salzburg possesses another 25 churches and several monasteries. From glorious palaces, gardens, and castles to medieval streets, museums, and abundant natural scenery, Salzburg holds the proud distinction as one of the most beautiful and romantic European cities, as well as one of the most sacred. No wonder the nickname of Salzburg is the "Rome of the North."

Getting to Salzburg

The railway station, the *hauptbahnhof*, is the main point of entry into the city, but Salzburg has its own airport as well. Several major highways in Austria and southern Germany lead into "Mozart's City." Fortunately, Salzburg received little damage during World War II, largely because the Allies recognized the city's historical and architectural value.

Photo by Brad Olsen

▲ The Iron Age burials at Lindholm Høje, Denmark predate the Viking Era. Both people revered the ship enough to represent it as their ultimate resting place.

Photo by Brad Olsen

▲ The hunnebeddens of northeastern Holland are the domain of the mythological "giant's beds."

Photo by Berill Johnson

▲ The approach into the althing, or the Viking Parliament, is filled with colorful mosses and wild flowers.

Photo by Berill Johnson

▲ Icelandic free men would converge once a year at the althing to pass laws and resolve differences. It is the location of the world's first true democracy.

Photo courtesy of www.SacredSites.com

▲ Votive items cluster around the Hill of Crosses, Lithuania.

Photo by Brad Olsen

▲ The Externsteine outcropping of five massive limestone
pillars was a pagan worship center and considered a
location of mystical power for thousands of years.

Photo by Brad Olsen

▲ Few pilgrimage locations can match the natural beauty of Saint Bartholomä on the shores of the Königssee.

Photo by Brad Olsen

▲ Martin Luther nailed his 95 grievances to the door of the Castle Church in Wittenberg, and from that day forward the concept of the Protestant Church was born.

Photo by Roy Tate

▲ The Throne Room in Knossos, Greece is partly restored. The throne, benches, floor and bowl are all original.

Photo courtesy of www.SacredSites.com

▲ The picturesque Moni Vatopediou is the only monastery at Mount Athós that keeps to the Western Gregorian calendar. All other Athonite monasteries operate under the Byzantine-influenced Julian calendar, which is off by 13 days.

▲ The Ggantija Temple on the Mediterranean island of Gozo is one of the oldest in the world.

Photo by Roy Tate

▲ The Lion's Patio at the Alhambra palace in Granada, Spain features exquisitely carved Islamic patterns and symmetry down to the smallest detail.

Photo by Brad Olsen

▲ The Imperial Temple within the old city of Évora is the best preserved Roman structure in Portugal.

▲ The old city center of Toledo, Spain features religious buildings of different persuasions.

Photo by Brad Olsen

▲ Strolling among the temples of Paestum, Italy
is like taking a walk through time.

Photo by Brad Olsen

▲ Montserrat, Spain occupies one of the most
spectacular settings for a sacred place in Europe.

GERMANY

The fierce Germanic tribes, believed to have migrated from Scandinavia, started their invasions of Germany around 100 BCE until 300 CE. Before then Germany was occupied by the Celts, who worshipped a pantheon of pagan gods in beautiful outdoor settings. The Germanic tribes were of partial Celtic stock,

193

or mixed quickly with Celtic ancestry to create the traditional German people, also known as the Saxons. The Saxons long avoided becoming Christians and being incorporated into the Frankish kingdom, but were decisively conquered by Charlemagne in a long series of annual campaigns (772 – 804). With defeat came the enforced baptism and conversion of the Saxon leaders and their people. Even their sacred tree, Irminsul, was destroyed.

Because the German tribes had no written language very little is known about their early history, except through their interactions with the Roman Empire and archaeological finds. Under Augustus Caesar, the Romans began to invade Germany via the Alps. Always industrious and willing to adopt new technology, it was from this period that the German tribes became familiar with Roman warfare tactics, all the while maintaining their national identity. The German tribes would use this knowledge of warfare to catch up militarily, which eventually led to the fall of the Roman Empire. In successful campaigns, starting in the early 1st century CE, German war chiefs drove the Romans out of north and eastern Germany, further strengthening the region's military prowess and preserving it from future Roman conquest.

The great German reformer Martin Luther would declare his own fight against the pesky Italians, namely the Roman Catholic Church. He cleverly used the example of Vatican domination to stress an urgent need for a renewal of German liberation. Similar to the Germanic tribes reasserting themselves, medieval Germans would use their superior army to enforce their will against Rome. When Martin Luther translated the Bible, he used the already developed German language, which in the 16th century was the most widely understood language in Europe. Today, the German language is spoken primarily in Germany, Austria, Liechtenstein, Luxembourg, and in two-thirds of Switzerland.

Aachen

The Romans were the first recorded settlers in the verdant green valleys of western *Germania*, but the Celts were certainly there long before. A major attraction to both the Roman and Celtic people was the presence of natural mineral springs at the location where the Netherlands, German, and Belgian borders currently meet. The Romans named their spa town *Aquae Granna*, or the "Springs of Grannus," after the Celtic god of water and health. The Roman municipality grew up around the warm baths. The Romans enjoyed bathing in the 30 thermal springs containing a high level of mineral content and other trace elements. The most famous spring, the *Kaiserquelle* (meaning "a source that springs here"), would one day become the most favored relaxation spot to the most influential man of medieval Europe.

In the 8th century, Aachen became the strategic hub of the great empire of Charlemagne. He chose the old Roman health spa for its central European location near relaxing springs.

As the medieval ruler of an empire stretching from Denmark to the Adriatic, Charlemagne amassed treasures from all over the known world. Among his favored items were books, jewels, ivories, and cameos. These treasures are now housed in Aachen's Cathedral Treasury (*Schatzkammer*), the richest museum of priceless artifacts in northern Europe. After visiting the Pope in Rome and being crowned the head of a new Holy Roman Empire in 800 CE, Charlemagne next became fascinated with architecture. On his return from Rome, he stopped in Ravenna, Italy and was awed by the octagonal San Vitale chapel with the magnificent mosaics of Justinian and Theodora. Charlemagne vowed to replicate San Vitale. He got pretty close with the chapel he built to himself at Aachen, regarded as one of the most famous examples of occidental architecture in Europe. Charlemagne kept his residence also at Aachen, mostly because he enjoyed swimming in the mineral springs.

The famous Palace Chapel of Charlemagne, now the octagonal building in the heart of the Dom, had to be enlarged by adding the Gothic chancel to accommodate the number of pilgrims who came to see the Holy Roman Emperors' throne. It was Charlemagne who laid the foundations for the Dom, one of the most important buildings north of the Alps. As Aachen grew in importance, subsequent kings added new features to the structure. It was the church of coronation for over 30 German kings and the burial site of Charlemagne. Also, it was a major pilgrimage location and, since 1930, named the Aachen diocese cathedral. In 1978, the Palace Chapel was the first German building appointed to

▲ The octagonal Palace Chapel was built first, then the gigantic Dom was added around on all sides.

the UNESCO World Heritage Site list. Only a few original furnishings remain from Charlemagne's time — the most famous are the enormous bronze doors. According to legend, you can still feel the devil's thumb in the right lion's mouth, which lends the portal its name: *Wolfstür*, or "Wolf's Door." The octagon still forms the center of the cathedral, but nothing remains of Charlemagne's residence. The Gothic town hall Rathaus was built on the foundations of his castle.

Getting to Aachen

The high amount of royal guests to Aachen over the years has given rise to the town nickname "Spa of Kings." The tradition continues today with about a dozen commercial spas in the city. The city of Aachen (in French, Aix-la-Chapelle) is easily accessed by the rail networks of Germany, Belgium, and the Netherlands. The city center, containing the Palace Chapel, the Dom, and Rathaus, is a 10-minute walk from the Aachen train station.

Altötting

This small Bavarian town was first mentioned in documents dating back to 748, when the first Christian missionaries of Germany built a baptistery in Altötting. The reconstructed baptistery is a tiny octagonal chapel, which houses a venerated statue of the Virgin Mary. It later became a pilgrimage destination known as *Gnadenkapelle,* or the "Chapel of the Miraculous Image," also called the "Chapel of the Blessed Virgin." This small town remains famous for the chapel, one of the most visited shrines in Germany. According to the pilgrimage legend, in 1489, a three-year-old local girl had accidentally drowned in the Inn River. The child was revived when her grief-stricken mother placed her in front of a wooden statue of the Virgin Mary at the high altar. News of the miracle quickly spread, and the chapel was immediately extended by the erection of a nave and a covered walkway.

> Altötting is home to a miraculous statue of the Virgin Mary, which has inspired centuries of pilgrimage, alongside some of Bavaria's finest religious buildings.

Altötting is the most important shrine of the Virgin Mary in the German-speaking region of Europe. Pilgrims have been traveling to this village for over 500 years. The chapel square, with its extensive lawns encircled by picturesque baroque buildings, ranks among the most beautiful city squares in Europe. The Monastery Church of Saint Konrad, with the saint's reliquary, is also a highly venerated destination for pilgrims. Additional sites include the late Gothic Collegiate Church and its treasure vaults, along with the *Goldene Rössl,* or Golden Horse, a masterpiece of French gold work dating back to the year 1404. Also in the Collegiate Church is the diorama display (with over 5,000 figures), the panorama "Christ's Crucifixion," and the Museum of Local History and Pilgrimage. Other architectural highlights in the town are the twin-towered *Stiftskirche*, a late Gothic church erected in the early 16th century to cater to oncoming pilgrims, and the huge neo-baroque *Basilika*, built at the beginning of the 20th century.

Getting to Altötting

The small southern German town Altötting is located roughly between Munich and Salzburg. It is located about 60 miles (100 km) directly east of Munich, which offers the quickest rail route. At Mühldorf, the rail line splits, with one branch line continuing eastwards to Altötting. Time of pilgrimage is Easter until Advent in October.

▲ Small yet charming, Altötting is one of Bavaria's oldest pilgrimage destinations.

Externsteine

Since prehistoric times, the outcropping of five massive limestone pillars was known as a pagan worship center and location of mystic power. This rock sanctuary was used by the Saxons as a solar observatory to predict the summer solstice and auspicious risings of the moon. Atop one of the rock pillars, accessible only by a narrow footbridge, is a tiny room cut from the living rock. Here in this rock-hewn chapel a strategic window was carved, facing the northeast, to receive the mid-summer sunrise on June 22nd. The window also captures a sighting of the most northerly rising of the moon. Other researchers suggest the chapel had additional functions, such as being part of a larger zodiac orientation. They suggest that the rays of the sun created a sundial at the Externsteine and once indicated a path through the zodiac. Unfortunately, much of the surrounding area and the site itself was destroyed when

▲ The Externsteine is a labyrinth of interconnecting passageways, rooms and terraces. It has been the site of religious activities since prehistoric times.

▲ The famous Externsteine bas relief of Christ being lowered from the cross also displays pagan imagery.

Charlemagne forbade the Saxons to use the site for pagan ceremonies any longer. Because the site was so close to Aachen, and because Charlemagne was on a crusade to extinguish paganism in his homeland, the site was completely denuded of all original buildings and non-Christian references. All that remains from the earliest era are carefully drilled holes, stairs that lead to dead ends, and platforms that seem to serve no purpose. Only recently have some of the pieces come together to suggest an elaborate solar observatory and ritual center. The apparently mysterious holes may have supported hanging structures or may have been carved into the stone to release earth energies. It is readily apparent that many wooden constructions were once attached to the rocks. What's more, geomancers have mapped out a network of Germanic chapels, hermitages, Celtic stones, and other sacred sites bound together by a series of straight lines, or "holy lines" called *Heilige Linien*. It appears that the original worshippers at the Externsteine detected a series of ley lines intersecting the site and designed their greater ritual center accordingly.

The site has also been associated with pre-Germanic people from the Celtic and Bronze Age periods. The main grotto was apparently carved for Roman soldiers who adhered to the Persian cult of Mithras. The Germanic deity of Teut, the Saxon Ostara, and the Nordic Wodan were all believed to have been worshipped at the Externsteine at different times. Some researchers suggest that the Bructerian prophetess Veleda, who came from a tribe along the lower Rhine, resided here, unseen by men. The Roman historian Tacitus wrote about Veleda living in the upper sanctuary. This same chamber, with the altar and solstice window, has been attributed to the Saxon Irminsul, a religious symbol destroyed by Charlemagne in 772 CE, according to the Carolingian annals. Since more theories than physical evidence remain, the Externsteine is the most disputed archaeological site in Germany.

> The Externsteine is a recognized pagan cultic center and mystical site. It was inhabited by pre-Germanic people, the Saxons, Christian monks, and today it is a popular New Age destination.

After the Externsteine was purged of its pagan influence, hermit monks settled into caves at the base of the rocks. Their task was to Christianize the site and to drive out the evil influences. During this period, the monks, with the help of a local bishop, rendered beautiful carvings to show the triumph of Christianity over paganism. There is no doubting the powerful symbolism represented in the central bas relief, the largest of its kind in Europe. The famous carving depicts the Tree of Life, a pagan representation of earth power, bowing down beneath the body of Christ being taken from the cross. Illiterate converts would have readily understood the various symbols represented, especially the weeping sun and moon — both important pagan fertility images of masculine and feminine. They would have seen the ancient tree of pagan knowledge submitting to the Tree of the Cross. Furthermore, the snake symbol of earth energies is seen being pushed underground beneath the feet of the disciples, entangling Adam and Eve. The snake in Christian and Jewish mythology represented the devil or the "evil one." This remarkable relief carving is unique because it is the only known German sculpture showing a distinct Byzantine influence. The hermits eventually abandoned the site in the 15th century, the chapel they built left to ruin, and the site was transformed into a small fortress. When this system of fortification was outdated, the counts of the region used the site for court banquets. After the death of Count Adolf in 1666, everything fell into decay. Over time, the legend of the Externsteine inspired a great number of books, paintings, essays, novels, and even several plays. In 1824, the famous author Goethe wrote an essay on the descent from the cross carving, even though he had never visited the Externsteine himself.

Getting to Externsteine

The park containing the Externsteine rock formations and twin ponds is located in northern Germany, near the city of Detmold. The nearest railway stop and local bus terminal is the small town of Horn-Bad Meinberg, only 1.3 miles (2 km) west of the Externsteine. Small inns and hotel rooms are within walking distance from hamlet Holzhausen Externsteine. Out of Detmold, there is a tourist bus that leaves every few hours, or take the local #782 bus from the Detmold Train Station which leaves on the hour.

Kelheim

If the ancient Greek term *genius loci,* or "power of place," can be applied in Germany, then the Michelsberg Hill, above the small Bavarian city of Kelheim, would qualify. Geomancers report that there is no other place in southern Germany with more accumulated earth energy. They claim powerful ley lines intersect directly on the hill. For one, the location of Michelsberg is the exact center of Bavaria. Two important rivers in southern Germany also connect here, the rivers Altmühl and Danube, making the location very strategic for the transportation of goods and ideas. Practically every culture from every era chose this spot for settlement. Stone Age people from 13,000 BCE hunted the big herds of animals that once roamed the narrow river valleys. The steep hillsides offered shelter in numerous caves and protection from predators. Prehistoric people quarried ample firestones nearby. Neolithic farmers utilized the fertile soil of Michelsberg Hill. Bronze Age tribes also thrived here. The most famous settlers were the Celts, an Iron Age community who loaned their name to Kelheim, literally the "Big Celt Ship." When the Romans drove out the Celts, they used the Danube River as an ideal defensive line which also denoted their northern border. Traces of the Roman fortified boundary walls called *limes*, the Latin word for "limit," can be found near Kelheim. The Roman bathing culture also thrived at the nearby spa called Bad Gögging. Next came the age of chivalry when medieval knights swore their allegiance to local kings, who erected a castle across from Michelsberg. Kings, dukes, and monks all favored the area. Finally, King Ludwig I of Bavaria recognized the importance of Michelsberg and erected the monumental Hall of Liberation between 1842 and 1863, which overlooks Kelheim.

> It is believed King Ludwig I chose the
> Michelsberg Hill above Kelheim for his
> Hall of Liberation because it had been a site
> famous for Celtic worship.

▲ Visitors to the Hall of Liberation may ascend the wrap-around staircase to the roof for fantastic views of the two rivers joining at Kelheim city.

The Celts called their city on the hill "Alkimoennis." The narrow valleys along the two rivers made the location easy to defend. The Celts also built vast fortifications surrounding the city. There are still remnants of the *Keltenwall*, or the "Celtic ramparts," across the sidewalk from the modern ticket office and bookstore. The spur of land extending out between the two rivers was naturally strategic, but the extensive earthen fortifications, with tall wooden walls, would have made it an Iron Age stronghold. The Celts mined iron ore in nearby quarries which they used for weapons, ornaments, toys, and tools. Mining and working the ore became the economic basis for their community. Alkimoennis was also a ritual site dating back to the 2nd century BCE. On the hill, human bones, showing signs of sacrifice, have been found, along with over 260 cremated bodies buried in funeral urns. Also uncovered were exquisite pottery fragments, bone tools, decorative items, and Roman coins. The best Celt artifacts and the reconstruction of homes, ships, and work places can be found in the Kelheim Archaeological Museum.

Dominating the Michelsberg for the last 150 years is the massive Hall of Liberation, or *Befreiungshalle*. It was completed 50 years after the Battle of Nations set an end to Napoleon's supremacy in Europe. King Ludwig I of Bavaria commissioned the work after visiting Tiryns in Greece and drawing a parallel between the destinies of the Greek and German peoples. Colossal statues, allegories of the Germanic tribes, crown the buttresses on the outside. Inside the monumental domed hall, fronting arcade niches, are 34 "victory goddesses" supporting gilded shields made from captured cannon bronze, with inscriptions denoting the victories in the liberation wars. The Hall of Liberation is 148 feet tall (45 m), with an outer diameter of 145 feet (44 m). The polygon building with 18 sides is based on a design from the Italian Middle Ages. The architect declared: "This is a triumphal monument for our times." Although the form and function of the building was designed as a monument to a political concept, the Hall of Liberation is one of the finest monumental buildings of the 19th century and an icon of Germanic pride and freedom. The peculiarly romantic patriotism of Ludwig I continues to inspire a feeling of German nationalism felt across the country.

Getting to Kelheim

The closest railroad station is at Saal, about 10 miles (16 km) east of Kelheim. There are frequent bus connections to Kelheim from Saal, and then buses leave from Kelheim to the Hall of Liberation quite frequently. It is also a pleasant walk of a little over a mile (2 km) from the Kelheim city center up to the Hall of Liberation. There is a superb "Archaeological Trail" that extends along the upper gorge of the Danube to the town of Weltenburg. By far the easiest way to arrive in Kelheim is by car, about 140 miles (260 km) northwest of Salzburg and 80 miles (125 km) due north of Munich. Once near Kelheim, the Hall of Liberation is easy to locate towering high on the Michelsberg Hill.

Königssee

Surrounded by nearly vertical rock faces, the *Königssee,* or "King's Lake," resembles a Norwegian fjord more than an alpine lake. Mighty waterfalls tumble into the emerald green lake from lofty mountain heights. Set romantically

▲ The pilgrimage church Saint Bartholomä occupies a beautiful location on the shore of Königssee.

in the Bavarian Alps and sculpted by glaciers during the last ice age, the Königssee is a remarkably pristine lake. The lake is five miles long (8 km), almost a mile wide (1.3 km) at its greatest width, and is situated 1,900 feet (602 m) above sea level. The lake is the cleanest in Germany and also the highest in elevation. Roughly following the craggy peaks that surround the lake on three sides is the Austrian border. One famous peak in Austria, visible from the lake, is the pyramid-shaped mountain called Schönfeldspitze, rising 8,755 feet (2,653 m) above sea level. No mountain surrounding the majestic King's Lake can compare to the formidable Mount Watzmann, the second tallest mountain in Germany, rising 8,953 feet (2,713 m) in height. According to legend, the tallest peak represents King Watzmann, the second peak his queen, and the smaller peaks between the two symbolize their seven children. The king was a notoriously cruel ruler to his subjects. As punishment, God turned the whole family into stone. The eastern face of Watzmann overlooking Königssee, featuring 5,940 feet (1,800 m) of sheer rock wall, is the tallest vertical cliff in the eastern Alps. Nearly 100 people have died trying to climb Watzmann since it was first conquered in 1881.

> Königssee is an inspiring location of natural scenery. Add in the pilgrimage church of Saint Bartholomä, the "ice chapels," and powerful energy paths coming down from Watzmann, and you have the perfect recipe for a sacred place.

The first chapel on the Saint Bartholomä Peninsula, jutting into the Königssee, was consecrated in 1134. It was replaced in the 17th century with the chapel of Saint Bartholomä and an attached house which still exists today. Until the beginning of the 19th century, it was the summer seat for the prince abbots of Berchtesgaden. Later, the Bavarian kings designated it as their hunting castle. Since the earliest time of its construction, it has inspired religious people to make a pilgrimage across Königssee to its onion-domed sanctuary. In 1688, a pilgrim's boat shattered on the cliff shore of Königssee and 70 pilgrims drowned. There is a small red cross on the Falkensteiner Wand (cliff face name) memorializing the tragic accident. The pilgrimage church of Saint Bartholomä is the destination of a traditional pilgrimage route that begins in Maria Alm, Austria. The route crosses over the Steinernes Meer (Stony Sea) in the high alpine wilderness above Königssee. Pilgrims used to hazard treacherous climbing conditions traveling overland, then risking the boat ride over frigid Königssee waters to reach the Romanesque and baroque style chapel on the lake shore.

▲ In the avalanche snow fields above Königssee are the "ice chapels," first worshipped by prehistoric pagan tribes.

From the Saint Bartholomä Peninsula, a trail snakes its way four miles (6 km) to the nearly vertical eastern rock face of Watzmann. Along the path is the chapel of Saint John and Saint Paul, erected from 1617 to 1620 in high Gothic style. It is believed to have been built on the site of a former pagan shrine. Because of the vertical nature of the eastern face, as much as 660 feet (200 m) of ice can accumulate in the large avalanche snow fields above the chapels. In mid-summer, until the next snowfall, enormous deposits of ice remain. The melting snow and flowing water creates large ice caves under the packed snow. These temporary caves are called *Eiskapelle,* or "ice chapels." Several are located at the base of Watzmann's east face. The ice chapel's size and shape change every season. Because of their unpredictable nature, it is advised not to walk into or over the ice chapels. Many people have died over the years when the ice collapsed. People have prayed and left offerings at these enormous dome-like ice vaults since pagan times. Geomancers claim there is a strong ley path, or energy line, coming down from the heights of Mount Watzmann, passing through the ice chapels, and continuing on to the chapel of Saint Bartholomä before recycling itself — like an "artesian spring" — back up to the summit of Watzmann.

Getting to Königssee

The majestic Königssee is located just south of the Bavarian town of Berchtesgaden, and is included in a national park of the same name. Approaching from the east Berchtesgaden is located less than an hour's train or car ride from Salzburg, Austria. Located to the northwest, Munich is an hour's drive away. Sightseeing boats leave for the Saint Bartholomä Peninsula regularly in the summer months and during select times in the off-season. Excellent hiking trails surround Königssee and connect to a wider network of trails in the Berchtesgaden National Park.

Wittenberg

The name Martin Luther is so synonymous with the city of Wittenberg that today they are considered one and the same. The official name of the city is Lutherstadt Wittenberg, or "Wittenberg, the city of Martin Luther." The great religious reformer came to Wittenberg originally as a monk and professor in 1511, not to antagonize the Catholic Church, but to profess its virtues as a devout follower. Already an ordained priest, Luther joined the monastery of the Augustinian hermit monks and in the following year obtained his doctorate in theology. He soon became a teacher of Bible studies at the University of Wittenberg, where he began to develop a strong dislike of the Church's practices. He outlined his 95 "theses" criticizing the abuses of indulgences and published it on October 31st, 1517. Luther himself nailed the grievances to the door of the Castle Church in Wittenberg, and from that moment forward the concept of the Protestant Church was born. Martin Luther would become world famous in his lifetime as a leading reformer.

Born in Eisleben, Germany in 1483, Martin Luther was a well-liked and studious child. At 22, he moved to nearby Erfurt to become a monk at the Augustinian abbey after his religious studies ended in Eisenach. He would return to the Wartburg Castle in Eisenach many years later after being forced into hiding for provoking the Catholic Church. While in seclusion, he became the first German to translate the New Testament from Latin into his native language. He published the New Testament in 1522, and the Old Testament was published in parts and completed in 1534. This translation work was so important to the literary development of Germany that Martin Luther has been called the "Father of the Modern German Language." The fifth city that played a pivotal role in his life is Torgau, the most important historical arena of debate during the early years of the Reformation. The chapel of Hartenfels Palace is the first ecclesiastical building ever built for the purpose of Protestant worship. It was in Torgau that Luther drafted the Augsburg Confession, the central creed of the Reformation. His birthplace, Eisleben, is also where he died in 1546. Each city played a critical role in the various chapters of Luther's life, but none were as important as Wittenberg.

> As a poet, writer, and translator, Martin Luther made a major contribution to German culture. But his life is inseparably connected with the Reformation, first in Wittenberg, then across northern Europe, and ultimately around the world.

It is rare that a person gains such influence during his or her own lifetime. Even rarer that such effects would continue hundreds of years later. Martin Luther was a learned theologian, powerfully eloquent speaker, teacher, preacher, and loving family man. He epitomized the ideals of a successful and introspective man of medieval Europe. His life included a wife and children, which he could not have had as a priest. In the year 1524, the Reformer cast off his monk's habit. He married a former nun named Katharina, who bore him three sons and three daughters. Still today, every June a Wittenberg festival commemorates a recreation of Luther's wedding. However, the good times were not to last in Luther's time. After he burned the canon law, the

▲ The Martin Luther statue in the Wittenberg city square is close to the Castle Church.

papacy publicly called for his excommunication at the Elster Gate in Wittenberg. Protestant iconoclasts then began destroying the interior of churches, first in Wittenberg, then all across the country. As retribution, Rome began to wage a war against the heretics in the north, forcing Martin Luther into years of seclusion. While hiding in the Wartburg Castle, he produced the first translated biblical versions of the Old and New Testaments. They first appeared in print in 1534, and the next year Luther delivered his first sermon in German at the City Church of Wittenberg. Doctor Martin Luther died a free and celebrated man. Under the beautiful pulpit in the Castle Church is the burial place of Martin Luther. On the bronze tablet over his tomb is the Latin inscription: "Here is buried the body of the Doctor of Sacred Theology, Martin Luther, who died in the year of Christ 1546, on February 18th, in his hometown Eisleben, after having lived for 63 years, two months and ten days." Martin Luther died one of the most important men of the Middle Ages. Pilgrims of the Protestant faith come to Wittenberg first, and some make the journey to the four other important cities of his life along the "Luther Route."

Getting to Wittenberg

The small city "Lutherstadt Wittenberg" is located about 60 miles (95 km) southwest of Berlin, or about an 80-minute train ride on the U-Bahn from Berlin Ostbahnhof Station. The #304 bus leaves the Wittenberg train station for the old town every 20 minutes, or it is a 30 minute walk to the old city. There is a Tourist Information Office at the train station and across the street from the Castle Church. Organized tour groups in the back of this book offer trips along the Luther Route cities: Wittenberg, Torgau, Eisenach, Erfurt, and the museum-homes of his birth and death in Eisleben.

SWITZERLAND

A lthough glaciers completely blanketed Switzerland during the last ice ages, geologists were either unable to recognize the signs of glaciation until the 19th century, or were simply too stubborn to accept this concept altogether. Thanks to the persistence of three Swiss geologists, the theory reached widespread acceptance in scientific communities. They presented evidence that ice had once lain heavily across not just the Swiss Alps, but over much of Europe, Asia, and North America. In 1837, one of the Swiss scientists, a botanist named Karl Schimper, was the first to coin the term "ice age," or *Eiszeit* in German. These conclusions suggest that when the ice retreated, the country became habitable, but not before. Thus, Switzerland was perhaps the last country in Europe to be settled by prehistoric people.

Einsiedeln

A Benedictine monk named Meinrad left the Island of Reichenau Monastery in Lake Constance and became a hermit in the "Dark Forest." The year was 835 CE when he decided to settle in a remote location — *Einsiedeln* (meaning "hermitage" in German). Meinrad founded his hermitage on the slopes of Mount Etzel, taking along with him a Black Madonna statue, which had supposedly performed miracles. First a few fellow monks followed him, and then a steady trickle of pilgrims came to view the miracle-working statue. Meinrad was killed in 861 by bandits, who coveted the treasures left at the shrine by devout pilgrims. According to legend, two crows that lived with Meinrad pursued his murderers to Zürich and helped assist with their capture. Meinrad's tragic death did not spell the end of his beloved hermitage. During the next 80 years, the spiritual site was never without one or more hermits emulating Saint Meinrad's example. One of them, named Eberhard, erected a monastery and church there, of which he became the first abbot. The baroque abbey of Einsiedeln, with its Marian shrine, became the focus of Swiss Catholic piety and has developed into an international pilgrimage site.

> Some contend that Einsiedeln rivals even
> Rome, Loreto, or Santiago as the top visited
> European pilgrimage destination of the last
> 500 years.

The pilgrimages to Einsiedeln have continued unabated since Meinrad was alive. Even today, over 150,000 pilgrims arrive annually, coming from all parts of the Catholic world. The miraculous statue of Our Lady, originally procured by Saint Meinrad, and later enthroned in the little chapel erected by Eberhard, is the object of their devotion. The "Lady Chapel" stands within the immense abbey church — a similar concept to the Holy House in Loreto, Italy. The chapel is encased in marble and intricate woodwork, elaborately decorated, and adorned with offerings from the pilgrims.

The learned and pious monks of Einsiedeln have been famous for over a thousand years, and many saints and scholars have lived at the abbey. Einsiedeln became a spiritual and cultural center for most of Switzerland. Its sphere of influence includes Bavaria in Germany and upper

▲ Einsiedeln is considered one of Europe's most beautiful Baroque churches.

Italy. The work of the Einsiedeln monks is divided chiefly between prayer, the confessional, and study. Some monks of Einsiedeln have gone on to become bishops, while others have helped establish and reform Benedictine abbeys elsewhere. Einsiedeln monks traveled to the United States from Switzerland in the 19th century to begin a new foundation. The Saint Meinrad Archabbey in Indiana was founded in 1854. By 1857, the Indiana monks were offering advance education courses in commerce, classics, philosophy, and theology. The Einsiedeln abbey in Switzerland has contributed largely to the advancement of the Benedictine Order.

Getting to Einsiedeln

Einsiedeln is located 32 miles (40 km) south of Zürich, with an impressive elevation difference of 1,550 feet (470 m). The town has a railway connection with Zürich and other large cities in Switzerland. It is situated not far from Lake Sihlsee in the foothills of the Alps. There are two main pilgrimage dates. September 14th is the anniversary of the miraculous consecration of Eberhard's basilica, and October 13th commemorates the transportation of Saint Meinrad's relics from Reichenau to Einsiedeln in 1039.

GREECE

He who exercises his reason and cultivates it seems to be both in the best state of mind and most dear to the gods.
—Aristotle

JUST THE NAME OF THIS ANCIENT COUNTRY conjures up images of mythical deities, spectacular architecture, emerging religious movements, and the early establishment of Western civilization. The powerful characteristics of Greek gods and goddesses became similar attributes for Roman deities during the Roman occupation of Greece, with some merely changing names and little else. Scattered across the country are numerous pagan temples and shrines. Of the 166 inhabited islands in the Aegean Sea, the island of Delos was considered the most sacred in times of antiquity, being the birthplace of Apollo and home to his famous sanctuary. Some early chroniclers of Christianity helped develop the new faith while residing in Greece. Christian saints proselytized from the secluded Aegean islands to the mainland crossroads of Europe. The predominant national religion remains Greek Orthodox, represented by thousands of monasteries nationwide, including more than 400 on the island of Kyos alone. Greece is the only country of "Hellenic Europe" and was the only European Union member country without a common land border to another EU country, until Bulgaria was accepted in 2006. Greece is sometimes associated with the Latin-based countries to its west, due to her geographical and cultural ties from the traditional sea routes in the Mediterranean. Other times the country is linked to the northern Slavic-Orthodox countries of Europe, because of its strong affiliation with the Greek Orthodox religion. The historic sites of Greece span four centuries of Western development.

The oldest Greek literary creations come from the eminent poet Homer, scribe of *The Iliad* and *The Odyssey* — both stories passed down orally for generations.

The Iliad narrates the circumstances and events of the Trojan War, which culminates in the destruction of a civilization. After the Greeks sacked Troy, by hiding in a wooden horse, *The Odyssey* continues the tale of the hero Ulysses and his long return home to the island of Ithaca. Homer's epic poems, describing a devastating feud between the ancient Greeks and the Persians, remain a potent warning to all humankind that war is both tragic and futile.

Athens Acropolis

The magnificent Acropolis is perched upon a limestone mount towering above the city of Athens. The ruins of the Acropolis consist of the Erechtheum, the Propylaea, the Temple of Athena Nike, and the magnificent Parthenon. The name Parthenon means "virgin's chamber," and was dedicated to the virgin Athena, the goddess of wisdom and patroness of Athens. The Parthenon was erected between 447 and 432 BCE by order of Pericles, and is considered one of the most perfectly proportioned buildings of all time. So precise was the Parthenon's architect, Ictinus, that a discernible indent was incorporated into the straight lines of the structure's long sides to lend the effect of appearing even straighter from a distance.

The ruins of the Acropolis are considered the most outstanding relics of the Classical Era. The ruins are the primary focus of Athens and remain the principal tourist attraction in the country. According to legend, when the ancient Greeks were planning to name their city, they called upon their two most potent gods, Athena and Poseidon, to hold a contest challenging each to procure the finest gift. Poseidon, the god of the sea, struck open a wall on the Acropolis with his trident and water poured out, bestowing a well. Athena acted quickly and formed an olive tree to grow from the well. The olive tree was considered a symbol of peace. The Greeks were so taken with this gift that they declared Athena the winner and named their city after her. The visible scratches on the lower Acropolis wall are Poseidon's trident markings, and below them grow Athena's many olive trees.

Long before the now-ruined buildings on the hill were constructed, the site was considered a sacred place. Around 3500 BCE, Neolithic people settled upon the hill and built small shrines to their many deities. By 1400 BCE, it had become the residence for all subsequent kings of Athens. In the sixth century BCE, the first temple honoring Athena was constructed here, and henceforth the "Citadel of the Gods" was considered a goddess shrine for many centuries. Byzantine priests wasted no time converting the various temples of the Acropolis to Christian worship after pagan worship was banned in 429 CE by the Christian Roman Emperor Theodosius. The last foreign occupiers, the Islamic Turks, established a garrison on the hill and converted the Parthenon into a mosque, replete with a call-to-prayer tower, which has since been removed.

SACRED PLACES OF GODDESS

The once sacred buildings of the Acropolis have endured many years of war and destruction. The remains, even impressive as ruins, continue to be Athens most everlasting symbol.

▲ The Acropolis is crowned by the Parthenon. This temple was dedicated to Athena, the patroness of Athens.

Some of the greatest damage to the 2,500-year-old Acropolis complex took place only in the last 350 years. In 1677, hostilities between the Ottoman Empire and Venice spiked when the Venetians lay siege upon Athens and scored a direct artillery hit on the Parthenon which, at the time, housed a Turkish ammunition dump. The explosion sent the roof and many pediment sculptures of Phidias hurling over the Athens sky. The goddess Athena undoubtedly wept on that infamous day when her Parthenon was largely destroyed by the folly of war. In the 1820s, the Greeks had been waging a violent War of Independence from the Turks, who again used several buildings of the Acropolis to store gunpowder and ammunition. Another explosion reduced the grand Erechtheum to a mere shell of its former self. Today, the greatest threat to the Acropolis complex is modern fossil-fuel emissions. Like the Taj Mahal in India, the corrosive effects of air pollution threaten to undermine these magnificent world treasures.

Getting to the Athens Acropolis

The Acropolis hill, or the "Sacred Rock" of Athens, is the most important site in Greece's capital, centrally located in the oldest section of the city. The site is a bustling tourist destination all year round and is nearly impossible to miss. A General Admission ticket is valid for all the archaeological sites of Athens: the Acropolis site and museum, Ancient Agora, Theater of Dionysos Kerameikos, Olympieion, and the Roman Agora.

Delos

It can be said that everything on the island of Delos was considered sacred in the eyes of the ancient Greeks. From the natural landscape to the marvelous buildings erected by humans, the geographical features of Delos determined the layout of the Sacred

Precincts. The small Sacred Lake is a topographical feature that dictated the placement of later structures. It was drained in 1925 to prevent the spread of malaria and remains dry. From the Sacred Harbor of Delos, two conical mounds on the horizon can be viewed as female breasts, identified as sacred to goddess worship as they have been similarly interpreted at other sites worldwide. One of the mounds, retaining its archaic name Mount Kynthos, is crowned with a sanctuary devoted to Dionysos, the god of wine and sexual revelry. At the base of Mount Kynthos is a cave long regarded as sacred. The Minoan Fountain was a rectangular public well sculpted into the rock denoting the sacred spring of Delos. According to a carved inscription, the cistern was first dug around

▲ The headless statue of Isis still stands in her temple on Delos. The entire island is a treasure trove of archaeological finds.

a central column in the 6th century BCE, and was reconstructed in 166 BCE. Well-preserved masonry form the walls of the well, and water can still be reached by a flight of steps down the south side of the cistern.

Because Olympian Greek mythology identified
Delos as the birthplace of Apollo and Artemis,
the island was revered as a holy sanctuary
for a thousand years.

In ancient times, Delos was mentioned in Homer's *The Odyssey* as a well-known religious center. The fame of the island was derived from the Greek mythological story of Leto giving birth to the divine twins Apollo and Artemis on the banks of the Sacred Lake. Worship of Leto was well established on Delos since 1000 BCE. There were several shrines and temples devoted to all three deities. The Sanctuary of Apollo dominates the approach into Delos from the Sacred Harbor.

Three more temples devoted to Apollo line the Sacred Way, the most important thoroughfare on the island. Remnants of the Temple of Artemis, or the Artemision, can be located just north of the Sacred Way.

With all its temples, mosaics, structures, and a superb museum, Delos is a treasure trove of sacred sites devoted to the Olympian gods, as well as to the deities of other settlers. In 478 BCE, Athens established an alliance known as the Delian League that gave them control of the lucrative trading routes passing by the island, but to do so they had to rid themselves of the original inhabitants. In that year, Athens expelled all the Delos residents, claiming that no one could die or be born on the sanctuary island. All former graves were dug up and removed. When the Romans took possession of the port in 166 BCE, people returned to live on Delos. Many of the new residents were foreigners who brought with them the deities of their faith. Near the base of Mount Kynthos are the sanctuaries of foreign gods, devoted to a host of religions, including several that came from Rome, Syria, and Egypt. The end of Delos as a sacred center was gradual, but accelerated after several raids on the island in the first century BCE left the city in ruins. As interest in the ancient religions began to wane, and Christianity began to sweep through the Mediterranean region, Delos became a haven for pirates and antiquity thieves. Only during the European Renaissance period was the antiquity value of the island recognized and Delos was afforded protection by the Greek government.

Getting to Delos

The island of Delos is located roughly in the center of the ring of islands called the Cyclades, only a few sea-miles west of Mykonos, in the central Aegean Sea. As one of the most important archaeological sites in Greece and also a World Heritage Site, Delos is inhabited today only by French archaeologists, island caretakers, and thousands of lizards. Overnight stays are no longer allowed. Almost all visitors arrive via the day ferry from Hora, Mykonos which departs and returns every hour from 9 am until 3 pm when the site closes for the day.

Delphi

In the 4th century BCE, Greek pilgrims rode wooden carts to Delphi seeking answers from the famous oracle. The Delphi religious complex contained more than 235 buildings and monuments, positioned beautifully to overlook the Gulf of Corinth at the base of Mount Parnassus. Individual temples at Delphi were ascribed to different Greek gods, including the circular sanctuary building dedicated to Athena. The most significant building was the Sanctuary of Apollo, bearing its famous inscription "Know Thyself." The Apollo temple dominates the Sacred Precincts area of the city, which was considered the exact center of the earth. Greek mythology relates how the god Zeus released two eagles from the eastern and western edges of the world and waited for the result. The two birds flew at exactly the same speed and met over Delphi. The spot is marked in the *omphalos* (meaning "navel") temple. Along with its abundance of temples, Delphi was renowned for the oracle, presided over by a priestess of the Delphic mystery school. The oracle was legendary for the accuracy of its predictions.

> Delphi was the most famous pilgrimage destination in ancient Greece. Pilgrims in antiquity sought a chasm of vapors where a priestess would recite divine direction.

Candidates seeking the enigmatic oracle, including foreign rulers, powerful generals, and everyday commoners would make the pilgrimage to Delphi from all parts of the Classical World. At the Temple of Apollo, pilgrims sought the oracle's advice on important matters such as war, worship, business, love, marriage, and vengeance. After a ritualistic cleansing in a nearby spring, they would sacrifice a ram in Apollo's name before entering the temple. Inside, they were directed into a subterranean vault where a local priestess (usually a young virgin), called the Pythia, sat suspended over a gas fissure in the rock. The foul smell of the gases, combined with the dim lighting and the multitude of high priests present in the chamber, must have been quite an amazing spectacle. Pilgrims would postulate their question to the priestess, who would enter into a trance and communicate with Apollo. Her answer, it would seem, came directly from the god Apollo himself through the fissures in the rock — from the very bowels of the earth. The priestess would utter a response and the assembled priests would translate her answer into pithy rhymes for the awaiting wayfarer. Those who purportedly consulted the Delphic oracle range from Oedipus and Agamemnon to Croesus and Philip of Macedon, as well as Philip's famous son Alexander the Great, who was told by the oracle, "My son, none can resist thee."

As Greek culture flourished in the Mediterranean region, Delphi became the premier pilgrimage destination for much of the ancient world. Festivals accompanied by athletic competitions took place regularly at the complex. Although Apollo was the primary deity worshipped at Delphi, many came to praise the goddess Venus. A

▲ Three columns are all that remain of the Athena Pronaia, a sanctuary at Delphi built in 360 BCE.

▲ The enigmatic Sphinx of the Naxians is a blending of Egyptian and Greek imagery.

festival was held at the temple complex every eight years to mark the completion of a "rose mandala" pattern made by the planet Venus. With each completed conjunction (a coming together with the sun), the planet Venus traces a five-pointed star within a circle pattern. The powerful connection ancient Greeks held with the cosmos climaxed in the eighth year at Delphi when Venus completed her cycle.

Worship at the various Delphi temples lasted for a thousand years before yielding to Christianity in the 4th century CE. In the following millennia, the old pagan sanctuary fell into decay. French archaeologists began to uncover Delphi in the late 19th century. They found the Sacred Precincts forming a square in the heart of Delphi, a place where the ancient Greeks believed gods and mortals could co-mingle. The Temple of Apollo dominates the Sacred Precincts, while the original theater, the stadium, and several various altars complete the square. Near the site is the Museum of Delphi, which contains more than 7,000 objects, including the famous bronze Charioteer, carved pieces from the Athenian Treasury, and the mysterious Sphinx of the Naxians sculpture.

Getting to Delphi

Delphi is conveniently located 108 miles (178 km) northwest of Athens, situated on the north shore of the Gulf of Corinth. The site is located on the lower slopes of 8,061-foot (2,457-m) Mount Parnassus. Athens is a major transportation hub with one of the busiest international airports in Europe. Buses and taxis ply the route every day from Athens, which is along the well-traveled road from Thebes (Thirai) to Amtissa. Local buses run regularly from the nearby train station Livadia to the Delphi archeological complex.

Epidavros

Sacred healing sites around the world have been a part of the human experience for thousands of years. In modern times, people continue to flock to locations such as Lourdes, France and Sainte-Anne De Beaupré in Quebec, Canada to pray for miraculous health-related cures. In times of antiquity, the motivations were no different than they are today. Epidavros was the most celebrated healing center in the ancient world. People from all over the Mediterranean region traveled great distances for the opportunity to be blessed by the radiance of the Sanctuary of Asklepios. The trickle of pilgrims soon became a steady stream, hosting visitors from as far away as Rome and Egypt. A small city was built to assist the pilgrims in their desire for better health. Within the Asklepios religious complex is the Sanctuary of Egyptian Gods, a throwback from the cult of Imhotep, who was similarly worshipped in Egypt for his own healing abilities. The cult of Asklepios at Epidavros took on a greater significance in the 6th century BCE when the older hill-top sanctuary of Apollo Maleatas was no longer spacious enough, forcing the confines of the sanctuary to expand. In the 4th and 3rd centuries BCE there was another building boom, this time to enlarge and reconstruct the monumental buildings.

In Greek mythology, Epidavros was known as the birthplace of Apollo's son Asklepios, whose mother was killed immediately after childbirth by a thunderbolt. Apollo rushed the infant to Mount Pelion where the physician Chiron instructed the boy in the techniques of the healing arts. As the most important healing deity of antiquity, Asklepios was renowned for bringing miraculous cures to the faithful who worshipped at his temple called the Asclepieion. Asklepios also represents the healing aspect of the medical arts, while his daughters Hygieia, Meditrine, and Panacea symbolize the forces of cleanliness, medicine, and cures respectively. One of the remedial practices at the sanctuary was reportedly for pilgrims to lick live snakes. Asklepios himself is often associated with the serpent. In modern times, most people would recognize the two snakes on the caduceus used as a symbol of the medical profession. The snake represents the regenerative ability to shed its skin and subsequently renew itself. Other known treatments at the sanctuary included herbal remedies, changes in diet, and even an occasional surgical operation.

> The Asklepios Sanctuary at Epidavros was the most celebrated healing center in the ancient world, a destination where mentally and physically ill people would risk a long journey in the hopes of being cured.

▲ The acoustically-perfect theatre at Epidavros is renowned as one of the finest buildings to survive from the age of Classical Greece.

217

The health spa and religious complex at Epidavros maintained living quarters for the priest-physicians, as well as various temples, long colonnaded buildings (stoa), a Mycenaean beehive-shaped tomb (tholos), a gymnasium, an athletic stadium, and a large theater. Epidavros was also renowned for a sporting and dramatic festival called the Asklepieia, held every four years. The exceptionally well-preserved theater at Epidavros continues to be used for modern productions of ancient Greek dramas. When sick pilgrims arrived at Epidavros they were welcomed with a separate bath house and several hotels. There are also mineral springs in the vicinity which may have been used for healing remedies. The myriad of therapies offered seemed to have been dependent upon the mind's influence over the body. To find the right cure, a pilgrim was instructed to sleep one night in the enkoimitiria, a large communal hall. In the pilgrim' dreams, the god Asklepios himself would advise what remedies needed to be applied to regain full health. Upon waking, a priest-physician would aid the pilgrim in interpreting the dream and offer assistance in finding a cure.

The cult of Asklepios brought prosperity to the small Peloponnesian town of Epidavros for nearly 1,000 years. Enthusiastic pilgrims continued to arrive throughout the Hellenistic period. In 87 BCE, the sanctuary was plundered by the Roman general Sulla, and in 67 BCE it was sacked by pirates. In the 2nd century CE, the sanctuary enjoyed a new upsurge of pilgrims under the Romans, but in 395 CE the Goths raided the sanctuary and left it in ruins. Even after the introduction of Christianity and the silencing of the oracles, the sanctuary at Epidavros was still renowned well into the 5th century. At that time it became a Christian healing center. Today it is known for the acoustically-perfect theater and is considered one of the finest classical buildings remaining in all of Greece.

Getting to Epidavros

The famous healing sanctuary is located on the eastern coast of the Saronic Gulf, just offshore the isolated Nea Epidavros Bay, on the Peloponnesian peninsula of Greece. The famous theater, archaeological site, health spa, and religious center are concentrated about five miles (8 km) west from the port town Epidavros (also spelled Nea Epidavros or Epidauros). Buses ply the route to Epidavros every day via the Greek capital Athens or Nafplio, the nearest city in the vicinity. Motorists will find Epidavros easy to reach by road via the Athens-Corinth Canal main highway, or along the scenic country roads from Nafplio or Kranidi.

Knossos

At a time on mainland Greece when the warlike Mycenaeans were fighting themselves into oblivion, another culture was blossoming on the island of Crete. They were the peaceful Minoans, who, along with the Mycenaeans, represented the last of the glorious Bronze Age Aegean civilizations. Many similarities exist between the two Archaic Greek predecessors, whose histories can be traced back to accounts given by Homer. The Minoans, named after their legendary King Minos, prospered on Crete between 2000 and 1400 BCE. They built thriving communities across the island without the fear of invasion. The foremost European city of its day was Knossos, of which Homer praised: "One of the 90 towns on Crete is a great city called Knossos, and there, for nine years, King Minos ruled and enjoyed the friendship of almighty Zeus."

> The ancient Minoans at Knossos helped form the structure of early Greece, until their civilization mysteriously ended.

The Minoans were a creative people and a maritime force on the high seas. They ruled the seaways from Asia Minor and Africa to Italy, and were among the first high civilizations to emerge in Europe. The legacy of the Minoans was their assimilation of great technological advancements made earlier in the East, particularly Egypt. They invented a written language of picture writing, much like Egyptian hieroglyphs. Their two linear scripts, called Linear A and B, were found on clay tablets at Knossos. Linear A, presumably the Minoans' own language, remains undeciphered, while Linear B was deciphered in 1952. It is an extremely archaic form of Greek. The Minoans at Knossos are credited with creating the oldest European alphabet. While similarities exist with Egypt, the Minoan civilization was essentially Mediterranean, and is sharply distinguished from any other culture of the Near East. Before its abrupt decline, the Minoan civilization largely shaped the development of early Greece.

The real glory of the Minoan people is found in the charred ruins of Knossos. Unlike the Mycenaean chieftains who lived in heavily fortified citadels, Minoan kings built the Palace of Knossos unfortified, brightly colored and open to the air. Devoid of the symmetry dear to the later Greeks, Knossos was a maze of apartments, corridors, colonnades, staircases, and light wells interconnecting over six acres and rising at least three stories tall. From

▲ The Palace of Knossos was partly reconstructed after it was excavated. Although unorthodox for an archaeological site, it does give the visitor a vicarious feel of the palace.

▲ The Palace of Knossos was unique in the Bronze Age because it was built without regard of fortifications. It was open to the air, defenseless and interconnected by roads to other Minoan cities on Crete.

its labyrinthine complexity came the myth of the Minotaur, a lurking half-man, half-bull monster slain by the legendary Theseus.

The Minoan civilization ended as mysteriously as it began. Sometime around 1400 BCE, most of its buildings were burned, destroyed, or abandoned. Possible explanations include a devastating earthquake, a seaborn invasion, or inundation by a tidal wave after a colossal volcano erupted on the nearby island of Thera, which was also inhabited by Minoans. Archaeologist K. T. Frost sums up the mysterious demise of the Minoan well: "As a political and commercial force, therefore, Knossos and its allied cities were swept away just when they seemed strongest and safest. It was as if the whole kingdom had sunk in the sea, as if the tale of Atlantis were true."

Getting to Knossos

The ruins of Knossos are easily located, three miles (5 km) uphill from the busy Cretan port city Iráklion. Buses and taxis ply the route to the site daily. It is also a pleasant walk, one surely trotted many times by the Minoans themselves, albeit without the souvenir stalls. The partially rebuilt Palace of Knossos is well worth a full day of exploring and wonder. An excellent museum of Minoan culture can be found in Iráklion, Crete's largest city.

Mount Athós

The enigmatic Mount Athós is one of the most unique sacred sites in the world, if not one of the most isolated. Mount Athós refers to the 6,670-foot (2,033-m) mountain, the Athós Peninsula it occupies, and the 20 Eastern Orthodox monasteries jutting from the mountain slopes. The semi-autonomous monastic

▲ The Simonos Petras Monastery towers dramatically from a cliff face overlooking the slopes of Mount Athós.

region, known in Greek as *Ágion Óros,* or "Holy Mountain," is strictly off-limits to all women and girls. Even female animals, including milk-providing goats, cows, and egg-laying hens are also prohibited! Only ten adult foreign men and 100 Orthodox men are allowed to visit per day. All visitors may stay only for a few days, and all are expected to live the ascetic life of the monks. The Athonite community still uses the Julian calendar, which is off by 13 days, a remnant of the long gone Byzantine Empire. The Mount Athós monasteries are truly a step back in time.

The official story of why women are not allowed on the Holy Mountain dates back two thousand years. The legend claims the Blessed Virgin Mary was sailing with Saint John the Evangelist on her way from Joppa to Cyprus to see Lazarus and some other apostles. When the ship was blown off course to the pagan Athós, it was forced to drop anchor near the port of Klement, close to the present monastery of Iviron. When ashore, a statue of Apollo started to speak and declared itself a false idol to the Virgin Mary. It then shattered itself, along with other pagan statues, in deference to the one true faith. The Virgin, overwhelmed by the wonderful natural beauty of the mountain, blessed it and asked her Son to preserve the peninsula as her garden. A voice was heard, "let this place be your inheritance and your garden, a paradise and a haven of salvation for those seeking to be saved." Since that day, the mountain was consecrated as the garden of the Mother of God and was off limits to all other females.

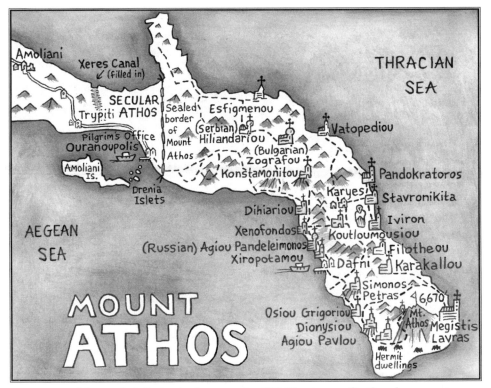

Labels on map: Amoliani · Xeres Canal (filled in) · THRACIAN SEA · SECULAR ATHOS · Trypiti · Sealed border of Mount Athos · Esfigmenou · (Serbian) Hiliandariou · Vatopediou · Pilgrim's Office · Ouranoupolis · (Bulgarian) Zografou · Amoliani Is. · Konstamonitou · Pandokratoros · Drenia Islets · Karyes · Stavronikita · AEGEAN SEA · Dihiariou · Iviron · Xenofondos · Koutloumousiou · (Russian) Agiou Pandeleimonos · Filotheou · Xiropotamou · Dafni · Karakallou · Simonos Petras · 6,670 · Osiou Grigoriou · Mt. Athos · Megistis Lavras · Dionysiou · Agiou Pavlou · Hermit dwellings · MOUNT ATHOS

Mount Athós is home to 20 Eastern Orthodox
monasteries and retains its own autonomous
governmental status under Greek sover-
eignty. It is the oldest monastic republic still
in existence.

The first monks to inhabit the Holy Mountain were Eastern Orthodox hermits
who withstood extreme austerities. The monks started to attract other hermits,
who in time became organized enough to establish their own monasteries. The
monastic rule of Athós was officially established in 963 CE, when a monk named
Peter the Athonite started work on the Monastery of the Great Lavra. At its peak
there were 300 monasteries on Mount Athós while, today, only 20 self-governing
monasteries remain. Of the 20 monasteries located on the Holy Mountain, 17 are
Greek and the other three belong to neighboring Eastern Orthodox countries. Of
the foreign three, the Chelandariou Monastery is Serbian, the Zografou Monastery
is Bulgarian, and the Aghiou Panteleimonos Monastery is Russian. Only males
over the age of 18, who are devout members of the Eastern Orthodox faith, are
allowed to live on Athós. In recent years, the Greek government has strongly discouraged any monks who are not Greek nationals from living on Athós.

Spiritually, Mount Athós comes under the direct jurisdiction of the Ecumenical
Patriarchate of Constantinople. The Holy Mountain is governed by the "Holy

Community" (*Iera Kinotita* in Greek), which consists of a representative abbot for each of the 20 monasteries. In turn, a Civil Governor, appointed by the Greek Ministry of Foreign Affairs, has the main duty of supervising the function of the institutions and keeping the public order. There are religious guards who are not monks but live there to assist the monks. The guards and any other people who are not monks are required to live in the peninsula's capital, Karyes. The current population numbers around 1,600. Inside the monastery complex, usually in the protected tower, are kept relics and treasures of inestimable value of devotional, artistic, historical, or national importance. Unfortunately, most of these items are difficult or impossible to access due security reasons.

Getting to Mount Athós

The Athós Peninsula, the easternmost "leg" of the larger Chalkidiki Peninsula, protrudes into the Aegean Sea for some 40 miles (60 km). Each monastery or cloister has a small harbor of their own to receive supplies by sea, but pilgrims must follow a strict protocol. Entry to the Holy Mountain is from the small port town of Ouranoupolis, from which special ferries go to Dáfni, the entry point of the monk's republic. There is no land entry to Mount Athós — all pilgrims must arrive by boat. In accordance with a *Chryssobul* or "edict" issued in 1060 CE by the Byzantine Emperor Constantine Monomahos, which still remains valid, the following basic conditions must be met for admission to Mount Athós:

1. A permit is required for both individuals and groups. This is issued by the Ministry of Foreign Affairs, Directorate of Churches (offices located at No 2, Zalokosta Street, in Athens; or by the Ministry of Northern Greece, Directorate of Civil Affairs at Diiki- tiriou Square in Thessaloniki).

2. Women are not admitted under any circumstances into the territory.

3. Overnight stays are forbidden except for those men who have proven religious or scientific interests, and are over 18 years old.

Mount Olympus

Atop the towering Mount Olympus, the tallest mountain in Greece, the ancient Greeks visualized the pantheon of their gods reigning over the world. Almighty Zeus hurled thunder and lightning from these heavenly heights and helped repel attacks from the mythical Titans and Giants to retain the Olympian's power over mortals. Although Zeus was the reigning god of the sublime ether, just as Poseidon was the ruler of the tumultuous sea and Hades the ruler of the somber depths of the earth, Mount Olympus was the dwelling place of all the gods. It was a supernatural location believed to be exempt of regular changes in climate. The eminent poet Homer spoke of Mount Olympus: "Never is it swept by the winds nor touched by snow; a purer air surrounds it, a white clarity envelops it and the gods there enjoy an eternal happiness."

▲ The summit of Mount Olympus was the legendary domicile of the Twelve Olympian gods.

In Greek mythology, Mount Olympus is home to the Twelve Olympians, the principal gods and goddesses in the Greek pantheon. Their exploits and deeds are legendary. There were, at various times, 17 different gods recognized as Olympians, although never more than 12 existed on Mount Olympus at any given time. The Greeks believed that incorporated into the mountain were fabulous crystal mansions where the gods lived and ruled over their own particular domains. They had workshops atop Mount Olympus, met amongst themselves, and judged the actions of the mortals. Among those ever-present were Zeus, Poseidon, Ares, Hermes, Hephaestus, Aphrodite, Athena, Apollo, and Artemis who were always considered Olympians. Hebe, Helios, Hestia, Demeter, Dionysos, Hades, and Persephone were the variable gods among the Twelve. Although Hades never ceased to be one of the principal Greek gods, his home in the underworld of the dead made his connection to the Olympians sometimes tenuous. Hestia gave up her position as an Olympian to Dionysos in order to live among humankind. Hestia eventually was assigned the role of tending the fire at Mount Olympus, while Dionysos sometimes would refuse the offer of being an Olympian god, preferring to live by himself among mortals. For three months a year Persephone spent her time in the underworld, thus causing the barren landscape of winter to appear in her absence. She was allowed to return to Mount Olympus for the other nine months in order to be with her mother, Demeter. The Olympian gods retained their own exclusive laws and society, with Zeus reigning supreme over all deities.

Mythology played an integral role in the ancient Greek belief system. So intertwined that myth is the very nucleus of Greek religion. Elements of pre-Hellenistic culture were infused to form the basis of an essentially polytheist and antropomorphical religion: polytheist, because numerous cults of various gods were created; antropomorphical, because the divinities were accepted and represented with human qualities, including anger, passion, virtues, and all of the deficiencies of their human counterparts. But the gods were immortal, always appearing youthful and physically fit, and possessing immense powers. Greek mythology is an expression of the beliefs underlying the civilization that produced it and is particularly rich since it developed all the way from primitive times to the most sophisticated period of ancient society.

GREECE

The deities who dwelled on Mount Olympus significantly inspired the ancient Greeks, forming the basis for their religion, mythology, warfare tactics and even political systems.

Because of the profound influence the mountain had on the lives of ancient Greeks, the whole surrounding area took on enormous significance. Everyday people felt intimidated to even look up at its summit. The neighboring Macedonians embellished the sacred city of Dion at the foot of Mount Olympus. The Olympian gods were worshipped at Dion, sacrifices were made to gain their favor, and fantastic temples were erected in their honor. Alexander the Great made a sacrifice at Dion before setting off on his historic conquest of Persia and the Near East. The founding of Dion is unknown, but it was likely an earth goddess of fertility shrine before being devoted to the gods of Mount Olympus.

Climbing Mount Olympus

Mount Olympus is the highest peak in Greece at 9,570 feet (2,919 m) in elevation and one of the highest in Europe from base to top, in real absolute altitude, since its base is located at sea level. The mountain is located on mainland Greece, southwest of Greece's second largest city Thessaloniki. On a clear day it can be seen for miles out to sea from the Thermaikos Sea. Mount Olympus is noted for its very rich flora with several endemic species.

Any climb of Mount Olympus starts from the town of Litohoro on the east side of the mountain, considered "base camp" for climbers. The village of Litohoro took the name "City of Gods," because of its location at the foot of the mountain. There are many cheap hotels, youth hostels, and camping areas in Litohoro. Hiking maps are available in the hostels or camping supply stores. The youth hostel is also the start of the well-marked E4 trail up the Mavrolongos canyon. While it is possible to trek the mountain in one long day, most hikers opt to stay in one of several refuges on the mountainside for an early morning ascent of the summit before the views are obscured by clouds in the afternoon. The highest peak on Mount Olympus is *Mytikas*, which means "nose" in Greek. There are two shelters on a plain that are about a 45-minute hike away from Mitikas.

Patmós

Strung out like a necklace of pearls along the western Turkey coast are the Dodecanese islands in the Aegean Sea. These 18 islands (including satellites) seem to be a separate entity of Greece altogether, perhaps because they were occupied by several invading forces over the centuries, including Italy, who held the archipelago until 1947. First inhabited thousands of years before Christ by pre-Minoan people, the ancient Greeks prized the islands for their beauty, proximity to Asia

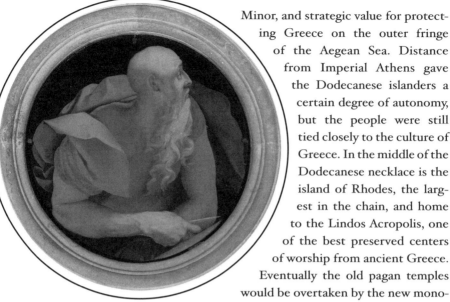

Minor, and strategic value for protecting Greece on the outer fringe of the Aegean Sea. Distance from Imperial Athens gave the Dodecanese islanders a certain degree of autonomy, but the people were still tied closely to the culture of Greece. In the middle of the Dodecanese necklace is the island of Rhodes, the largest in the chain, and home to the Lindos Acropolis, one of the best preserved centers of worship from ancient Greece. Eventually the old pagan temples would be overtaken by the new monotheistic faiths emerging out of the Middle East. Islamic Turks would hold a firm grip on the Dodecanese islands for many

▲ Saint John the Theologian wrote the Book of Revelation while in exile on Patmós. His brief stay has made the island the goal for pilgrims.

centuries, but no single island would possess the spiritual influence of Patmós, a "Holy Island" to the Christian Orthodox Church.

> Patmós is described as the "Jerusalem of the Aegean" because of the countless pilgrims who have come to the island for nearly a thousand years.

Any approach to Patmós by boat arrives at the port Skala, dominated by the towering monastery dedicated to the memory of Saint John the Theologian, or *Agios Ioannis o Theologos* in Greek. Saint John was banished to Patmós by the Roman Emperor Domitian around 95 CE. At that time, the island was one of three remote locations used by the Romans to exile political dissidents. Uninhabited and lacking proper shelter or regular food supplies, indeed this picture-postcard paradise could also be viewed as harsh and damning. Inside one of the many caves on the island Saint John had a vision of the Apocalypse, which became known as the Book of Revelations in the Bible. Because of his title and accomplishments, Patmós became a top destination for Christian pilgrims. Several other monasteries scattered across the island are also dedicated to Saint John.

When the first hermit named Ossios Christodoulos arrived on Patmós in 1088 CE to establish a monastery devoted to Saint John, the island was completely deserted. Construction of the monastery was financed by the Byzantine Emperor Alexios Komnenos. For centuries, the monks were the island's only residents, and for 700 years they administered the island autonomously. Because Patmós, now governed by modern Greece, holds the title of a Sacred Island, the Monastery of Saint John must be consulted on

▲ The landmass of Asia Minor can be seen from Patmós on a clear day. Although only a few sea miles away from western Turkey, Patmós can also feel very remote.

important matters of state. The Blessed Christodoulos also founded the now-famous monastery library. When he arrived on the island, he brought with him his personal library, including manuscripts from the monastic area of Mount Latmos. The library is home to more than 3,000 printed books, 900 manuscripts, and 13,000 documents, most dating back to the 11th century. Perhaps the library's most important document is a parchment of Saint Mark's gospel dated from the 6th century. Saint Christodoulos is buried in the main monastery church.

Getting to Patmós

Patmós is an island made up of rocks and bays, its atmosphere biblical and peaceful. Ferry boats arrive daily at the port, Skala, which is connected to Hora by a paved road. The Greek Orthodox Monastery of Saint John in Hora is supposedly built around the grotto where the Apocalypse was written. The monastery library is not open to the public except by special permission, usually for Byzantine officials or biblical scholars.

ITALY

AND MALTA

The Great Book of Nature can only be read by those who know the language in which it was written.
—Galileo Galilei, Italian Astronomer

T HE PEOPLE OF ITALY AND MALTA HAVE LONG SHARED a cultural link with each other, mainly due to their proximity. Malta is a small and densely populated island nation in the southernmost reaches of Europe. The Mediterranean archipelago is located directly south of Sicily, its closest European neighbor, and north of Libya. From Turks to crusader knights, Malta has long been dominated by colonial masters. These strategically located Mediterranean islands, including Italian-controlled Sicily and Sardinia, have been ruled by various powers over the centuries. Malta is the smallest European Union country in terms of both population and area. Similar to Italy, Malta has many museums, shops, beaches, and archaeological sites. Both are well-known popular vacation destinations among European and international visitors. Much like Italy, Malta has a long and colorful history dating far back into prehistory.

ITALY

The long boot-shaped peninsula, jutting into the Mediterranean Sea, was geo-graphically strategic for cultural dissemination. Starting with the artistically gifted Etruscans, co-existing with Greek colonists, to mighty Imperial Rome morphing into the seat of the Holy Roman Empire, much of Western Civilization originated or passed through Italy. In Roman times, the statesman Julius Caesar praised his countrymen for "imitating whatever was worthwhile in the culture of other nations." From the early inhabitants of Italy, particularly the indigenous Etruscans, the Romans inherited a taste for honest portraiture, superb metal-work, and lavish jewelry. The Greek settlers in southern Italy and Sicily imported their heritage of architecture, marble sculpture, and mural paintings, which the Romans admired and copied. Benefiting from the rich culture that Rome absorbed from its empire, Roman art and architecture took on an imitated look that became uniquely Roman. Its common language, Italian, developed directly from the Latin of Imperial Rome. The religion is Roman Catholic.

Assisi

North of Rome, in the quiet Umbria countryside, is the charming hill-top town of Assisi. Although its early founding remains questionable, there seems to be evidence that the town was inhabited by the Etruscans in prehistoric times. The Romans occupied the hill next, leaving behind the still-intact Roman temple of Minerva. Although other parts of Assisi have great historical value, most of us today would associate Assisi as being the birthplace of a legendary saint.

▲ Saint Francis gained a sizeable following during his lifetime. After death he became legendary.

Like the young Buddha, who left his princely confines in Nepal to seek enlightenment, a fellow seeker named Francesco Bernardone suffered a similar change of heart. One day, while dressed in his finest clothes, he met a poor man whose needs seemed greater than his own. Francis (his English name) gave the poor man his cloak and that night dreamt that he should rebuild the Celestial City of God. In the coming months, he gave away his earthly possessions so liberally that his father, a rich cloth merchant in Assisi, disowned him. This inspired Francis to then give away absolutely everything he owned while making a vow to pos-sess nothing in life. The next three years he spent in abject poverty, looking after lepers, feeding the poor, and rebuilding old churches with his own hands. Disowned by the community as the "Fool of Assisi," Francis left the city to walk the hillside of Mount Subaso as "God's Beggar." He believed that wealth corrupts and that being in the company of anyone poorer than himself was discourteous.

While living an ascetic life in the woods near Assisi, Francis assembled his first 12 ragged disciples. This rag-tag group decided to pay a visit to the Pope in Rome. Against all odds, they not only gained access, but left with Pope Innocent III's permission to found an order. This was an astonishing feat, considering that the soon-to-be religious founder was a layman with no theological training.

> Inspired by Christ's teachings, Saint Francis advocated a life of communal poverty. Shortly after he died Saint Francis became a wildly popular saint, inspired millions, and has generally become regarded as the greatest religious genius that Assisi, and all of Europe, has ever produced.

By founding the Franciscan order, Saint Francis strove to return to Christ's own principles by rejecting opulence and wealth. He instructed his friars to live in poverty with ordinary people, preaching the gospel barefoot and sparsely clothed. His creed of living close to nature, befriending and even speaking to wild beasts, led Francis to become regarded as the patron saint of animals. Indeed, Francis considered himself one with all of nature. When his followers were hungry he told them: "when we must eat, God will provide as he does for our brothers and sisters the birds. So go and ask for food in the name of God. And if they offer you wine, tell them you're already intoxicated with the light of Jesus." The new way of living together, that Francis proposed, was to create a fraternity that was like a family, not monastic, and based on individual and communal poverty.

Despite widespread popularity in Europe, it is surprising that Saint Francis' cult of poverty did not survive — in fact, it did not even last his lifetime. It was officially rejected by the Church, mainly because the Church had already become part of the international banking system that originated in 13th century Italy. This connection, for seven hundred years, fueled Western capitalism into its present proportions. Those of his disciples who clung to his doctrine of poverty were

▲ The basilica, monastery, and tomb of Saint Francis dominates a large section of Assisi. It is a suiting tribute to the city's most famous son.

denounced as heretics and many were tortured or killed. Yet it is clear that Buddha and Francis held the same convictions. In order to free the spirit, seekers must first shed all earthly belongings. By enacting this truth, with such simplicity and grace, Saint Francis could sincerely feel a kinship with all created things — not only living entities, but with "brother fire and sister wind," as he referred to the forces of nature.

He died in 1226 at the age of 43, utterly worn out by a lifetime of vigorous work. On his deathbed, he asked for forgiveness of "poor brother donkey, my body" for the hardships he made it suffer. He also received the stigmata before his passing. Six years earlier, he wisely relinquished control of the order that had grown into a great institution with hundreds of followers. In his humility, Francis chose never to be ordained a priest, and desired that his community of hundreds of followers live as "lesser brothers."

In the decade following Saint Francis' death, an enormous Gothic basilica and monastery were built in his honor within the city walls of Assisi. Emphasizing Saint Francis' desire for peace and tolerance of all beings, along with its fantastic architecture, Assisi and associated Franciscan locations in Italy are included as UNESCO World Heritage Sites.

Getting to Assisi

The old town of Assisi, located on the slope of a hill, is accessed by city buses and taxis from the train station 3 miles (5 km) to the east. The four traditional pilgrimage routes to Assisi are from the central Italian cities of Gubbio, Nocera Umbra, Spoleto, and Cortona. In times past, pilgrims traveled on foot and received food and lodging from other Christians along the way. The goal for all visitors is the multi-leveled Basilica of Francis and the Sacro Covento, dating from the 13th century. The bi-level basilicas are lavishly decorated in frescoes, while the lowest level contains the tomb of Saint Francis.

Damanhur

In a deep valley, situated in Italy's northwest Alps region of Piedmont, are the "Spiritual People" of the Damanhur Federation. This group has developed its own art, philosophy, social system, university and even its own complimentary currency. The people form a collective entity, born out of the union of human spirituality, society, and emotions. Entry into Damanhur is open to all spiritual seekers, no matter where they are from or what race, as long as they have a desire to grow, improve themselves, and aspire to create a better world. The Spiritual People recognize the critical moment where we find ourselves today. We continue to witness the disappearance of more and more languages, depriving humanity of its memories and cultural wealth. Becoming a Damanhurian implies that new applicants share the same ideals, culture, and artistic appreciation. Total members of the Federation number over 1,000, with

▲ Above ground architecture at Damanhur mimics the underground temples.

over 600 living on site. 86% are Italian with a low turnover rate of 10% since 1978. The people grow most of their own food, create most of their own energy, have their own schools, and provide community assistance in the form of fire protection, volunteers in case of an emergency, and assistance to the elderly.

Damanhur is a new and experimental way of living and thinking. The first and most important principle of Damanhurian philosophy is that everything changes. They have evolved through the years, from the first single community of a few dozen people to the complex organization of today's Federation. Their Constitution has changed many times, which reflects the dynamic growth of the community. The model of decision making is an effective democratic system with elected representatives and the lively participation of its citizens in the public debate. The homes and companies of the Federation are not concentrated in one single area, but are scattered all over the Valchiusella Valley around Damanhur. The citizens are committed to creating a sustainable way of life reflecting their fundamental belief that the planet is considered a living being to be respected and preserved. Established in 1975, the Federation of Damanhur is today known throughout the world as a center for spiritual, artistic, and social research. Damanhur is an eco-society, a federation of communities and eco-villages with a continuously evolving social and political structure.

Spiritual pilgrims worldwide come to
Damanhur to experience the Temples of
Humankind, the amazing underground work

of art dedicated to humanity, built by the citizens of the Federation. The vast underground temple complex is considered by many to be the "Eighth Wonder of the World."

In the esoteric traditions, there are only three ways to transmit knowledge: by word, by art, or by architecture. The Temples of Humankind are designed like an enormous three-dimensional book, telling the story of humanity in pictures and sculptures. Historical and allegorical stories are told in the Hall of Water, Earth, Spheres, Mirrors, Metals, and the Blue Temple and Labyrinth, along with several more temples currently under construction. Indeed, the entire complex is only 10% complete; yet, already it holds the Guinness Book of World Records for the world's largest underground temple. The total volume at the time of the record is 780 cubic yards (600 m3), and certainly this number will continue to grow. The choice of establishing Damanhur in the Valchiusella Valley was not made by accident.

▲ The Federation of Damanhur promotes the arts, both above and below the ground.

The valley was chosen for both its energetic and mineralogical values. The rock contains the highest concentration of different minerals on the planet, including a very rare mineral called mylonite. The Temples of Humankind are built inside a vein of this very special rock. This vein of rock also represents the meeting of the Eurasian and the African continental plates. Within this confluence of rocks is the flowing energy of four Synchronic Lines, known as "Energy Rivers," that surround the planet and link us to the universe. According to the Damanhurians, Tibet is the only other place where four Synchronic Lines meet. The temples are specifically orientated to tap into this earth energy. Some of the Damanhur University courses, along with meditation sessions, are held in the temples because the energy flows catalyze the forces in the universe and effect positive change. Tapping into the Synchronic Lines can assist in one's inner growth or help in bringing forth world peace. The lines can modify events and carry ideas, alter thoughts and moods; thereby influencing all living creatures.

The Spiritual People consider the Temples as a living entity. Before visiting or meditating in the Temples, visitors must undertake a series of guided exercises in order to prepare them for this profound and unique experience. Damanhur also offers such classes as "Astral Travel," "New Mediumism: Past Life Research," and "Contact with the Vegetal World: Speaking with Plants." A minimum of three days is recommended for a visit, and reserving a tour of the Temples in advance is required.

Getting to Damanhur

The Federation of Damanhur and the arts center of Damanhur Crea are both located just outside the small village of Baldissero in the foothills of the far western Italian Alps. The nearest railway station is Ivrea, 11 miles (18 km) downhill from Damanhur. If taking the train into Ivrea, hire a cab or take the Blue suburban bus "Traversella" to Baldissero with a stop at the Damanhur Visitor's Center. The Blue buses travel infrequently from Ivrea, every two hours or so. By car from Turin, follow the signs for Rivarolo and Castellamonte, then to Baldissero. Damanhur is located 26 miles (42 km) from Turin, and 75 miles (120 km) from Milan. Check the www.damanhur.org website for contact information and reservations.

Loreto

Since the 15th century, and possibly even earlier, the Holy House (or *Santa Casa*) of Loreto has been among Italy's most famous shrines of pilgrimage, outside of Rome. The settlement is set prominently on a hill overlooking the harbor town of Ancona. Visible from afar, the most conspicuous building in Loreto is the basilica. This domed edifice took more than a century to build and decorate under the direction of many famous artists. The beautiful dome serves as the setting for a tiny cottage standing within the basilica itself. Inside the cottage, a Madonna statue has welcomed visitors for over 700 years.

The original Holy House was brought by crusaders to the *Colli del Lauri* in 1294 and, in the 15th century, a basilica was built over it like a fort. Eminent masters participated in the planning and construction of the basilica. The marble facing on the inside is especially impressive. The relief work was completed by master sculptors Lombardo and Della Porta. The treasury in the Holy House contains frescoes by Roncalli, called the *Pomarancio*. The little building has been raised in height, but the rough walls remain, while the interior measures only 31 x 13 feet (9 x 4 m), covered externally in richly sculptured marble by Bramante. An altar stands at one end beneath a statue, blackened with age, of the Virgin Mother and her Divine Infant, carved of Lebanon cedar and adorned with jewels. Legend attributes Saint Luke as carving the statue, however its workmanship suggests it was created in the 15th century.

> The Holy House in Loreto has been a primary destination for Catholic pilgrims since it arrived from the Holy Land.

▲ The Loreto "Holy House" is located within another holy house. Pilgrims continue to arrive barefoot to demonstrate their humility and poverty of spirit.

The venerated Holy House in Loreto comes from Nazareth, and is reportedly the same dwelling where Mary was born and raised. In this home, Mary received the annunciation and lived during the childhood of Jesus. After the ascension of Jesus, the apostles converted Mary's house into a church. In 336 CE, the empress Helena made a pilgrimage to Nazareth and commissioned a basilica to be erected over the Holy House. Worship continued until the fall of Jerusalem in 1291. Threatened with destruction by the Turks, it was taken by crusaders from the Holy Land to Italy, where it continues to be venerated by thousands of Catholic pilgrims every year. Pilgrimage season is from Easter to October, with the annual Venuta celebration occurring on the 9th and 10th of December.

Getting to Loreto

Loreto is perched on a hill 417 feet (127 m) above sea level on the right bank of the Musone River. It is located 15 miles (22 m) southeast of Ancona. Like many places in the Marche region, it provides good views of the Apennines Mountains to the Adriatic Sea. Years ago, pilgrims would have approached the Holy House by boat, and then hiked to Loreto from Ancona. A local train service now eliminates the leg work.

Mount Etna

The Romans considered it Vulcan's forge. Arabs from the 9th century envisioned its snow as sweet, flavored ices. To the ancient Greeks, it was the realm of gods and monsters. Mystical Mount Etna, the untamed volcano that dominates eastern Sicily, has inspired legend and fear from ancient times until today. On a clear day the vast bulk of Europe's largest active volcano can be seen for a hundred miles across the central Mediterranean basin. The towering mass rises 10,086 feet (3,315 m) directly from sea level. Long called the "Myth of Europe," Mount Etna has periodically cast destructive lava down its slopes. Sicily's eastern Ionian coastal communities have been threatened or overrun a half dozen times since documenting lava flows began in 1381. The devastating four-month eruption in 1669 breached the city walls of Catania, continued to submerge the western half of the city before pushing out to sea. Always smoking, Mount Etna has been increasingly active in the last 50 years. Although the volcanic activity rarely takes human lives, the last major eruption in July, 2001 shocked and awed local Sicilians. Meanwhile, the crater continues to emit a plume of smoke and gas every day, suggesting this sleeping giant could wake from a nap at anytime.

> A spewing volcano that has previously wiped
> out cities, crowned with a blanket of snow,
> has elevated Mount Etna to legendary status
> among countless generations.

The ancient Greeks were particularly enamored with Mount Etna. The famous philosopher Plato sailed from Greece in 387 BCE just to gaze upon the peak with his own eyes. In Greek mythology Mount Etna was home to a fierce one-eyed monster called Cyclops. The brave Odysseus was forced to do battle with Cyclops, during his voyage from Utica to Ithaca, in Homer's famous epic *The Odyssey*. The enormous monster hurled boulders from the lofty heights, which Odysseus had to dodge on his climb up the mountain. Odysseus blinded Cyclops by thrusting a lance into his one eye, dropping the massive beast, and thus freeing the passage for our hero to return home to Greece. The fiery crater of Etna represented the one eye, and the red lava was the legendary blood of Cyclops pouring forth. Sicilian myths from Magna Graecia describe the legendary giant men of the mountain doing battle with the all-powerful Greek gods near Mount Etna. The most outstanding of the Sicilian giants, Encelado, took part in a battle with his brothers against the mighty Zeus and the gods of Mount Olympus. Not surprisingly, the Sicilian giants were no match against the omnipotent gods. Zeus struck Encelado so hard that it thrust him into the deepness of Mount Etna. From deep inside the crater, Encelado cast up fire to the sky in the throes of his prolonged death.

▲ Mount Etna has been in an erratic state of eruption for thousands of years. Such a force of nature has awed countless generations.

When the ancient Greeks came to settle in Magna Graecia, Mount Etna was a different mountain, featuring abundant life-sustaining resources. The first Greeks in Sicily found a moderately hilly land, whose highest peak culminated in the two-mile-high Etna volcano. Elsewhere on Sicily and southern Italy, there are no mountains exceeding a mile above sea level. The long, sweeping slopes of Etna are of moderate steepness, today covered with grass and shrubs. There are trees in the valleys, but in the time of the Greeks it is likely all of Etna's slopes were forested. In Sicily, as elsewhere around the Mediterranean, 3,000 years of tree cutting, together with the destruction of grazing animals, have deforested vast areas and reduced once pleasant woodlands to steppe or semi-desert. Sicily still contains broad valleys and flat fertile plains, which enticed the bread-loving Greeks and modern Sicilians to grow wheat. For generations of farmers, the productive soil enriched by volcanic ash was a trade-off for living in the precarious shadow of Mount Etna.

Ascending Mount Etna

Mount Etna is first and foremost an active and unpredictable volcano. If not in a state of dangerous eruption, an exhilarating hiking trip is to the craters near the summit. Approach the upper slopes with a good map or guide, preferably in a sturdy 4x4 vehicle, to discover the breathtaking panorama at the volcano's three highest summits. On the upper slopes the aftermath of the violent 2001 and 2002 eruptions are easily sighted. Those less inclined to rugged hikes can enjoy the beauty of Mount Etna on the Circumetnea Round Etna Railway trip. Trains leave in the morning from Catania Borgo Station and snake upward through the foothills, into valleys, around the mountain, and back to the sea before returning to the same station. Another option is to drive the many roads that ascend the flanks of Mount Etna. Local road SP92 climbs as high as 63,000 feet (1,910 m), the altitude of the Etna Rifucio Sapienza resort. Other roads skirt the volcano, such as route SS284 which joins the coastal route SS114 after circling the mid-level western and northern slopes of Etna. The train route and roads pass picturesque vineyards, pistachio plantations, citrus groves, Norman castles, baroque cathedrals, and other breathtaking panoramas.

Padua

Soaring over the Piazza del Santo is the basilica of San Antonio, or the Il Santo. The basilica is undoubtedly the most famous and artistically important building in Padua. Architectural students marvel at how the building harmonically blends together Romanesque, Gothic, and the Oriental Venetian styles in a seamless way. The inside of Il Santo has been enriched over the centuries through the acquisition of artistic masterpieces, including frescoes by the venerated Giotto school, sculptures on the high altar by Donatello, and marble statues by Parodi.

Pope John Paul II declared the Basilica of San Antonio an international shrine in 1993. The Pope went on to describe the magnificent building: "As everybody knows, it holds the body of the great teacher and miracle worker. Of all the shrines in the world, the basilica dedicated to Saint Anthony, as proved over the centuries, is of special importance. We hereby announce and declare that the basilica in Padua, dedicated to God and in honor of Saint Anthony, priest and doctor of the Church, is an International Shrine, whose importance is amply demonstrated by the large number of pilgrims from all over the world who continue to visit it, inspired by their great devotion."

> Millions of annual pilgrims from all over Italy, Europe, and the world come to visit Saint Anthony's Basilica in Padua. 15 cities in North America and 44 cities in Latin America are named after him.

How did a simple friar from Portugal gain such intense devotion centuries after his death? The answer is in his extraordinary life. He was born around 1195 to a noble and well-to-do Lisbon family. As a young man, he studied theology and joined the Augustinian Order of monks. Upon meeting Franciscan monks traveling from Italy, he became fascinated with the philosophy of the new order. It didn't take long before he joined the order and changed his name from Fernando to Anthony. He eventually traveled to Italy and befriended Francis. He became the first Franciscan who was promoted by Saint Francis himself to teach theology to his brother monks in Italy. He tirelessly preached with the gift of simple speech and the ability to individually impress upon his listeners many fundamental Christian concerns, especially the danger of heretics. He helped mend disagreements, voiced his

S·ANTONIUS·DE·PADUA

▲ Saint Anthony was a follower of Saint Francis. Like his mentor he too became a mythical figure after his death.

239

▲ The Donatello sculpture in front of Il Santo is a priceless work of art.

opinion on church reforms, and defended people in debt. He performed four recognized miracles during his lifetime and is attributed to many more after his death.

When he died in 1231 outside of Padua, his body was deposited in a marble tomb in the Monastery of the Franciscans. Three years later, the fantastic basilica was started to meet the demands of the already growing numbers of pilgrims coming to Padua to pay their respects. 80 years later, Il Santo was completed and Saint Anthony's tomb was moved from the central nave to the north transept, where it remains today. Huge numbers of pilgrims continue to stream into the basilica to touch the tomb. Most pray for miracles, such as cures for a particular illness, or appeal to Saint Anthony to help them find something. He is especially popular with young women hoping to find a husband. An unusual ex-voto is the custom of publishing testimonies in newspaper classified sections thanking Anthony for favors received. The Chapel of the Saint was built for the countless pilgrims who arrive daily to pray in front of the monumental façade.

Next to the basilica is the Franciscan Monastery, a complex of buildings around five cloisters where monks continue to live and greet incoming pilgrims. Outside the basilica is a Donatello sculpture called the Monument to Erasmo da Nardi. The bronze statue of the commander on his horse had been the first of its kind cast in Italy since Roman times. It seems unlikely that Anthony himself would have understood the worldwide devotion and artistic masterpieces dedicated to his life. After all, in his mind he was but a humble monk of the Franciscan order, serving God unselfishly. 11 months after his death he was declared a saint.

Getting to Padua

The Basilica di San Antonio is located about a mile (1.6 km) due south of the Padua train station. Padua is on the main train route between Milan and Venice in northern Italy. Venice is located 25 miles (40 km) east of Padua. The Tourist Information Office at the train station, or elsewhere in the city, has free maps of Padua to help visitors find their way to Il Santo.

Pompeii

Nearly 2,000 years ago Mount Vesuvius violently erupted over a period of two days. The outflow of thick ash buried everything in its path. Several Roman towns to the south of the volcano — Herculaneum, Boscoreale, Oplontis, Stabiae, and Pompeii — were completely covered in volcanic debris. The cataclysm occurred so suddenly that the activities of thousands of people were frozen in time. Some escaped by boat into the Bay of Naples, but those who stayed in their homes were buried alive. Pompeii is a snapshot of a Roman city whose daily life in August 79 CE came to an instant standstill. Illustrating the suddenness of the deadly catastrophe, archaeologists have produced exact-likeness plaster casts of Pompeii citizens gasping for air as they attempted to survive the deadly gas.

> The well-preserved city of Pompeii gives the visitor a vicarious feel of what it was like to walk down an urban Roman street and visit its many sacred sites.

According to Roman city design, Pompeii centers itself around a large rectangular open-air plaza called the Forum. This square denotes the center of the city, in most cases founded at the confluence of important old communication routes. The Roman Forum of every city played a fundamental role in politics, economics, and religion. Situated prominently around the Pompeii Forum are most of the important religious buildings in the city, including the temples of Apollo and Jupiter. Near the Forum are the opulent baths, the House of the Vetii and the Villa of Mystery, where pagan cults met and mysterious rituals took place. The unusual Temple of Isis is located in a sacred area, bounded by a high wall near the Large Theater and the Triangular Forum. Inside the Doric-pillared temple are

▲ The Isis Temple at Pompeii is a direct import from the Isis cult of Egypt.

▲ This sculpture of a Pompeii goddess was found amid the rubble of the ruined city.

the statues of Harpocrates and Anubis, divinities connected with the cult of Isis. The walls are frescoed with five panels of sacred subjects in Egyptian style with dual representations of Io in Egypt and Io in Argos. The large hall in the temple is where the cult of Isis met and initiations were performed.

The Mount Vesuvius eruption that destroyed Pompeii also buried Herculaneum — a smaller city, persevered in its entirety. About 5,000 people lived in Herculaneum at the time of the eruption. Great care has been taken in the excavation of the two cities and the outlaying villas. Herculaneum was a residential suburb of Naples, rather than a resort town like Oplontis, and because it was buried in mud lava, it remained in a better state of preservation than Pompeii. About 3,360 people died in the eruption from poisonous gases, ash flows, and falling rocks in all the impacted towns. Approximately 90% of the population survived the explosion by leaving in time. Those left behind were prisoners, slaves, children, or adults who refused to vacate.

All trips to Pompeii should include a visit to the famous museum within the archaeological park, where exhibits include plaster casts of people and animals found during excavations. Archaeologists created the casts by pouring liquid plaster into hollow cavities containing bones. When the plaster dried, a statue of the deceased person or animal was rendered in its exact likeness. Also on display in the museum are stoves, altars, cooking utensils, tools, coins, fossilized bread loaves, and many accessories from everyday life in a Roman municipality. Other fantastic finds from Pompeii and Herculaneum are exhibited in the *Museo Archaeologico Nazionale*, which fronts the Plazza Cavour in the old section of Naples.

Getting to Pompeii

The archaeological ruins of Pompeii and the modern town spelled "Pompei" are located about 10 miles (16 km) southeast of Naples. Public buses and local trains access Pompei with Naples and most southern Italian cities. Pompeii has its own direct train stop and, like so many other famous archaeological sites, a modern tourist town has developed around the ruins. Herculaneum, once a seaside village, is now surrounded by the modern city of Ercolano. If possible, visit Pompeii on a night when the site is illuminated.

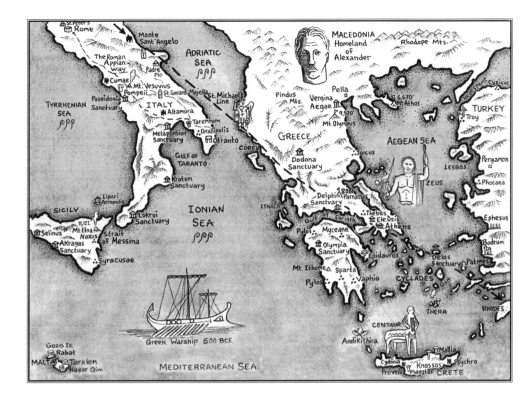

Poseidonia (Paestum)

Around the middle of the 7th century BCE, ancient Greece experienced a population boom. There was not enough fertile soil for growing crops to feed the burgeoning population, so the Greeks did what most people do throughout history when faced with the same problem — they migrated. The Greek colonies were founded by a voluntary migration of the population, not moved by conquest, but out of necessity for new lands. The foundation of any Greek colony preserved political, cultural, religious, judicial, and economical traditions of the mother country. At first the Greeks turned west to a land very similar to their own, southern Italy, which they named *Magna Graecia*. The southern tip of Italy was first colonized with a city called Sybaris, and within a generation colonists of Sybaris started their own new colonies. Around 600 BCE, the Achaean Greeks from Sybaris, perhaps having already explored the west coast of Italy and having chosen a suitable location, did what all ancient Greeks did when confronted with a major decision — they consulted the oracle at Delphi. The Sybarians would have appointed an "Ecista" (a leader who could guide the colonists to their new destination), but only after the oracle determined the move to be a wise and auspicious one.

The Achaeans from Sybaris founded a city which they called Poseidonia to honor the sacred god of the sea. The first thing they did was erect a sanctuary

▲ The ekklesiasterion was an assembly area for the Greeks, only to be buried by the Romans. It remained completely lost until excavators chanced upon finding it a few decades ago.

called the Heraion, dedicated to the goddess Hera, situated next to the River Sele about 5 miles (8 km) north of Poseidonia. Old writers tell that, for many centuries, the sanctuary had been one of the most important religious centers in Magna Graecia. Its legendary construction was attributed to Jason and the Argonauts.

As the sanctuary to Hera was being built, so were the imposing walls of Poseidonia, which remain intact today. These impressive fortifications hold the distinction of being called the finest walls preserved from ancient times. The continuously reinforced walls featured four gates facing the four cardinal directions. With the security of the city intact, the *polis* would soon blossom. Situated on a critical trade crossroad, accessible to ocean and river routes, and within close proximity to fertile growing lands, Poseidonia soon reached a high degree of richness, renowned in the ancient world.

> The city of Poseidonia features three magnificent Doric temples, an incomparable inheritance from Greek civilization. A few centuries later the Romans conquered the city, redesigned it, and renamed it Paestum.

In each Greek community there existed a sacred area consecrated to the gods, often surrounded by a wall. The crowning achievement of Poseidonia was the construction of three temples devoted to the worship of Athena, Poseidon, and Hera respectively. The Athenaion, built around 500 BCE, was a Doric temple with some Ionic features. It connects to the other two temples by the road called Via Sacra. The Temple of Poseidon is the best preserved today, a temple originally designed on the Doric rules of the mother country, specifically modeled after the Temple of Zeus in Olympia. The Temple of Hera, dedicated to the goddess of women and marriage, is the oldest temple in Poseidonia. It is also of the pure Doric order. However, this temple didn't correspond to the rules of sacred architecture, because it features an odd number of columns. All three temples are situated in the city center with an east-west orientation.

When the Romans occupied the city, starting in 273 BCE, they added many constructions of their own, but left the temples standing. The pious Romans would never have dismantled them, but rededicated them to their own divinities. Under the Romans, the tangible signs of Greek civic life were eventually removed. The *ekklesiasterion* was filled in and replaced by the Roman assembly area to the south. The new Roman Forum

▲ The Temple of Poseidon is a copy of the Temple of Zeus at Olympia. It is the best preserved of the three main temples at Poseidonia.

replaced the Greek *agora*, again situated to the south. The Romans enriched the city with large buildings, the Forum, the *thermae*, the amphitheater, and the so-called *Tempio della Pace* (the "Temple of Peace"). Such an overlap of civilizations can make the city somewhat confusing to visit.

Paestum, as Poseidonia was soon renamed, flourished as a Roman city until the Late Empire, when Rome turned its seat of power towards the east. This left Paestum and other coastal communities with little influence, just as Christianity was taking hold of the Italian peninsula. For a while the Athenaion served as a burial site in early Christian times and was converted into a church during the Middle Ages. After successive outbreaks of malaria and additional invasions, Paestum was finally abandoned of its permanent population. It was only "rediscovered" in the early 18th century as writers, poets, and artists began to visit the renowned Greek city on their "Grand Tour," while consequently propagating its fame all over Europe.

Getting to Paestum

The train station and the modern community, surrounding the archaeological park, still retain the Roman name Paestum. A few trains per day stop at Paestum station along the Salerno to Sapri route. The nearby Capaccio Scalo station has more frequent train stops, but is not as close to the ruins as the Paestum station. Heading west out of the Paestum station, it is only a 10-minute walk to the entrance of the park. Also near the entrance is the wonderful Museo Archeologico Nazionale, featuring some of the best finds from Paestum, including the famous Diver's Tomb. The Heraion Sanctuary, north of Paestum, consists of little more than a base today, but can be reached via the coastal road.

Ravenna

The exact time when Ravenna was founded as a town is lost in legend. It was likely inhabited by the pre-Roman Umbrian and Etruscan people. There is, however, evidence that in the 2nd century BCE, a large part of the Po River valley was colonized by Rome. Ravenna was situated at that time on several small, sandy islands in a lagoon, its position making it strategic from enemy attack, while remaining linked to the mainland. It rose to prominence in 402 CE when it became the capital of the Western Empire. Emperor Honorius moved his court from Rome, to this obscure town on the Romagna coast, after being increasingly alarmed with the armies of barbarian forces invading from the north. The location was ideal, because it was easy to defend. The Emperor's anxiety proved well-founded when Rome was sacked by the Goths in 410, but Ravenna, too, would soon fall to the barbarians. In the 63 years it was the capital, Ravenna became the heir to all the greatness of Rome. After capture, the Ostrogoth Kings, rather than destroy Ravenna, continued to beautify the city, proclaiming it as their royal seat. This reign also would prove to be short-lived, as the Byzantine army captured Ravenna in 540 and put an end to the Goth rule of Italy.

> Within the span of 140 years, Ravenna went from the last Roman capital of the Western Empire, to a city of barbarian rule, to re-capture by the Eastern Empire. No city of its time possessed an equally rich heritage, in terms of artistic quality and religious imagery.

During the "Dark Ages" of Europe, when much of the continent was in a state of chaos following the vacuum of Latin dominance, Ravenna flourished. Even the great cities of the East (Constantinople, Antioch, Jerusalem, Alexandria), or the re-emerging cities of the West (Rome, Milan, Trier, Cologne), could not compete with the splendors being created in Ravenna. The city prospered during the rule of Justinian, whose main ambition was to reunite East and West both culturally, politically, and artistically. The Byzantine art, particularly the mosaics, are so important that they are considered the origin of Christian iconology. But Justinian's dream was destined to failure as Ravenna slowly fell into

▲ The octagonal Basilica of San Vitale is the crowning jewel of Ravenna.

decline. The city was poorly administered, the great Porto di Classe harbor began silting up, and when the city was captured by the Longobard barbarians in 751, the history of Ravenna seemed to come to an ignoble end. Fortunately, few Byzantine religious buildings were altered or destroyed by Ravenna's many occupiers. Over the centuries, the city has become a time capsule of art treasures. The city's many mosaic decorations are regarded among the crowning achievements of Byzantine art.

The artistic technique of mosaic design was popular with the ancient Greeks and Romans, while this tradition was passed on to the early Christians of the Eastern Empire. The finest Ravenna mosaics are located in the Basilica of San Vitale, a church finished by Justinian in 548 CE. Justinian used San Vitale to form the model for his masterpiece, Hagia Sophia, in Constantinople 15 years later. Charlemagne, the first Holy Roman Emperor, was equally inspired by San Vitale and modeled his 8th century palace / chapel in Aachen, Germany after passing through Ravenna.

The octagonal San Vitale church in Ravenna is fairly plain on the outside, but the inside is considered among the best examples of Byzantine art in the West. The mosaics are located in the apse of San Vitale, arranged in a rigid hierarchy, with Old Testament scenes shown across the dome in the choir. It features a beardless Christ in the center, presenting a crown to San Vitale, who is accompanied by an angel. Below, on each side, there are two fantastic imperial mosaics: on the right, the empress Theodora is accompanied by court dignitaries; on the left, Justinian is surrounded by two patricians and the Imperial Guard armed with shields and lances. These mosaics are

▲ The San Vitale mosaics are world renowned for their exquisite detail. This mosaic of Justinian is one of the best portraits of the Byzantine emperor.

so detailed that they show the three wise men offering their gifts on Theodora's purple gown, various expressions on all the faces represented, and the symbolism of Justinian's foot resting atop the foot of his leading general, who liberated the city.

While San Vitale receives the lion's share of attention, several other buildings in Ravenna contain equally impressive mosaic designs. Across the grounds from San Vitale is the tiny Mausoleum of Galla Placidia, featuring Roman, Christian, and naturalistic mosaic motifs. The same entrance ticket to the mausoleum and San Vitale also gains the visitor entrance to the stunning Neonian Baptistery, Basilica of Apollinare, and the Museo Arcivescovile, all incomparable mosaic sites. These locations, including three other mosaic baptisteries and two dozen other monuments in Ravenna, are listed on the UNESCO World Heritage list.

Getting to Ravenna

The municipality of Ravenna consists of Roman, Gothic, Byzantine, medieval, Venetian, as well as contemporary buildings. Ravenna has a compact city center with a centrally located train station. Many tour groups of Italy feature Ravenna in their itinerary of destinations. Catch connecting trains to Ravenna in Bologna or Ferrara.

Rome

With religious sculptures, churches, shrines, and ancient pagan temples around every corner, it would be possible to write an entire book on the sacred sites of Rome. The city has been a pilgrimage destination for over two millennia and has been continuously inhabited for 3,000 years, making it one of Europe's oldest cities. Despite its age and importance, Rome did not become Italy's capital city until 1871.

Some of the most important ancient remains in Italy are within the city limits of old Rome. The ruins are of extraordinary archeological, cultural, and artistic value — the Coliseum, the Roman Forum, and the Area Sacra, to name a few, give a glimpse of its former splendor and glory. Juxtaposing hundreds of historical monuments, spanning three millenniums, Rome certainly lives up to its nickname as the "Eternal City."

Starting this survey in Classical times, few structures in Rome, or even worldwide, can compare to the splendor of the Pantheon — the most complete Roman structure in the city, finished around 125 CE. The name of Agrippa, which can be read on the outside façade, commemorates the son-in-law of Emperor Augustus, who built the temple "to all the gods." The reason the pagan temple survived, after Christianity became the official religion of Rome, is due to Phocas, the Byzantine emperor. He gave the building to Pope Boniface IV, who turned it into the present church of Santa Maria of the Martyrs. For the solemn consecration of the new

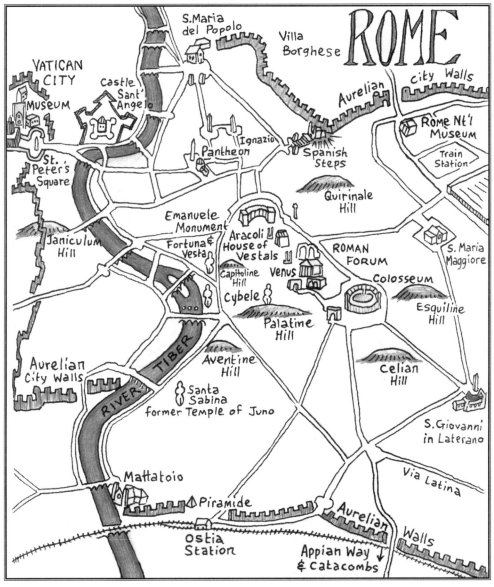

church, the pope had 28 cartloads of martyr bones brought from the catacombs to be placed underneath the altar. A formidable achievement, even now, the Parthenon remains the largest dome ever created out of concrete. The dome is 146 feet (43.3 m) in diameter, while the hole in the domes' center measures a full 30 feet (9 m) across. The entire building is designed as a perfect geometric figure — a sphere inserted in a cylinder — incorporating the dimensions of the dome and height as precisely equal.

Nearby the Pantheon, running through the core of the Roman Forum (the political, economic, and religious center of Imperial Rome), is the Via Sacra.

▲ The twin goddess temples of the Vestal Virgins and Fortuna reside not far from the Roman Forum.

Flanking this best-known street in ancient Rome are the remains of many pagan temples and shrines. Among the most important is the House of the Vestal Virgins. Six women had the responsibility of keeping the sacred flame of vesta alight. The women lived on four floors of rooms around a central courtyard, with the round Temple of Vesta at the near end. The Via Sacra continues towards the Coliseum under the Arch of Titus, one of the most famous arches in Rome. The arch was erected to commemorate the capture of Jerusalem by Vespasian and Titus himself. According to tradition, Jewish people do not pass underneath the arch, so as not to pay homage to those who had destroyed their temple in Jerusalem. Inside the Arch of Titus is a bas-relief depicting the Romans carrying off booty taken from the temple, including silver trumpets, the golden table, the ark that contained the sacred scriptures, and the seven-branched candelabrum.

The Via Sacra extends outside the city walls to the Appian Way, the first and most important of the great roads built by Rome. A journey along the Appian Way (largely preserved today), passes important Roman and early Christian sites, through the suburbs of modern Rome and into the southern Italian countryside. Within the first eight Roman miles are 50 preserved monuments, protected by the Appian Way Park Authority. Among the most important buildings are: the small church of Quo Vadis, commemorating the spot where Saint Peter returned to Rome after having a vision of Christ; at Mile II is the entrance to the Jewish catacombs, just beyond the Christian catacombs (the most important burial place for early Christian popes and martyrs); elaborate tombs and mausoleums for the Roman emperors and their family members; the remains to the temple of Jove is just past Mile IV, along with the Villa Dei Quintili (which is among the largest villas in suburban Rome); and lastly, just before Mile VIII, are the remains of the temple of Hercules.

The Basilica of San Giovanni in Laterano
houses many relics from Rome's exquisite
past, while also being a significant place for
the emerging Christian faith.

Apart from Saint Peter's Basilica, in the autonomous Vatican City, the second most important church to the Roman Popes is the Basilica of San Giovanni in Laterano. The first church on this site was established in the 4th century by Constantine, the first Roman emperor to be Christianized. The present basilica was re-worked by the master Borromini in the 17th century. Despite changes, it can be seen as a snapshot of Rome's history since Christianity embedded itself into this once

▲ An Egyptian obelisk dominates the plaza in front of San Giovanni in Laterano.

deeply pagan city. The church's prize relics are the heads of Saint Peter and Saint Paul, kept behind the papal altar. San Giovanni in Laterano was Rome's cathedral and seat of the Pope until the unification of Italy. Pilgrims have been coming here for many centuries to ascend the 28 steps of Scala Santa on their knees — the only way permitted. The staircase is supposed to be from Pontius Pilate's house in Jerusalem, which Christ walked after his trial. Next door to the church is the Baptistery, established by Constantine in the 5th century, making it the oldest surviving baptistery in the Christian world. Many other relics in this church attest to the staggering history of Rome: the doors were taken from the Curia in the Roman Forum; fragments of Giotto's frescoes proclaim the first holy year in 1300; and the bones of Constantine's bishop Sylvester I are said to sweat and rattle when the current Pope is about to die. Fronting the basilica in the Piazza San Giovanni in Laterano is an original Egyptian obelisk, one of 13 standing in Rome. The emperors of Rome, starting with Augustus, brought back the obelisks from their military campaigns in Egypt. It is interesting to note that in ancient Egypt and now in Rome, the obelisks were erected in holy sanctuaries and in front of their most important religious buildings. Little wonder Rome contains more obelisks than any other city in the world.

Getting to Rome's monuments

As the capital of Italy, Rome has an international airport, a domestic airport, and several train stations. The Pantheon faces the Piazza della Rotonda, almost directly centered in the old city. The Roman Forum is located just east of the Coliseum, one of the most visible landmarks in Rome. Beginning at the Porta San Sebastiano, connecting to the Aurelian Wall, extends the Appian Way. Be sure to stop at the Appian Way Park Authority, at the beginning of Appia Antica, for a route map of the antiquities and historical sites. The Piazza San Giovanni in Laterano is easily located at the end of the road of the same name, intersected by Via dell'Amba Aradam. There is a metro stop named "San Giovanni" at the plaza.

Saint Peter's Basilica

Approaching the autonomous state of Vatican City (Holy See) has been the focus of Catholic pilgrims for many centuries. Crossing the Tiber River, on the Ponte Sant'Angelo bridge in central Rome, the visitor is welcomed to the world's smallest nation (106 acres / 43 ha) by beautifully rendered marble angels. Soon the visitor enters the Piazza San Pietro, fronting Saint Peter's Basilica, which was created by renaissance sculptor Bernini. It is one of the most renowned squares in the world. Twin colonnades, featuring statues of various saints and martyrs, flank either side of the square, with an 85-foot (26-m) obelisk rising from the center. It is the Piazza San Pietro where the masses gather to receive the Pope's blessing every Wednesday.

> The Vatican City is its own autonomous
> political entity within Rome. At its center,
> the towering Saint Peter's is the heart of
> Christianity and the most venerated basilica
> to Catholics.

Standing before Saint Peter's Basilica, the largest and most awe-inspiring church in Christendom, it is easy to grasp the enormous spiritual history of this site. Here is the church that kept alive the flame of Western Civilization long after the demise of the Roman Empire in Italy. Christians believe Jesus sent the apostle Peter to Rome, the "rock" upon which his church would be built. When Europe descended into the Dark Ages, it was the ecclesiastical scribes who patiently copied manuscripts to preserve Western culture. During the Italian Renaissance, when Saint Peter's was constructed on the exact spot where a 4th century church built by Constantine stood, a rare configuration of brilliant minds gathered to add their gifted influence. The fathers of the church (the visionary Saint Ignatius Loyola, Saint Francis Xavier, and the eminent poet of mysticism Saint John of the Cross) are all represented as marble statues inside the church. These statues, and the church itself, were designed by leading artists of the age. Bernini, Raphael, Michelangelo, Borromini, and Bramante were indeed renaissance and baroque masters, who dedicated much of their lives to Christian art and architecture — including Saint Peter's magnificent church.

Many people believe Saint Peter's Basilica contains the most beautiful collection of artwork ever assembled in one place. Inside and out, thousands of magnificent pieces of art and sculpture decorate the walls, floors, and halls of the church. Most famous are Michelangelo's *Pietà,* the highly adored statue of

Saint Peter, and the spectacular papal altar. The Pietà, just within the entrance of the basilica to the right, is an exquisitely rendered sculpture of Mary, grieving over the body of Jesus after the crucifixion. In the central nave is the statue of the seated apostle Peter. His one foot is worn thin from the faithful kissing and touching it over the centuries. Front and center in the basilica is the high altar, where the Pope celebrates mass.

▲ Saint Peter's Basilica is one of the most famous religious buildings in the world.

Perhaps the most outstanding aspect of Saint Peter's Basilica is the dome. Designed by Michelangelo and finished 24 years after his death by Fontana and Della Porta, it holds reign over the enormous interior of the church, which at capacity can accommodate 100,000 standing people. Four massive pentagonal pillars support the dome. Each gilded pier is a reliquary, containing very sacred Christian objects. The colossal space created by the dome allows spectacular shafts of light to flood into the basilica. Vatican City's other attractions include galleries, museums, the papal library, and the amazing Sistine Chapel adorned with famous Michelangelo frescos.

Getting to Saint Peter's Basilica

Saint Peter's Basilica comprises a sizable amount of the area in the tiny autonomous state of Vatican City. After several days of sightseeing in Rome, be sure to save at least a full day for the Vatican City. Like most of the attractions in the old section of Rome, *Citta del Vaticano* is easily reached by bus or on foot. From the center of Rome, usually demarcated by the first century CE Coliseum, head east and cross the Tiber River. The dome of Saint Peter's dominates the eastern skyline and is easily located. Most visitors arrive at Saint Peter's in the morning for the elevator tour to the top of the dome for the commanding views of Rome.

Shroud of Turin

According to Christian tradition, Jesus was taken down from the cross and wrapped in a burial cloth. The Gospel of Matthew says that Joseph of Arimathea laid the body of Jesus in a tomb, after wrapping it in a "shroud." Such a relic would be a prize possession of the Church, if not the most valuable item of Christendom. A remarkable life-sized shroud, bearing the likeness of a bearded man with clear signs of being crucified, was located a few centuries after Jesus' death, eventually finding its way to Turin, Italy. Unfortunately there is

▲ The busy entrance to the Turin Cathedral.

no conclusive way to determine if the man on the imprinted image really is Jesus Christ. Some critics have declared it an outright fake. True believers call it the necessary evidence to prove the legitimacy of the Gospels.

The Shroud of Turin is 13.5 feet (4.42 m) long, 4.25 feet (1.13 m) wide, and depicts a man who would have stood five feet seven inches (170 cm) in height. The first mention was described in 544 CE in the town of Urfa, Turkey. The shroud was reported as an extraordinary image of a man imprinted on cloth, which was "not made by hand." It cannot be verified if this is the same shroud mentioned by the crusader Robert de Clari, who wrote in 1204 that a holy shroud disappeared when Constantinople was sacked. The sacred relic, now known as the Shroud of Turin, first appears conclusively around 1360 in France, but in 1578, after being rescued from a fire, it was taken to the cathedral of Turin, Italy. During the late Middle Ages, the shroud was considered authentic and large numbers of pilgrims came to Turin just to be near it, especially after Pope Sixtus IV (1471 – 1484) called it "the portrait of Jesus Christ himself." Today, the sacred relic is exposed for veneration only on very rare occasions. Popular devotion to the Shroud continues in Turin, with many thousands per year coming to behold the cloth. Faith or no faith, the holy relic raises as many questions as science has been able to put to rest.

From the time the shroud was in France numerous challenges to its authenticity have been made. The bishop in Troyes denounced it in 1389 as an artist's rendition and forbade priests from claiming it as the true shroud. Such pro and con views continued for hundreds of years. It was not until Church authorities allowed the shroud to be carbon dated by several independent authorities that a new opinion emerged. Both independent studies concluded that the cloth samples sent in were manufactured between 1260 and 1390. Such hard evidence forced the Church to accept the test results and reverse its decision. Now the Catholic Church says the Shroud is a representation of the passion of Christ, but not the original burial shroud of Jesus.

The Shroud of Turin is perhaps Europe's most famous religious relic. Untold millions have made a pilgrimage to Turin to be near the prized cloth, showing the imprint of a man who appears to have been recently crucified.

The advent of photography in the 19th century led to a new discovery regarding the portrait on the fabric. It appears to be a negative image and when reversed it reveals an image never before seen. The reversal of the Shroud offered a likeness of Christ, especially the face. A century of scientific research also concluded the following tantalizing tidbits: the Shroud is not a painting; traces of real human blood appear in several different places; the blood stains involve gravity, suggesting a real death; the eyes are covered with coins, one of which has been identified as the "widow's mite" minted under Pontius Pilate; and finally, pollen embedded in the cloth has been extracted and can be dated to the 1st century Palestine, implying that the Shroud passed through the region of the eastern Mediterranean. Some of these details could not have been faked, say the die-hard believers. For example, how could people in the Middle Ages have anticipated 20th century image analyzers that show specific details, which would otherwise be undetectable?

Viewing the Shroud of Turin

Due to the immense popularity of the Shroud, it is not available to be viewed unless by special arrangement. Instead the masses are directed to the Museum of the Turin Shroud (Via S. Domenico, 28), where an exact replica is on display. The Shroud narrowly missed total destruction in 1997 when the Guarini Chapel in the Turin Cathedral was gutted by fire. The Shroud was rescued by Turin firemen and later determined to be undamaged. The Cathedral of Turin has been restored and features an exhibit about the Shroud. The Cathedral and museum are located in the old city about a mile from the Stazione Porta Nuova train station. Turin also hosts the second most important Egyptian Museum in the world after Cairo. Also worth seeing in Turin is the famous self-portrait of Leonardo da Vinci, the opulent palaces of the Savoy royal family, and the National Museum of Cinema.

Valley of the Temples

The Greek colonization of Magna Graecia extended from Asia Minor to southern Italy. "Akragas" was the largest Greek city built on the southern coast of Sicily. The Romans changed the name to "Agrigentum," while much later the Italians modified the name to "Agrigento." The ancient Greeks imparted their refined cultural and social models upon all their oversea colonies. They imported advanced metal processing techniques, new wine and oil production methods, and introduced the alphabet and writing. Such sophistication certainly influenced the Romans who, at the time of the Greek arrival, were little more than unorganized farming communities, ruled by warriors. Centuries later the Romans designed their cities based upon the model they inherited from the Greeks. Especially important was the administrative model of the *polis*, the Greek city-state. Greek colonies like Akragas were enclosed by strong walls, which included residential areas, public spaces, and holy districts.

The account of Akragas has been handed down to us by the historian Thucydides, who speaks of its establishment by colonists from Rhodes and Crete. Akragas would become one of the last Greek colonies founded in Sicily. The location was chosen for its fertile farmlands, strategic position overlooking the Sicilian Channel, and the sacred landscape where the Valley of the Temples was to be located. In the 5th century BCE, the city was organized politically, the great public works established, and the construction of the monuments began in earnest. When completed, the famous Greek poet Pindar praised Akragas as the "most beautiful city of mortals." Positioned along the Via Sacra roadway are ten Doric temples, three in a fairly decent state of preservation today.

The Valley of the Temples is a breathtaking sacred city of temples overlooking the Mediterranean Sea.

Greek mythology determined the location, size, and interior decoration of all the temples. Each was dedicated to a particular god or goddess. The omnipresent deities had a variety of duties: they controlled the forces of nature, intervened in people's everyday lives, and determined the political life of the city. Depending on the circumstances, a mortal could appeal to a particular god to remedy a situation through intense prayer or sponsoring a ceremony. For matters of farming, people would pray at the Temple of Demeter and Persephone, two native female divinities related to the earth and particularly popular in Sicily. Women who wanted help with their marriage or an upcoming childbirth worshipped primarily at the Temple of Hera. The goddess Hera is best known for her marriage to the almighty Zeus, father of all the gods. Zeus was known for his many amorous adventures and his ability to control the weather. Due mostly to his supreme status, the Zeus temple at Akragas was the largest Doric temple ever built by the Greeks.

▲ The modern city of Agrigento overlooks the Valley of the Temples.

The son of Zeus was Heracles, who was intensely worshipped at Akragas for his attainment of purification through suffering. The cult of Heracles, the strong hero and conqueror, was especially popular in Sicily. His powers were evoked when the Greeks made their many incursions to the interior of the country.

The Temple of Concord, completed in 430 BCE, is one of the best-preserved buildings of Greek antiquity. It was spared destruction by the Carthaginians and Christians only because they converted it to their own religion. When it was a Greek temple, it was covered in white stucco and painted in vivid colors. Like all the Greek houses of worship in the Valley of the Temples, elaborate prayers and sacrifices took place. Prayers were spoken standing up and out loud; and, if a prayer was directed to the gods at Olympus, a person would turn their palms to the sky. Sacrifices were an involved ceremony. Libations such as honey, wine, cakes, produce, and even hair were offered for divine favors. Animals were brought on special occasions and killed by the priests in accordance with carefully handed down traditions. The meat was roasted and offered to all those present. The immortal and untouchable gods received the rising smoke from the altars.

The prosperity of the Greek colonies lasted only a few centuries. Throughout the 3rd century BCE, Akragas was the scene of many battles between the Romans and the Carthaginians from North Africa. The Romans finally conquered Akragas in 210 BCE, changed the constitution, repopulated it, renamed it, and added new structures. The Romans did not believe in dismantling Greek temples, but merely rededicating them to their own divinities with very similar attributes to the Greek gods. After annexation, Agrigentum was again a flourishing city under the domain of the Roman Empire.

Getting to the Valley of the Temples

The modern city of Agrigento is perched on a hill, overlooking the ancient Valley of the Temples, or *Valle dei Templi* in Italian. A road winds down to the archaeological park from Agrigento. The #1, #2, or #3 buses make a stop at the Valley of the Temples car park. The city buses originate at the Agrigento Train Station. Long distance trains and buses travel connect Agrigento several times per day from Catania or Palmero.

MALTA

Long before humans inhabited the Maltese archipelago, when ocean levels were much lower, a land bridge connected Malta to Sicily and mainland Europe. Large mammals migrated over during the last ice age. Bones of elephant, rhinoceros, deer, and foxes have all been found on Malta from an era when the climate was much cooler. At the end of the Pleistocene Era, the Mediterranean basin filled with water and the islands were formed. At one point a massive tidal wave swept over the islands and deposited the remains of many now-extinct animals under deep levels of sediment.

The official language is Maltese, originally derived from the Semitic-Phoenician peoples who settled here in the millennium before Christ. The language evolved and assimilated with other foreign languages, depending on who was occupying Malta at the time. In the Middle Ages the most influential were the Knights of

Saint John, who introduced their distinct languages from eight different regions: Auvergne; Provence; France; Aragon; Castile; England; Germany; and Italy. Today the official second language is English; yet, most Maltese are also fluent in Italian. As a result of so many racial and cultural influences, the Maltese have a very diverse appearance, with features ranging from dark-skinned Mediterranean to fair-skinned northern European.

Today, the three inhabited islands of the Maltese archipelago form an independent republic, currently a member of the European Union. Hosting a population of around 400,000 people crowding into an area of 150 square miles (320 sq. km), Malta can make the claim of being the most densely populated country in Europe. As tiny as it is, Malta is loaded with thousands of years of historical sites and cultural influences.

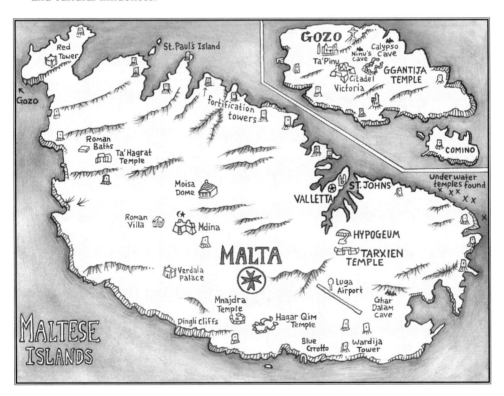

Ggantija

Malta loans its name to the entire Maltese archipelago, a string of islands that consist of Malta, Gozo, Comino, and two uninhabited rock outcroppings. Centrally located in the Mediterranean Sea, about 55 miles (90 km) south of Sicily and 175 miles (290 km) to the north of the African mainland, Malta hardly seems far from civilization. Yet 5,000 years ago this was a rather isolated location. Scattered across Malta and Gozo are numerous megalithic temples dating from 3600 to 2200 BCE. The earliest arrivals were a puzzling tribe of skilled masons, known as the "Beaker People." How these earliest arrivals learned to move massive slabs of stone and build enormous circular temples remains unknown. Also puzzling are several underwater "temples" discovered in 1999. By mapping peculiar shapes in aerial photos, divers discovered interesting features carved into the bedrock offshore Malta's northeastern coast. These features include trough-like structures, cart rut tracks, straight lines, circular holes, and a ceramic plate.

▲ The softly rounded contours of Ggantija, along with the numerous artifacts found, suggest this Neolithic temple was devoted to goddess worship.

It seems evident that the Maltese temple builders took many factors into consideration prior to the commencement of construction. First, the proximity to fresh water and fertile growing areas was necessary. This is apparent at all temple sites ensuring adequate water for daily use. It was also necessary to have large boulders available nearby, due to the lack of efficient transport. Cave shelters were also important. The area near Ggantija contains the highest concentration of caves on the island of Gozo. Finally, almost all of the temples featured sunlight entering the temple on the winter solstice sunrise, a similarity to Newgrange, Ireland and other megalithic temples in Europe. Archaeoastronomers map nearly all the Maltese temples with a southeast orientation, determining that the ancient builders intentionally designed the layout of their temple entrances to capture the sun's most southerly position around the days of December 21st. Both the north and south temples of the Ggantija complex allow the winter solstice sunrise to enter the doorways and illuminate altars in each temple's apse. The sunlight penetrates all the way through three chambers in the larger southern temple of Ggantija to the rear wall. What rituals were performed here 5,600 years ago had to include some aspect of solar worship.

> Along with their enormous dimensions, the Ggantija Temples are recognized on the World Heritage list as "the oldest free-standing stone structures in the world."

The Ggantija megalithic complex consists of two temples surrounded by undressed coralline limestone blocks. Some of the blocks exceed 16 feet (5 m) in

▲ The enormous blocks used, along with the scale of Ggantija, makes this one of the most remarkable temples of prehistory. It is a "must see" for any trip to the Maltese archipelago.

length and weigh over 50 tons (45,350 kg). The southern temple features altars, relief carvings of spirals, libation holes, and a wall 26 feet (8 m) tall, the highest in all the Maltese temples. Both Ggantija temples show a corbelling effect on the upper walls, which consists of placing the large blocks inclined slightly inward. This technique was employed to reduce the roofing span. The temple roofs most likely consisted of wooden beams covered with branches, reeds, animal hides, and with a layer of blue clay to prevent rainwater penetration. The interior of the walls were plastered and painted with red ochre.

The massive outer wall is one of the most striking features of the entire temple complex. The huge megaliths were stacked alternately, with one rectangular slab placed upright, the next horizontally. The enormous boulders inspired the local population to create folkloristic legends involving gruesome monsters doing the stacking. The name *Ggantija* is the Maltese word for "giant's grotto." Such epic proportions and mythical notoriety makes Ggantija the most famous of all the Maltese temples.

Getting to Ggantija

The island of Malta is only 16 miles (25 km) across at its widest point. The nearby island of Gozo is even smaller, and is accessible only by a regular ferry. The dozen or so ruins on Malta and Gozo are easy to locate and accessible by road. Gozo does not have the extensive bus system like Malta does so it is best to hire a guide, take a taxi, or be part of a tour group. It is possible to hike from Gozo's Mgarr Harbor up Highway 1 to Highway 4, but the two roads are very busy and the days can be extremely hot. Although Ggantija is only 3.5 miles (6 km) from the harbor, the hike consists of two steep hills.

Hypogeum

Similar to other religious hierarchies, it was likely that a few high priests of both sexes controlled the population in prehistoric Malta. These individuals were thought to hold the key to health and prosperity, and thus wielded great power. A tremendously organized workforce must have come from a blend of individual vision and communal effort to create the various temple complexes on Malta. Among the most important sites are Mnajdra, Tarxien, Hagar Qim, Mgarr, and Skorba on Malta, and Ggantija on Gozo. The Hypogeum megalithic temple complex is perhaps the apex of temple design and best preserved of all. Almost all Maltese prehistoric temples feature their interior chambers decorated with numerous spiral carvings and elaborate altars for animal sacrifice. An unknown, yet highly organized religion was clearly at hand, whose practice included worship of fat-bodied asexual statues and naturalistically rendered female goddesses.

The "Sleeping Lady" statue is a unique creation representing a singular achievement in the development of prehistoric art. This beautifully rendered figure of a reclining woman, with the head intact, was found in a pit in one of the galleries of the Hypogeum. Often hailed as the "Sleeping Mother Goddess," the figure may well be an eloquent representation of death or the eternal sleep. Another find in the Hypogeum, an asexual human figure represented face down (the head is lost), may also represent sleep or death. A third find, often interpreted as a fish, may be the base that was used to receive a human figure. Similar to the Hypogeum's "Sleeping Lady," other ancient Maltese figurines were often represented as resting on a bed. There is much conjecture about the significance of

▲ The "Sleeping Lady" is in her eternal rest at the National Museum of Archeology in Valletta.

▲ The Hypogeum near Valetta has produced more corpulent goddess statues than any other Malta temple site.

these obese lady statues found in most Maltese temples. The leading theory is that they are examples of female fertility deities, prevalent throughout the lands bordering the Mediterranean in Neolithic times.

The expertly carved underground area of the Hypogeum, a reflection of the above surface temple, has been called the "Holy of Holies" for its fantastic features.

The earliest period of Maltese temple building was the rock-cut tombs and burial facilities of the Zebbug phase, estimated construction around 4,000 BCE. This form of structure culminated in multilevel underground cemeteries that mimicked surface architecture. Foremost in this tradition is the Hal Saflieni Hypogeum, where surface architecture and underground structures converged. Around 1800 BCE, the Hypogeum and most other Maltese temples were abandoned for unknown reasons. About 200 years later, the temples were reused by the Bronze Age culture as crematoria and as repositories for the ashes of the dead. It is interesting to note that the temples originally began as tombs, developed into temples for the living, and then were brought back into use as a necropolis for the dead.

Getting to the Hypogeum

There are regular flights to Malta from Italy and most European cities. The most popular Maltese route for backpackers is the ferry from Catania or Pozzallo, Sicily to Valletta. Contact Virtu Ferries at www.virtuferries.com for schedules and information. For public transportation information to the Hypogeum, see the "Getting to" information for Tarxien, below. Reservations for the Hypogeum must be made weeks in advance. The National Museum of Archeology in Valletta contains a rich collection of prehistoric artifacts from the temples, including the best spiral motifs, the Venus of Malta, the Sleeping Lady, and many other fine artifacts.

Saint John's Co-Cathedral

The Christian faith has been an integral part of Maltese religious tradition since 60 CE, with the arrival of Saint Paul the Apostle, who was shipwrecked on Malta. He was later arrested and transported to Rome, where he was scheduled to be judged before the Roman emperor Nero. Amongst the other prisoners was the physician Saint Luke, who recorded the account of that eventful journey in some detail in the Acts of the Apostles.

Saint Paul is credited with sowing the first seeds of Christianity during the three months he stayed on Malta. Although Saint Paul was kept as a prisoner in the catacombs of Melita, he is reputed to have cured the island chief's father from a terrible fever. Before Saint Paul left Malta, he ordained the chief as the first bishop of the island. He sailed to Rome loaded with gifts from his Maltese friends, but was subsequently martyred shortly after his arrival. Tradition has it that a church was built on the site where Saint Paul cured the chief's father. Many times rebuilt, the site is now occupied by the cathedral dedicated to Saint Paul at Mdina.

Despite continued occupation by the Romans, followed by an Arab conquest, the Maltese held on to their Christian faith throughout the tumultuous Middle Ages. After the Muslims were expelled, Malta became the possession of various mainland European countries. Finally the Knights of Saint John inherited the archipelago from the King of Spain. As a military order, the Knights took part in the crusades of the Holy Land, but were driven out in 1291 only to spend time on Cyprus and Rhodes before establishing a permanent base on Malta. Their official name became the "Sovereign Military Order Hospitalliers of Saint John." The order could be described as a multi-national force divided into Langues, or tongues, according to the eight nationalities of its members. This is the basis for the eight-pointed cross, known as the Maltese Cross — the national symbol to this day.

Knowing that the Ottoman Turks had their eye on the strategic Maltese archipelago, the knights established the capital Valletta to protect the two harbors on either side of the rocky peninsula on which it was to be built. Among the first buildings to go up was the Saint John's Co-Cathedral, dedicated to the protector of the knights. It was named a co-cathedral, because the Cathedral to Saint Paul already existed at Mdina, and the order of Christian knights deeply venerated the tradition of Saint Paul on Malta. Nevertheless,

▲ The tombs of many of the Knights of Saint John are interred under the co-cathedral's floor.

the new co-cathedral in the walled city of Valletta became the place of pride for the Knights of Saint John.

Saint John's Co-Cathedral was embellished
by successive Grandmasters where the
Knights of the Order were bound by stature
and eventually buried.

▲ The Saint John Co-Cathedral is located in the oldest section of Valletta.

The plain exterior of Saint Johns belies its fantastic interior. Inside, no space is left unadorned. The walls are gilded and ornately carved. The painted vaulted ceiling is considered a masterpiece of Mattia Preti. On the floor, 400 slabs of graphic inlaid marble pave the church like a mosaic of Afghan rugs. Buried underneath each emblazoned slab are the most important members of the Order from years gone by. The rectangular baroque interior features several paintings depicting the life of Saint John the Baptist, patron saint of the Order. One picture by Caravaggio depicts the beheading of Saint John, considered a masterpiece and the first intentional representation of "chiaroscuro," or the light and dark painting technique.

Such treasures were jealously guarded against attacks by the Arabs, but when Napoleon came to the island in 1798, the Order was at its weakest and had to surrender without a fight. Part of the surrender treaty stated that Napoleon would leave the co-cathedral treasures intact. First stripping the palaces and churches of Valletta bare, Napoleon conveniently forgot his promise by looting everything of value except those articles indispensable for the "exercise of the cult." Priceless articles of gold and silver were melted down into ingots, but one ornate silver grating was saved because it was painted black. The British expelled the French in the following year and Malta became a British possession until independence was granted in 1964. Through all the modern changes, Saint John's Co-Cathedral remained a centerpiece of the knights who first asserted Maltese independence.

Getting to Saint John's Co-Cathedral

Located nearly dead center within the high walls of Valletta's old city, Saint Johns is on Triq San Gwann, or Saint Johns Street, fronting the square called

Misrah San Gwann. Ferries from Sicily arrive just below the Co-Cathedral in Valletta's Grand Harbor. The National Museum of Fine Arts on South Street houses paintings, sculptures, furniture, and objects connected to the Order of Saint John.

Tarxien

The Tarxien sanctuary was completely buried under field soil until 1914, when a farmer mentioned to the curator of a nearby museum that his plow continued to hit rock at a certain depth. While nothing on the surface pointed to its existence, the site was completely excavated in six years. What emerged was an intact stone temple that is among the largest, and oldest, ever discovered in the world. The Tarxien monument is composed of three interconnecting main temples and the remains of an original temple. The older temple may be the first religious building ever constructed in Europe.

The central temple of Tarxien is composed of six oval apses, all interconnected. This is the only known example of such a layout and it represents the final phase in the long evolution of the Maltese temple plan. The oldest temple at Tarxien, now in a state of great disrepair, dates back about 4,800 years old, while the newer temples transformed in a blaze of splendor some 700 years later.

▲ The Earth Mother sculpture at Tarxien features the characteristic wide hips, bulbous legs, and a pleated skirt. Only the lower part of the statue remains. If still intact she would be an 8-foot (2.4-m) tall giant.

▲ A Tarxien spiral motif.

Tarxien is unique because it features the highest concentration of decorative art found in any of the Maltese temples. The carved megalithic stones, popularly referred to as altars, are mainly clustered within Tarxien's first temple. The exquisitely carved spirals appear strikingly similar to those found in Ireland's Boyne Valley, or they may have been developed independently on Malta and then traveled overseas with their masons. The spiral, as a decorative motif, is found in several places across Europe, from the North Atlantic seaboard to the Aegean.

> Tarxien once hosted a mysterious Neolithic cult who performed frequent sacrifices, tracked the sun's alignments, and worshipped a corpulent goddess figure.

The ancient Maltese inhabitants worshiped an overabundant female deity — called the Earth Mother, or Great Goddess. She is represented in many statues across the islands, with similar characteristics such as wide hips, bulbous legs, and a single folded arm. Judging from what's left — only the lower part of a pleated skirt and two massive legs — one statue at Tarxien depicts her as a giant who would have stood 8 feet (2.4 m) tall. This mysterious cult of the Earth Mother may be a result of the Maltese people's fear of starvation, a depiction of an earthly Venus, a fertility symbol, or simply a profound respect for powerful women. Whoever she was, the Earth Mother was highly venerated for about 800 years before the Maltese temples were abandoned and their users vanished. Drought, plague, famine, relocation, and invasion are among suggestions as to the cause of their disappearance. Others say it was the planetary cataclysm associated with the sinking of Atlantis that destroyed the ancient Maltese culture. Nevertheless, successive settlers used the ruins of Tarxien as a cemetery for cremated remains, and the Romans used part of the temple as a wine cellar. Shortly after the Roman era it was covered with topsoil and forgotten.

Getting to Tarxien

Most of the Maltese ruins, including Tarxien, are scattered around the suburbs of the capital Valletta. From Valletta city center, take a local bus or taxi to Tarxien and the Hypogeum. The Valletta Main Bus Terminus surrounds the Triton Fountain just outside the Valletta city gate. Take any city bus out of town and change to either the #427 or #627 bus at Hamrun or Marsa. These two buses access both the Hypogeum and Tarxien temples. The two historic sites are within a few city blocks of each other.

SPAIN

AND PORTUGAL

I remember the black wharves and the slips,
and the sea-tides tossing free;
And Spanish sailors with bearded lips,
and the beauty and mystery of the ships;
And the magic of the sea.
—*Henry Wadsworth Longfellow,* My Lost Youth

C IVILIZATION TOOK A GREAT LEAP FORWARD with the advancement of Spanish and Portuguese navigators, who charted global sea lanes and opened up the planet for exploration. Within a century, these brave explorers changed their perception of the ocean from mystifying superstition to golden opportunity based on navigational skills. Prince Henry of Portugal (1394 – 1460), one of the truly great minds of the 15th century, is often credited with perfecting the understanding of latitude — how far north or south of the equator any given place is located. His cartographers knew that the height of the North Star above the horizon gives a close approximation of latitude. At Sagres, on the Portuguese coast, Henry created a school for navigators and scholars. Here he ambitiously collected all the maps, globes, and accounts of exploration that could be purchased. His brother, Pedro, is known to have returned from Venice with two gifts for Henry: a collection of world maps and a copy of the account of Marco Polo's recent travels to the Orient. Through education, ambition, and bravery Prince Henry boldly ushered in the European Age of Discovery.

16 years after Prince Henry's death, in 1476, Christopher Columbus was shipwrecked off the coast of Portugal. He was rescued and nursed back to health by a colony of Italian countrymen from his home city of Genoa. Columbus began a new career in the service of Portugal and settled down in Lisbon to become a mapmaker with his younger brother, Bartholomew. He married into a wealthy family. Nowhere on earth could he have been better situated to begin his famous voyage westward. Ferdinand Magellan was born into a noble Portuguese family in 1480 and, like Columbus, sailed in the service of Spain after having learned his trade in Lisbon. Columbus and Magellan, trained in Portugal and financed by Spain, helped establish trade routes that would usher in the complete mapping of the planet. In a century, Spanish and Portuguese influence would be global and in turn make these two home countries fabulously wealthy.

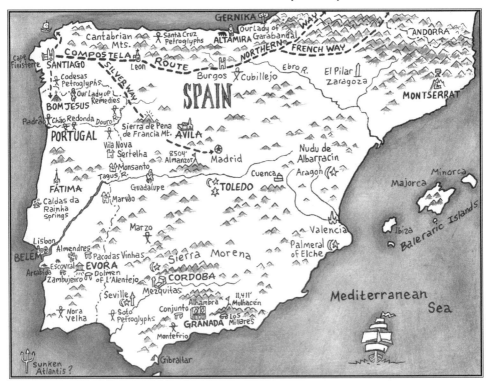

PORTUGAL

Portugal has always been a country turned toward the sea. Since the earliest times, fishing and overseas commerce were the main economic activities. Prominent explorers, such as Henry the Navigator, Bartolomeu Dias, and Vasco da Gama, left the shores of Portugal to establish global trade routes. Following its heyday as a world power during the 15th and 16th centuries Portugal began to lose much of its wealth and status as a result of three major events: the destruction of Lisbon in the earthquake of 1755, occupation during the Napoleonic Wars, and the loss of its Brazilian colony in 1822. Today, it is a shadow of its former self, but is still a fascinating country with many highlights to please the visitor.

Belém

The Portuguese people emerged emboldened from the Middle Ages. They were victorious against the Spaniards in a major sea battle — thus securing their independence. Their next task was to evict all the Islamic Moors, which they did successfully. The country was theirs, but more importantly, so was the sea.

At the time Henry the Navigator set up his school for long-distance sea travel in Sagres, almost everyone in Europe was superstitious about sailing too far away from the land. In the 13th century, most believed the earth was flat and the seas were filled with ferocious monsters. Prince Henry and a few of his understudies sought to challenge these misperceptions. They also wanted to locate a sea route to the Far East in order to avoid the overland trade tariffs imposed by the Muslims.

It cannot be overstated how important these initial Portuguese discoveries were to the development of Europe in the coming centuries. International trade, colonialism, untold wealth, and the spread of Western culture around the globe commenced from the shores of Portugal. The era began in 1497 when Vasco da Gama set sail from Belém around Africa's Cape of Good Hope to India. He returned to a hero's welcome two and a half years later. King Dom Manuel "The Fortunate" lavished Vasco da Gama with prestigious titles and a large income. Then Manuel went on to impose a 5% tax on all spices other than pepper, cinnamon, and cloves, whose import became the sole preserve of the Crown. With the newfound wealth, King Manuel began construction on Portugal's finest religious monument: the Monastery of Jerónimos at Belém.

> The Monastery of Jerónimos at Belém was constructed on the site of an earlier church, Santa Maria de Belém, where the monks had a tradition of giving aid to sailors in transit. The new monastery continued the tradition and became the national symbol of Portugal.

The Portuguese trade routes to India, Brazil, China, and Japan continued to pay off handsomely for the Crown. King Manuel channeled enormous sums of money into the making of the monastery. Although work commenced in 1501, it took nearly a century to complete. All the while, *vintena da pimento*, or "pepper money," which amounted to the equivalent of 155 pounds (70 kg) of gold per year, continued to pay the bills. The location was very symbolic: Belém is the gateway to the

▲ The Monastery of Jerónimos is a direct recipient of the riches acquired during the Age of Discovery in Portugal.

Atlantic, on the banks of the Tagus River at the entrance to the bay fronting Lisbon, the capital. Another reason for building the monastery was the king's desire to make it the pantheon of the new royal house of Aviz (Aviz-Beja), of which he was the first monarch. Manuel and his descendents were all laid to rest in marble tombs inside the adjoining church. Vasco da Gama and other famous or influential Portuguese patrons were also buried in the church. The monastery has been closely related and linked to the Portuguese royal family, and thus has a lasting image of nationalism. The power of the Crown, combined with the Hieronymite Order and its close ties to Spain, made the royal seat at Belém one of the most powerful in the world. When completed, the Monastery of Jerónimos and Belém Tower became the symbol of maritime discoveries. It was the first landmark sighted by returning sailors, before their welcome home in the capital Lisbon.

The Monastery of Jerónimos and nearby Belém Tower are both considered masterpieces of Manueline architecture. Both structures survived the devastating earthquake of 1755 that leveled Lisbon. These two monuments are listed as UNESCO World Heritage Sites and many consider them the crown jewels of architecture from Portugal's golden age of exploration. The Manueline architectural style is unique to Portugal, being named after King Manuel himself. The Moorish influence is readily seen in both buildings, as are the references to maritime accomplishments.

The main entrance to the church features several statues, with Henry the Navigator in the center. The ceilings of both buildings have a wave-like and flowing style, typical of Manueline architecture. This ceiling is designed to evoke ropes, anchors, and the sea. Other maritime imagery, along with a healthy dose of late Gothic and Renaissance styles, combined with Moorish elements, defines the Portuguese Manueline style. When King Manueline granted the monastery to the monks of the Order of Saint Jeróme, he insisted that they pray not only for the soul of the king, but also for the sailors and navigators who set out from Belém to discover new worlds. Perhaps the monks' spiritual succor to the seamen gave them the courage to usher in the Age of Discovery.

Getting to Belém

The Monastery of Jerónimos and the Belém Tower are within 1/3 mile (500 m) of each other, and 4 miles (6.5 km) west from the old city of Lisbon. Tram #15 or Bus #27 each leave regularly from Praca do Coméercio for Belém. The *Torre de Belém*, or Belém Tower, was built by Dom Manuel to guard the entrance to the port. It has become a symbol of Portugal and tours of both the monastery and tower are available every day. The tower is worth a look just to see the delicately arched Moorish style windows. Unlike the monastery, the interior of the tower is unremarkable.

Bom Jesus

If the saying "build it and they will come" is true for sacred places, then the sanctuary called Bom Jesus, near Braga, would be a perfect example. In the 18th century, the arch-bishop of Braga commissioned a vast ornamental staircase up a wooded mountainside high above his beloved city. Along with the grueling 654 steps to the church, each corner features a unique chapel and each level has an ornate fountain. The famous staircase winds up the hill among many varieties of trees. Eventually, the staircase leads to a wide patio halfway up, from which it is said affords one of the finest views in all of Portugal. On a clear day, the view extends as far away as the ocean.

The "Staircase of the Virtues" is designed in the elegant Louis XVI style. Inside each chapel are life size statues representing the different scenes of the "Holy Way," or the last days of Jesus' life in Jerusalem. The first scene begins with the Last Supper and the last scene is the crucifixion of Christ, which is located inside the sanctuary at the top of the staircase. The fountains are also significant. There are five primary fountains, each bearing a figure pouring water from one of the five senses. The figure pouring water from

▲ The steps of Bom Jesus extend from the outskirts of Bragga to one of the highest rises in the region.

▲ The object of devotion looms above as a pilgrim ascends Espinho Hill.

their eyes is the "Sight" fountain; their ears, the "Hearing" fountain; their nose, the "Smell" fountain; their mouth, the "Taste" fountain; and the final fountain is a figure holding a jar representing the "Touch" fountain. In the event a pilgrim had a problem with any of these five senses, they could stop and pray at the corresponding fountain.

All this makes Bom Jesus a very inspiring site. A pilgrim would be overwhelmed by the view, the chapels, the fountains, the lush scenery, and certainly the physical exercise required to climb all the steps. Although Bom Jesus was never the site of a recorded miracle, vision, nor home to any holy relics, it does remain a vastly popular sacred site with the Portuguese people.

Bom Jesus do Monte, or "Good Jesus of the Mountain," is positioned on a mountain slope overlooking the Portuguese countryside. For the last 500 years, its steep trail and sanctuary has been the object of devout pilgrimage.

Originally Bom Jesus was merely a wooden calvary scene set atop a mountain by an unknown hermit. In the 16th century, a small hermitage was built there, which stood until the late 18th century when the present church was erected. The top has always been a sanctuary for prayer and contemplation. From the earliest time of the hermitage, devout people from the neighboring villages would ascend Espinho Hill to visit whatever shrine was there at the time. The foot path became crude steps, which were finally replaced by the grand staircase. Devotees soon began climbing the stairs on their knees.

A popular rest stop along the modern steps is at the platform containing the statues of Faith, Hope, and Charity, the "Three Virtues." For the faithful climbers, there are many places to stop and pray. Ascending the stairs is meant to convey a slow and thoughtful experience. Reaching the summit, like so many other temples and pyramids worldwide, would be the ultimate climax. The staircase finishes in the "yard of Moses" at the base of the impressive church. Also near the church complex is the small Museum of the Brotherhood of Bom Jesus. Few people outside of Portugal have ever heard of Bom Jesus, but it is quite renowned to the devout Catholics of northern Portugal.

Getting to Bom Jesus

From downtown Braga, follow the signs north 3 miles (5 km) to the base of the grand staircase. It is another half mile (.8 km) to drive the winding road to the sanctuary gardens on top. From here, it is usually easy to park and wander around the beautiful grounds, including manicured gardens and a small lake surrounding the church. On weekends, this is a popular picnic destination so parking may be difficult. A city bus accesses the site regularly. There is also a pedestrian tram that runs parallel to the staircase.

Évora

The greater Évora region, called the Alentejo, is the largest province of Portugal, yet has one of the smallest populations. Defined by picturesque rolling plains leading up to small mountains, the landscape alone would be enough incentive for a visit. Perhaps that's why the original colonizers on the Iberian Peninsula settled here in the Paleolithic Era. Remarkable traces of prehistoric etchings and paintings grace the walls of the Escoural Caves, dated at 18,000 BCE. These early hunter and gatherers settled permanently and became classified as Neolithic people known for their megalithic architecture, examples of which are scattered across the Alentejo. Surely these earliest inhabitants were drawn to the Évora region for the same reason the Romans were — the river headwaters of the Tejo, Sado, and Guadiana all originate here, creating natural river routes to inland Portugal.

The city of Évora holds a commanding position on a small hilltop overlooking vast areas of the Alentejo. Following the Romans were successions of artistic cultures, which have constantly been renewed over time and throughout history. The Moors were forced out in the 12th century, but left their mark in Évora. A building boom of medieval Christian architecture replaced Roman and Moorish structures. The dominating cathedral and Episcopal Palace now occupies the site of a Moorish mosque and the old Roman Forum. Because of the cathedral's enormous scale and influence, it was an important pilgrimage location for many centuries. Évora was the second largest Portuguese city in medieval times, thus becoming home to the royal court where the king, nobles, scholars, and

▲ The Zambujeiro dolmen is the largest in Portugal.

▲ Two concentric circles of menhirs were erected at Almendres, near Évora. Whatever kind of prehistoric rituals took place here remain a mystery.

notable artists all resided. Due to its important role in maritime discoveries, Évora became a cultural center during the 16th century Renaissance, which can be seen in its numerous palaces, fountains, and churches. Baroque architecture is also featured in Évora, as well as some tastefully designed contemporary buildings.

At Almendres, near Évora, two concentric circles of menhirs were built as a ritual site in the 5th and 3rd millenniums BCE, respectively. The inner circle was erected first, with the second added two centuries later. The site was frequented by many people over long periods of time. The ancient visitors left carved crook designs, abstract lines, and snakes carved onto the stones. Towards the end of the Neolithic Era abstract faces were etched. There are 92 menhirs with different shapes, but originally the Almendres cromlech site contained over 100. The enclosure is considered one of the first public monuments in human history, and remains the largest and most important group of menhirs on the Iberian Peninsula. Today, more than a dozen carvings can still be seen on the stones. They show depictions of serpents, faces, circles, crescent moons, and dimple marks. Both enclosures are aligned according to the equinoxes, making it a primitive astronomical observatory with religious functions. It is 8 miles (14 km) from Évora near the town of Guadalupe.

Branching out in another direction from Guadalupe, 4 miles (6 km) away near the town of Valverde, is the impressive dolmen called Zambujeiro — the largest dolmen on the Iberian Peninsula. Its corridors are 43 feet (14 m) long and lead to an enormous chamber 19 feet (6 m) in height. The earth that once covered it is still partly intact. Furthermore, Zambujeiro is integrated into the regional alignment system of the area's impressive cromlechs. Rounding out some other sites on the "Neolithic Route" are single menhirs, other stone circles, and a scattering of dolmens. Most are positioned on strategic hilltops and feature astronomical alignments, suggesting a much larger ritual area that once existed throughout the Évora region.

Including Stone Age cave art and megaliths to modern architecture, Évora and its immediate surroundings have one of the longest

> uninterrupted human occupations of any
> location in Europe. From prehistoric ritual
> sites, a Roman temple, to medieval pilgrim-
> age centers, Évora is a complete snapshot of
> history spanning the ages.

Because Évora contains buildings of so many different cultures within the confines of its city walls, UNESCO dedicated the whole city a World Heritage Site in 1986. Of its many impressive monuments is the Imperial Temple, generally regarded as the "Diana Temple," as it was once thought to be dedicated to the goddess of the moon and the hunt. Now archaeologists tell us it was built in the 1st century CE to honor the mighty Emperor Augustus himself. The Imperial Temple of Évora is the best preserved Roman structure in Portugal. Julius Caesar considered Évora so important that it was designated as a "municipium," an important city to Rome's administrative structure. Portions of the Roman baths can still be seen, along with an original gate and a villa called Tourega, among the Roman road to Alcacer do Sal.

Unfortunately, little is left of Islamic Évora, except the extensive stone wall surrounding the city. The imposing cathedral built atop the mosque dominates the city skyline and influenced the city's political climate immensely. Inside are two statues (of seven worldwide) depicting a pregnant Mother Mary. In this cathedral, the flags of Vasco da Gama's fleet, bound for the Orient, were blessed in 1497 — thus beginning the great Portuguese exploration of the world.

As it became fabulously wealthy through trade, Évora also blossomed during the Renaissance and baroque periods. Dozens of ornately decorated monasteries, palaces, chapels, and convents grace the city, attracting many pilgrims. Indeed, the city of Évora is a living museum of architecture and spiritual sites.

Getting to Évora

A train station was added in 1860, connecting the city to Lisbon, only a few hours away. Most people arrive by car, which is the best option for visiting the Neolithic sites. Follow the road to Montemor-O-Novo and follow the signs to Guadalupe and the "cromlechs of Almendres." From there, the signs lead to Valverde and Zambujeiro. Traveling west from Valverde is the Brissos chapel, constructed from the remains of a megalith. It is a short distance (5 km) from there to the Upper Paleolithic Escoural Caves, on the way to Montemor-o-Novo and back to Évora. Along this route, in the village of Alto da Portela de Mogos, are two cromlechs (megalithic circles) about a mile apart. Heading from Évora to Estremoz is the Dolmen do Paco das Vinhas. Other monuments are scattered about the region. Detailed road maps can be obtained at the Tourist Information Office in Évora.

Fátima

As World War I was devastating Europe, three illiterate children in a poor Portuguese village experienced visions of the Virgin Mary. The news spread quickly from village to village. Within months other townspeople observed aspects of the apparition and the legend of Fátima began. Despite only the three children bearing as direct witnesses, thousands of others experienced a variety of miracles and strange sightings. Perhaps the most astonishing came when 70,000 people filled the valley, during a heavy downpour, for the sixth apparition. After the sightings, as soon as the sun burst through the clouds, the people became miraculously dry. After this event, the three youngsters became world-renowned and the atmosphere of their peasant village would never be the same.

The famous story begins early in 1916 when nine-year-old Lúcia Santos was sent to tend her family's sheep in the hills near Fátima. Her cousins Francisco Marto, aged eight, and his six-year-old sister, Jacinta, also accompanied her. The children were walking along a hillside when they saw a vision of a human figure. Writing many years later of the event, Lúcia remembers, "It was a figure like a statue ... a young man, about 14 or 15, whiter than snow." The figure spoke to the children, directing them to pray three times with him, "My God, I believe, I adore." Yet the children kept their first encounter a secret. The next year, in 1917, the Marian series of apparitions appeared to the children near the same location. The children first saw two flashes of lightning and then a "Lady, brighter than the sun, shedding rays of light," who said she was from heaven. Lúcia — the only one of the three children who ever spoke to the visions directly — asked, "What do you want of me?" The Lady answered, "I want you to come here for six months in succession. Then I will tell you who I am and what I want." The Lady also directed the children to pray every day for world peace before she departed in a blinding light.

The children, unsure of what had happened to them once again, promised to keep quiet as they had before, but later Jacinta let the subject slip to her parents. Soon the entire village knew of the supposed apparitions and started making fun of the children. Yet the children knew the apparitions were to continue through October, always on the 13th of each month. The second vision came to the children again on the prophesized date in front of 60 onlookers. After the second Marian sighting, the apparitions were widely reported.

▲ The religious city of Fátima hosts five million visitors per year.

The information Mary conveyed to Lúcia during the apparitions remains a mystery. The three secrets of Fátima came during the

July appearance when the lady prefigured the coming of World War II, another identified Russia's "rejection of God," and the final secret became a "sealed message" recorded by Lúcia, for the Pope's eyes only. Also prophesied by Mary, both Francisco and Jacinta died soon after the apparitions ended during the worldwide influenza epidemic of 1918 – 1920. Church officials opened the third secret in 1960, but only the Pope knows the letter in its entirety. Part of the third message describes the 1981 assassination attempt on Pope John Paul II. Apparently the final secret of Fátima foretells of major events that will shape the world.

> Fátima is one of the most visited shrines in the world devoted to the Virgin Mary. The site draws some five million visitors per year, putting it on par with Lourdes in southern France.

One of the final requests of the Virgin Mary was to have a place of worship devoted to her in the valley. A small chapel once stood at Cova da Iria (where the children experienced the visions) to commemorate the apparitions. The original chapel was destroyed by skeptics in 1922, only to be replaced by a massive square and towering church. In 1930, after thoroughly investigating the events of 1917, the Vatican authenticated the apparitions. Uncomfortable with all the attention, Lúcia left Fátima and became a nun in 1926. In 1948, she joined a Carmelite monastery in Spain. She died in February, 2005 at the age of 97. She had only returned to the Fátima shrine a few times during her long lifetime.

Getting to Fátima

Located in west-central Portugal, in the region of Leiria and approximately 87 miles (140 km) north-northeast of Lisbon, Fátima is a small rural village in a rocky region, whose main export is olive oil. A train runs daily from Lisbon to Chão de Maças, 12.5 miles (20 km) outside Fátima. From there, a 30-minute bus ride takes passengers from Chão de Maças into Fátima.

SPAIN

Richly endowed by both nature and history, Spain is a sun-baked land of castles, dramatic coastlines, snow-capped mountains, lively festivals, and proud traditions. The Pyrenees form its mountainous backbone border with France. Portugal is the only other country it neighbors on the Iberian Peninsula. From prehistoric cave dwellers, numerous empires and invaders, to eight centuries of Moorish (Muslim) influence, Spain has been on the forefront of Western Civilization's development. Spain was a first-rate power in developing the New World, and as a result, Spanish remains one of the top languages spoken in the world.

Altamira Cave

The first modern humans in Europe, the hunter and gatherers of the Upper Paleolithic period (35,000 – 30,000 BCE), produced the continent's earliest recorded art. This art, mostly found painted on cave walls in northern Spain and southwestern France, is believed to have played an important role in religious rituals, such as hunting, fertility, and the initiation of young tribal members. The cave art of this period is often located in extremely inaccessible locations of the cave, where few could have viewed the art. Torch lighting and the erection of scaffolding would have been required for the creation of this art.

> The Paleolithic cave art of Altamira is an evocative monument to early humanity and represents the earliest exploration of the sacred.

Altamira Cave is 890 feet (270 m) long, and consists of a series of twisting passages and chambers. The main passage varies from 6 to 20 feet (2 to 6 m) high. This 14,000-year-old masterpiece was discovered in 1879, but its authenticity was not recognized until 1902. Altamira (Spanish for "high view") was discovered by an amateur anthropologist and his eight-year old daughter while they were out exploring near Santillana del Mar. They spotted an opening to a cave that had been exposed a few years before by a landslide. A hunter had initially found the opening a year before, but finding no bears or wolves, he continued on his way. Filled with curiosity, father and daughter lit their charcoal lamps and climbed in through the entrance. As the anthropologist scoured the floor for bones and arrowheads, his daughter looked up to the cave's ceiling and exclaimed, *"Mira, papá, son bueyes,"* or "Look father, they're cows!"

Human occupation was limited to the cave mouth, yet the paintings were created throughout the length of the cave. The painted ceilings and walls in Altamira Cave depict near life-sized animals and strange symbols all through its labyrinth. Altamira is regarded as one of the best-preserved and most prolifically painted prehistoric caves in Europe. Bison dominate the animal compositions, but other interesting depictions include horses, red deer, boars, stags, felines, and woolly mammoths. The narrow corridor at the back of the cave was crowded with images, suggesting an area of special significance. This area is called the "Polychrome Ceiling," depicting a herd of bison in different poses, two horses, a large hind, and what is most likely a wild boar. Small totem figurines have also been discovered at the site.

The paintings were saved from the ravages of time and erosion by a landslide about 13,000 years ago, which sealed off the cave and protected the art for posterity. Experts were amazed at the life-like details of the animals and the sense of perspective, the same perspective that was supposedly "invented" during the Renaissance. The artists used charcoal and ochre, or haematite, to create the images, often scratching or diluting these dyes to produce variances in intensity and creating an impression of chiaroscuro (the technique of using light and dark elements). They also exploited the natural contours in the cave walls to give a three-dimensional effect to the animals. The animals appear to come to life through the careful selection of uneven wall surfaces. Everything is achieved with just three colors: ochre, red, and black.

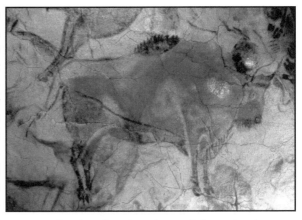

▲ The detail and realism of the animals painted on the cave walls of Altamira is truly remarkable. The Upper Paleolithic school of religious, magic-evoking art sprang up roughly 30,000 years ago, flourished for 20,000 years, then vanished from the sight of humans for over 10,000 years.

The Altamira site is considered one of the greatest collections of prehistoric cave paintings ever discovered. One critic declared the cave the "Sistine Chapel of the Quaternary." At first, the cave paintings were visited by a trickle of inquisitive locals, anthropologists, and artists. A long line of great 20th century artists from Henry Moore to Miquel Barceló have been astonished and inspired by the paintings. Joan Miró, for instance, painted an abstract work entitled "Altamira" in 1958. When Pablo Picasso viewed the paintings, he proclaimed, "After Altamira, all is decadence."

In an age of mass tourism, the trickle of visitors soon became a flood, and finally the cave had to be closed to only limited public access. The carbon dioxide in the visitors' breath was corroding away the paint. There is presently a three-year waiting list, as the caretakers are currently allowing 30 people into the real cave per day. Most sightseers visit a realistic reconstruction of the cave built next to the site, along with a multimedia exhibition and interpretative center. Altamira Cave has been declared a protected UNESCO World Heritage Site.

Getting to Altamira Cave

Altamira Cave is close to the beautiful Bay of Biscay coastline. It is located just outside the town of Santillana del Mar in Cantabria, Spain, 18 miles (30 km) west of Santander. The cave is well-marked with signs on the roads leading towards the site. There is public bus service to nearby Torrelavega, then a transfer can be made to Santillana del Mar. The cave is just 1.3 miles (2 km) outside of the Santillana town center.

Avila

Two main features of Avila make it an outstanding city. One is the completely intact city walls, considered among the best preserved in Europe. Second are all the saints who have lived there, especially the mystic Saint Teresa. Approaching from afar, the soaring cathedral of Avila can be seen interconnecting with the battlement walls to create the impression of an imposing medieval fortress. The rectangular perimeter of the walls is 1.5 miles (2.5 km) long, has nine gates and 88 turrets, all pristinely preserved. The walls were built upon earlier Roman fortifications, which were themselves built upon the site of an ancient Veton hill-fort. Little remains of these earliest cultures, but what does can be found incorporated into the fortifications. In the walls are traces of the earliest dwellers: Veton *verracos*, Roman funeral urns, steles, and keystones. And, while the walls have repelled many enemy forces (mainly the Muslim foes), the walls allowed the city to flourish without being captured for almost 1,000 years. The old city of Avila sheltered some of the most illustrious sons and daughters in Spanish history, such as John of the Cross and Sister Teresa. These saints were known to profess the belief that "God alone is enough." God perhaps, but don't forget the impregnable walls.

▲ Good walls make good neighbors at Avila.

Royal Avila began in 1090 when King Alfonso VI conquered the city and ordered it to be repopulated with knights, artisans, and agricultural workers. Fantastic churches, palaces, wall gates, and the grand cathedral were all started under Alfonso's rule. The master stone masons, hired from across the country, incorporated star alignments and sacred geometry into their constructions. This Romanesque building boom was followed by other architectural periods, but few could rival the earliest constructions. The artistic qualities represented, along with the fine state of preservation, have earned the city of Avila the UNESCO distinction "Heritage of Mankind." As a further compliment, UNESCO reminds us that Avila was nicknamed the "land of songs and saints." Inside the walled city, time seems to have stopped for hundreds of years in favor of history, art, and religion.

In an age when men dominated religion and society, one woman would break the mold and become the most celebrated saint of the Spanish Middle Ages. Saint Teresa of Avila was a nun, writer, mystic, and a leading reformer of the Catholic Church.

Saint Teresa was born in Avila to a noble family in 1515. Deeply religious, by the age of seven she ran away from home to fight the heretic Muslims. It was her desire to be killed in battle and become martyred. She was captured with her brother by the Moors, only to be recaptured and brought back to town. When young Teresa joined the Carmelites in 1535, without her father's permission, the convent was one of the most populated in the city. During her 27 years in the Encarnacion Convent, Teresa knew of the Inquisition in Spain and the Reformation taking place in Germany. As the Reformation began spreading in northern Europe, the idea of reforming the convent system manifested itself in the

▲ The Avila Cathedral was a great inspiration to Sister Teresa.

restless mind of Sister Teresa. Together with John of the Cross, they described and clarified the "Path of Perfection" in their writings. These works struck a chord with the Spanish people and soon Avila found itself as a center for unrivaled spiritual thinking and Christian mysticism.

In 1562, she left Encarnacion to start the first of several of her own convents in Avila. At the first convent of San Jose, Teresa instructed the architects and assisted in building the chapel with her own hands. She also helped care for the sick and poor. Her compassionate reputation attracted people from near and far to witness this amazing disciple of God. Teresa was also a mystic who claimed to have levitated. Deep in reverie, people would test her transcendental state by pouring hot wax on her hand, but she never flinched nor showed pain. To certain people, she would expose a burned stigma above her left breast, featuring a heart with an arrow piercing it.

Although sometimes at odds with local authorities, Teresa was enormously popular with the ordinary people. Along with establishing many convents on her own, she was one of the leading figures of the Counter-Reformation. When she died at the age of 65, pilgrims were already coming to Avila to walk the Teresa Route. Over the years, more monuments were added and even more pilgrims began arriving annually. The Church of La Santa was built at Santa Teresa's birthplace, the Church of San Juan where she was baptized, and the several convents she founded are all part of the pilgrimage route. Other martyrs, mystics, and saints also hail from Avila, but it is Santa Teresa who deeply captured the hearts and minds of her fellow Spaniards.

Getting to Avila

The walled city of Avila is located 70 miles (113 km) northwest of the capital Madrid. Trains from Chamartin Station in Madrid service Avila several times per day. Avila is the Spanish Provincial Capital situated at the highest altitude of all provincial capitals: 3,600 feet (1,130 m) above sea level. It is one of the nine provinces which make up the famous Castile-León autonomous region. The annual feast of Santa Teresa on October 15th attracts hundreds of pilgrims to Avila from all over Europe.

Córdoba

The small city of Córdoba in southern Spain is a minor provincial capital today, but in times of old it was much more influential. Many archaeological and architectural treasures attest to its former glory. It was the largest city on the Iberian Peninsula during Roman rule. In the early 8th century, the Moors conquered Córdoba and for the next three centuries it formed the heart of the great Caliphate Empire. The Moors were a mixed race of Arabs and Berbers who crossed into Spain from northern Africa. They brought with them the new faith of Islam. Within a century, Islam had spread from Arabia to the far reaches of Indonesia in the east, to the Caspian and Black Sea regions in the north, to virtually the entire northern half of Africa, then across the Strait of Gibraltar to Portugal and nearly all of Spain.

Muslims worldwide pray in mosques and focus their prayers toward the city of Mecca on the Saudi Peninsula. In Córdoba, the Moors built the grandest and most beautiful mosque in all of Spain — the Mezquita. Upon recapture in the 15th century, nearly every Moorish building was destroyed, but the Mezquita miraculously survived. The Moors were far more tolerant of Christianity, allowing Christian worship during their reign. They also permitted the Jews to live and worship in Córdoba, and although both Jews and Muslims were expelled from Córdoba in 1492, a labyrinth of narrow streets comprising the Jewish Quarter borders what is left of the Moorish

▲ The Moors built the Mezquita following Islamic design. After the Christian reconquest it was converted into a cathedral.

Quarter. The Juderia, Córdoba's old Jewish Quarter, contains a synagogue, one of only three from the Moorish Era in Spain that survived the expulsion. The other two surviving synagogues are in Toledo. After the Christians reestablished themselves in Córdoba, they completely modified the city, including the redesign of the Mezquita into a cathedral. Several new churches, squares, palaces, chapels, plazas, and city fortifications became integrated into an already magnificent city.

> By far, the most important religious building
> in Córdoba is the Mezquita. It is a building of
> exceptional mystical and aesthetic power.

The Mezquita is the largest Moorish mosque in Europe and the only one of its kind in Spain. The lavish building has been embellished with Gothic, Plateresque, and baroque elements to become a combined cathedral-mosque. It is a fascinating building which offers surprising light and color effects at various times of the day. Also outstanding are the beautiful doors and the nearly 1,000 columns holding up the roof. Each marble column supports the characteristic red and white twin-layered arches, which in turn support the ceiling. The columns and pillars create a mesmerizing effect on the visitor, focusing the symmetry (before modification) to the exquisite *Mihrab*, aligned to Mecca for prayer. The Mihrab, or prayer niche, is considered the finest surviving example of all Moorish religious architecture.

Although subsequent Moorish rulers continued to make additions to the Mezquita for some 350 years, it was the conquering Christians intent on converting the building into a cathedral that altered it most. The Renaissance choir is now in the center of the mosque, diminishing the position of the Mihrab. To the left of the choir stands the Mudéjar Capilla de Villaviciosa, built by Moorish craftsmen in 1371. Fortunately, the approach into the mosque via the Patio de los Naranjos was not lost or altered. This classic Islamic court still has orange trees

▲ The Córdoba Roman Bridge is still in use.

and the fountains used for ritual purification before prayer. In its original state, all 19 naves opened upon the courtyard, lending the effect that the columns were an extension of the trees.

Because the Mezquita is so magnificent, the rest of Córdoba can seem anticlimatic. The best walk in Córdoba is along Rio Guadalquivir, featuring the city fortifications and the interesting Arab waterwheels. The Roman Bridge retains its original foundation stones, constructed following Caesar's victory over Pompey. The Calahorra Tower, across the bridge and opposite the Mezquita, is now the Museum of Three Cultures (Jewish, Christian, and Muslim). The fortified palace called Alcázar de los Reyes was built for Ferdinand and Isabella, but was later used during the Inquisition. Dozens of other churches and palaces scatter around Córdoba, making it an excellent city for long walks. No other city in Europe preserves the transition from Romanesque to Gothic style, overlaid on earlier Arabic constructions and Roman designs, quite like the old city of Córdoba.

Getting to Córdoba

Along with its old city attractions, Córdoba is also a university city, making it a bustling travel destination. The city is linked by road and rail, has a good range of renovated and affordable hotels, and also features a rich cultural calendar for year-round activities. The train station and the main bus terminal are located a few blocks west of the old city.

Galicia region

In the far-western Galicia region of Spain is a mystical land which long predates the Christian era. The countryside of Galicia features impressive megalithic dolmens, menhirs, and cromlechs — dating from the era of Britain's Stonehenge and France's Carnac. The original settlement of Santiago de Compostela fascinated pagans, similarly to the way the city later attracted medieval Christians, who made countless pilgrimages there to honor the remains of Saint James the Apostle. Another term for "compostela" refers to energy line paths, the same paths that became the Way of Saint James. Perhaps the earliest prehistoric settlers recognized the ley lines of Galicia and followed them to Santiago, only to be transformed into well-trodden roads by the Christians of a later era. The large amount of megaliths and rock engravings near Santiago indicates that it was a sacred place throughout ancient times. It is believed that the earliest pilgrims would have been able to find this farthest point on the continent by taking bearings from the Milky Way galaxy.

Near the holy city of Santiago is a lone mountain peak known as Pico Sagro, another venerated site from pagan times. The Santiago cathedral was supposedly laid out in accordance to the angle of the sunlight as it shines across the lone mountain peak. In the age of flat earth believers, Galicia was literally considered Land's End, and the actual edge of the world was supposedly visible from nearby *Cabo Fisterra,* or Cape Finisterre. Interestingly, Galicia is also renowned for its numerous UFO sightings.

The Galicia region was a sacred land to
Neolithic dolmen builders, Bronze Age petroglyph carvers, and the Celtic people, who
were eventually conquered by the Romans.
Abundant remains of all these cultures can be
found in Galicia.

Easily the oldest and least understood monuments in Galicia belong to the
Neolithic Era. Some researchers consider the dolmens to be strictly burial tombs,
while others describe them as solar temples. The dolmens were likely both,
becoming funeral monuments after they had been abandoned as temples. Indeed,
most of the entrances are orientated to view the sunset to the west or situated to
observe prominent stars, while also found containing burials. Literally thousands
of megalithic monuments were once scattered across the Galicia region, but now
only about 100 remain.

All locals know of the *mámoas*, those mounds of earth that usually hide a dol-
men-like structure related to curious legends. The builders were described as
mythical beings of the past, associated with alchemy, magic, giants, or treasures.
In most cases, the mounds were dismantled, the smaller stones removed, the
burials looted, only to leave the skeletal core of the megalithic dolmen. From this
same period are menhirs, or *pedrafitas*, which usually had some astral significance
in agriculture, fertility, or were possibly used as markers to predict the seasons.
The dolmens and menhirs are usually clustered together like a ritual site, or perhaps they were positioned to create a relationship of visibility and proximity. One
of the most important megalithic concentrations in Galicia can be found in the
interior of the Sierra do Barbanza, consisting of no less than 35 barrows. Many of
these preserve the original mound and the undisturbed dolmen and passageway.

The Neolithic people eventually settled in different areas of Galicia and adopted
different customs. Along with farming, Bronze Age people took to raising livestock and melting tin and copper together to make stronger weapons and tools.
During this period, a different and ambiguous type of monument appeared: the
petroglyph. These engravings depict animals, weapons, hunting scenes, and geometric motifs. The most common geometric motif is the deer, sometimes being
hunted by a human. The abstract motifs are circular combinations of concentric
circles, circles with lines, or circles with bowls. Incidentally, some of the abstract
petroglyph designs are remarkably similar to modern crop circle designs!

The only ancient people with a historical record in Galicia are the Celts. They
fought many battles against the history-minded Romans. The best account of Celtic
military might is recorded by Julius Caesar, who wrote in his Commentaries, Book
III, that the Celtic ships were able to travel on the open ocean and were strong
enough to withstand storms and high seas. "They were like swans, high-prowed and
graceful with tall masts and billowing sails." Celtic sailors were skilled at harness-
ing the power of the wind. Caesar was amazed that they could even tact into the

▲ The dolmens of the Galicia region are some of the best preserved, and least visited, in all of Europe.

wind. The Celts were certainly a warlike people and their settlements reflect their priorities. They constructed *castros*, or round houses of stone, with thatched roofs, clustered together in hill fort settlements. The hill forts were placed in strategic locations, such as at the summit of a natural rise or at the end of a peninsula. Concentric circle ramparts, with high fences, originally protected the settlements.

The Iberian Celts mastered the craft of smelting iron, making intricate baskets, and producing other fine textiles. Their farms and livestock were located outside the hill forts, but never too far away in case war broke out. Eventually, the Celts of Iberia, France, Belgium, and Britain were subdued by the Romans, but some think the "lost" Celts immigrated to North America before subjugation. It is interesting to note that many Mississippian mound sites closely resemble the design of Celtic hill forts. Around 300 CE, the Celts all but disappeared from the Galicia region. The Romans replaced Celtic culture with orderly roads, fortified cities, and much larger monuments. In Galicia, over 5,000 castros have been excavated.

Getting to Galicia region monuments

Only a few dolmen and petroglyph sites are marked with signs off the main roads. The rest are rather difficult to find without a guide. A good starting point is the Centro Argueolóxico du Barbanza near the city of Boiro. This museum is built next to a Celtic hill fort and offers detailed maps, guided trips, and an excellent interpretive center. From the road, the Dolmen de Axeitos and the petroglyph Pedra das Cabras are well-marked near Ribeira. A Guarda, at the southernmost tip of Galicia, contains a hill fort ruin, as does Porto do Son in the Barbanza region. Both of these are well-marked from the road. Having a car is essential to discovering the remains of prehistoric Galicia.

Gernika

The Basque are an indigenous people who have long inhabited territory in both Spain and France. They are predominantly found in an area known as "Basque Country," a two-country region situated in the western Pyrenees and fronting the Bay of Biscay. They consist of four provinces in Spain and three in France. The Basque Country corresponds more or less with the historical homeland of the Basque people and language. Their territory is an autonomous community within Spain, the capital of which is Vitoria. From ancient times, the town of Gernika has been considered the spiritual center of Basque cultural tradition.

The Basque are a very unique grouping of people. It is widely believed that they have continuously occupied their single region of Europe longer than any other identifiable ethnic group. There is also considerable evidence that the Basque language was once spoken over a much wider area than the modern day Basque Country. Besides Spanish or French, about a quarter of Basques speak their own ethnic Basque language, referred to as Euskara, which is not only distinct from French and Spanish, but apparently unrelated to every other language (both modern and historical) in the entire world. The Basque people are widely thought to be descended from some of the earliest human inhabitants of Europe, possibly originating as far back as 40,000 years ago when Cro-Magnon hunters were exterminating the last of the Neanderthals. Their closest genetic markers show a very strong relationship with the Celts.

> Gernika is renowned as the home of Basque
> liberation where, before the famous oak
> tree, rulers of Spain took an oath to observe
> Basque local rights.

The Gernika Tree (called *Gernikako Arbola* in Basque) is an oak tree in the center of town that symbolizes traditional freedoms of the Basque people. The Lords of Biscay swore their respect to Biscayne liberties under it for centuries, along with the kings of Spain, who traditionally took an oath to assure the democratic rights and privileges (*fueros*) of the Basques in return for their allegiance. In 1476, Ferdinand and Isabella, after hearing mass in the Church of Santa Maria de la Antigua, came to the tree avowing the Basque right to maintain their fueros.

The ancient oak of Gernika is the most venerable natural monument to the Biscayan people, and still holds importance today. Certain trees, especially as they grow old and large, attract veneration and legend. It was a known practice in ancient times to replace sacred trees in decay with saplings of their own seed. The current Gernika tree is a direct descendant of an earlier one, known as the "old tree," whose trunk is conserved in the surrounding garden. The site of the old tree may have been rooted in pre-Christian times when the Basque people were still pagan. In 2004, the current Gernika tree was declared dead.

The gardeners of the Biscayne government keep several saplings growing from the original tree acorns.

During the Spanish Civil War, Gernika was heavily bombed by Nazi Germany, which was an ally to the dictator Francisco Franco. They chose Gernika to prove their air superiority. In the span of almost four hours, on April 26, 1937, the *Luftwaffe* unloaded many bombs on the defenseless town. It would appear that the motivation of this particular attack was simply to terrorize the civilian population and to demoralize

▲ A sapling tree of the original Gernika Tree grows in front of the former Basque parliament building.

the Republican side. Amazingly, nearly the entire village was destroyed, except for the Gernika Tree and the adjacent Basque parliament building. Today, the former Basque parliament, the Casa de Juntas (or *Juntetxea*), is the principal attraction in town. Outside are the remains of the ancient communal oak tree, symbol of Basque independence. As a testament to its importance, an oak tree is depicted in the heraldic arms of Biscay, and an oak leaf logo is used to represent the local government of Biscay.

Getting to Gernika

The town of Gernika is located in the province of Vizcaya in northern Spain. Vizcaya is the northwestern province of the autonomous Biscayne community. Gernika is situated 18 miles (30 k) east of Bilbao, in the heart of Basque Country. It is located 266 miles (428 km) north of Madrid, and 52 miles (84 km) west of San Sebastián. The Gernika Tree is easily located in the center of the village. From the train station, head up Calle Urioste.

Granada

Southern Spain has always been a crossroads of diverse races and cultures. The mountainous region has made it easy to defend — or to hide. Archaeological remains in the fertile mountain area of La Alpujarra confirm it had been inhabited by prehistoric people. The Phoenicians, Greeks, and Carthaginians settled in the same region centuries later. Isolated by towering mountains, the tallest on the Iberian Peninsula, the Alpujarra has served as a refuge throughout history. Of all the transient people in the region's early history, the Romans were the first to establish a settlement in Granada. They called their city "Albayzin."

▲ The Alhambra is perched high upon a hill over-looking Granada.

Most of the original Roman ramparts stood in the 8th century when the Moors stormed through southern Iberia and established an empire that lasted over 700 years. The Moorish ruler Ased-ibn al Rahaman chose the site for the first Muslim fortress, called the Alcazaba Qadimo. Using the Roman walls as protection, the Moorish rulers felt confident enough to expand the city. Water reservoirs, market places, city gates, and the Grand Mosque were added, along with a new name for the city — Granada.

In the late Middle Ages, Granada was one of the most prosperous cities in Europe. The pre-existing fortifications on the hill expanded into an elaborate palace and garden for the Moorish rulers, called the Alhambra. Each successive ruler added a new wing, which in time would be regarded as one of the most splendid palaces of all time. The age of Moorish rule in Spain would climax in the art and architecture of Granada.

> The Moors of Granada maintained their autonomy the longest. They surrendered in 1492 to Ferdinand and Isabella's army of 150,000 troops. The Christian reconquest of Spain was complete. To Muslims worldwide, Granada represents a symbol of resistance and strength.

Ferdinand and Isabella were so enchanted with the Alhambra that they decided to live there for a while. While taking up residence in the grandest of all Moorish palaces, the famous Spanish king and queen directed all Muslim religious buildings in Granada to be either destroyed or Christianized. Meanwhile, all the Jews and the Moors were being expelled from Spain, unless they converted to Christianity. An Italian explorer named Christopher Columbus was granted ships to explore a possible westerly route to India in the same year. Ferdinand and Isabella were ferocious Inquisitors, followed by their grandson Charles V, who was even more violent. Charles V removed a section of the Alhambra to create a lackluster Renaissance palace. His wanton destruction at Córdoba and Seville was even worse. Not surprising, the Grand Mosque in the old city of Granada was replaced with a cathedral, and the settlement around the *medina* ("city" in

Arabic) was leveled. In light of all these changes, it is amazing the Alhambra even survived. Few traces of the Moors remain in Granada; yet, the Alhambra is the only medieval Muslim palace to remain largely intact.

The Alhambra was built within the confines of an impregnable fort, which protected the sultan and his harem. The site enjoys commanding views of the surrounding countryside. It was designed to be the paradigm of an Islamic city: surrounded

▲ The Alhambra was designed to be a city within a city. It takes a full day to visit all the attractions.

by walls, it is a city within a city. Importance is given to enclosed areas inside the buildings, rather than the exterior design and symmetry. The intricate interior carvings, some of the finest ever rendered, feature stylized Arabic writings within the patterns. Most all of the verses are quotations from the *Koran*. The carvings, along with paintings, woodwork, and the refined techniques of Granada Islamic architecture represent the peak of Moorish art.

As a religious site, the Alhambra palace contained a mosque that was destroyed by the Catholic monarchs. It also contained ritual bathing centers that, fortunately, have survived. The Muslims in this part of Spain believed in ritual bathing for spiritual cleansing. Like Jewish or Christian baptismal rituals, the Moors also believed water could symbolize purification — a cleansing from sin and regeneration. After ritual bathing, came freedom from any impure acts, which the bather may have committed against the *Koran* precepts. When the Alhambra fell to the Catholic monarchs in 1492, the clerics, or *imams*, were not initially persecuted. Within the first year, the Muslim nobles began to sell their property and moved to northern Africa. Shortly after, if the imams didn't convert (*conversos*) to Christianity, they were forced out. Such was the fate of the last enclave of the Muslim empire on the Iberian Peninsula.

Getting to Granada

Granada is the capital city of Andalusia, located in the southernmost part of Spain. Granada is easily reached by private car, train, or bus. The Alhambra dominates the skyline in the center of the city. Crowds can be a factor when taking a tour of the Alhambra, especially on weekends. Sometimes making a reservation for the Alhambra tour is necessary. The old city section of Granada is a charming maze of narrow streets and small plazas.

291

Montserrat

The Montserrat monastery in the Pyrenees Mountains is a sacred Christian site central to several religious legends and Christian achievements. It is here that Saint Peter is said to have deposited a statue of the Virgin Mary 50 years after Christ's death. The statue was given to Peter by Saint Luke and hidden in one of the mountain caves. The 12th century "Black Madonna" statue earned fame for being the catalyst of many miracles. So popular was the sculpture that several of the first Spanish missionary churches in Mexico, Chile, Peru, and a Caribbean island of the same name were dedicated to the Virgin of Montserrat. In King Arthur's legend, Montserrat is where Parsifal ended his arduous journey from England and discovered the Holy Grail. The famous Ignatius Loyola spent much of his life in Montserrat writing his spiritual exercises and establishing the Jesuit order.

Among its many mysteries, Montserrat is also reputed to contain the biblical Ark of the Covenant. The ultra-sacred Ark first appears in the story of Exodus and returns about 200 times in the Old Testament. Sacred to Jews and Christians alike, the Ark is said to possess supernatural powers and is where Moses symbolically placed a copy of the Ten Commandments. As the legend goes, an earthquake and a hurricane hit Jerusalem around the time of Christ's crucifixion and exposed the Ark inside Solomon's Temple. In the Montserrat version of the story, the Ark was taken to the Phoenician port of Catalunya, where it was transported by the Essene Brotherhood to a secret cave underneath the monastery. The symbol for Montserrat is three mountain peaks, with an elevated "Ark" over the center peak.

▲ Montserrat is situated atop a mountain plateau surrounded by serrated sandstone cliffs.

The legendary Montserrat is a famous mountain, sanctuary, monastery, and spiritual community, which currently attracts more than a million visitors per year.

Based on its reputation, Montserrat is one of the most popular pilgrimage destinations in Spain. The Benedictine monastery and spiritual community is perched high upon a 4,200-foot (1,300-m) saw-toothed mountain. The name *Montserrat* literally means "jagged mountain" and refers to the peculiar aspect of the edifice, which is visible from a great distance. Montserrat is popular for mountain biking, hiking, spelunking, and rock climbing, but the real attraction is a serpentine trail leading to the 11th century sanctuary of Our Lady of Montserrat. This pilgrimage destination is home to the 12th century statue of *La Moreneta* (Black Madonna), which resides near the *Santa Cova* (Holy Cave) where the relic was originally housed. The statue is now located above the high alter in a mountaintop basilica, which is open to the public. The cave,

▲ Saint Ignatius inspired the founding of the Jesuit order.

statue and basilica are all blackened by the smoke of countless candles. Many miracles have been attributed to the Black Madonna, and it has attracted untold millions of pilgrims over the centuries.

Getting to Montserrat

Montserrat is 35 miles (56 km) northwest of Barcelona. The best approach from the city is the *Ferrocarriles Catalanes* train line that terminates at a cable car station for an exhilarating ride up the mountain. The trains to Montserrat leave Barcelona from beneath the Placa de Espanya five times daily and take about 90 minutes each way. Tour buses also make the round trip from Barcelona along the A2 road toward Tarragona, then turning west on the N11 and following the signs to the monastery.

Sagrada Família

Antonio Gaudí started work designing a building in 1883 he originally termed the "church of the poor." After disagreements between the founding association and the original architect, Gaudí was assigned to lead the project in 1884, and thus produced an entirely new design. Already a famous architect for his unique designs in Barcelona, Gaudí had in mind something spectacular, which he would eventually achieve. In his later years, he abandoned all secular work and devoted his life to the basilica called *La Sagrada Família,* or "The Holy Family." Gaudí was an ardent Catholic and a fervent Catalan nationalist. He worked on the project for over 40 years, devoting the last 15 years of his life entirely to this endeavor. When questioned about the extremely long duration of construction, Gaudí is said to have joked, "My client is not in a hurry."

Together with other artists, he supervised the work until his death on June 7, 1926, when the eminent architect was run over by a city tram. Because of his ragged attire and empty pockets, several cab drivers refused to pick him up for fear that he would be unable to pay the fare. He was eventually taken to a pauper's hospital in Barcelona. Nobody recognized the injured Gaudí until some friends located him the next day. When they tried to move him into a better hospital, Gaudí refused, reportedly saying, "I belong here among the poor." He died two days later and was buried in the crypt underneath his unfinished masterpiece, Sagrada Família.

> Integrated into the curvaceous architecture of Sagrada Família are subtle details of Christian symbolism. It is a church like no other. Because of its unique appearance the unfinished basilica is the single most visited destination in Spain.

▲ The distinctive architecture of Antonio Gaudí can be found all around Barcelona. He was a successful architect until he devoted himself to his life's work.

The church was originally conceived by Josep Maria Bocabella, the founder of the spiritual Association of Devotees of Saint Joseph, and his desire to promote Catholic values at a time of social and religious instability in Spain. Antonio Gaudí met this objective by designing a church dedicated to the Holy Family. He wanted Sagrada Família to establish a religious bond between the ordinary people and God. Every detail, from the colors used to the rich sculptures, all contain deep religious symbolism. As for conceptualizing the church, he originally got his inspiration from neighboring Montserrat, the famous pilgrimage destination atop a craggy peak. The three façades at the church represent birth, death, and resurrection. Every part of the design is rich with mystic Christian symbolism, as Gaudí intended the church to be the "last great sanctuary of Christendom." Perhaps the most striking aspects are the spindle-shaped towers. A total of 18 tall towers are featured in the finished design, representing in ascending order of height the 12

Apostles, the four Evangelists, the Virgin Mary, and — tallest of all — Jesus Christ.

Sagrada Família is still under construction, and will remain that way for several more decades. The enormous structure must be financed entirely by personal donations as required in the original concept. The ongoing construction of Sagrada Família is paid for almost exclusively by the nearly 2.5 million people who visit each year. It is a Roman Catholic basilica, not to be confused with a cathedral. Barcelona's Cathedral of Santa Eulàlia is a Gothic building constructed in the late Middle Ages. By one estimate, the completion of Sagrada Família may come as soon as 2026, corresponding with the 100th anniversary of Gaudí's death. It has recently been declared a UNESCO World Heritage Site.

▲ The Sagrada Família is Gaudi's real gift to the city of Barcelona. Even unfinished it is a masterpiece.

Getting to the Sagrada Família

When ground was broke in 1883, the basilica stood in an empty field over a mile away from urban Barcelona. That is not the case anymore. The towering Sagrada Família is located at the *Placa de la Sagrada,* with its own metro stop. Many Barcelona city buses also pass the basilica. Sagrada Família is open for tours in the summer months from early morning to mid-evening, in the winter it is open about half the time.

Santiago de Compostela

Biblical tradition relates the story of Saint James the Apostle traveling to the Galicia region in 40 CE to spread the gospel of Jesus to the farthest reaches of western Europe. He died a martyr's death upon returning to Jerusalem, and his remains were eventually returned to Spain and laid to rest in the sacred city of Santiago de Compostela. Through many centuries, his shrine has attracted more pilgrims than that of any other Christian apostle. The end-point of Christian pilgrimage is the cathedral where the relics of Saint James reside in a bejeweled altar. Devout pilgrims can follow the centuries-old tradition of climbing the stairs behind the altar to kiss the golden cape on the life-size statue of the saint. Directly below the statue is the famous crypt. His bones are contained in a silver reliquary.

> The monumental cathedral at Santiago de Compostela was the terminus of the most important pilgrimage destination of medieval Europe, second only to Rome.

▲ The shrine of Saint James is the ultimate destination for all who travel the Camino to Santiago.

The Cathedral of Santiago, whose construction began in 1075, is one of the finest monuments in Europe, both from an artistic and symbolic viewpoint. It was started in the Romanesque style, but over the centuries evolved to incorporate various other styles. The cloister is Gothic-Renaissance, Neo-Classical makes an appearance, yet it was the splendid baroque style that dominates inside and out. The High Altar was originally Romanesque, but was redesigned in the 16th century with baroque decorations. The baroque additions reached their culmination with the façade of O Obradoiro, installed between 1738 and 1750.

Upon finishing their trek, road-weary pilgrims initially performed the ritual of visiting the chapel and crypt of Saint James to put closure on their journey. Some pilgrims were convicted criminals. They had to bring back a certificate of arrival so the judge would abdicate their sentence. Certificates in Latin, called a *Compostela*, are still given out at the Saint James shrine. From medieval times to the present, a pilgrim would also acquire a scallop clam shell, the universal image of a journey to Santiago. This clam shell was usually painted with symbols, attached to a backpack or could embellish the top of a walking stick. When Saint Francis himself came to Santiago he was so inspired that he founded the Saint Francis' Convent at nearby Obradoiro Square. Countless others have gained profound inspiration upon reaching the cathedral, some after hiking 700 miles (1,000 km) from the French border.

Santiago de Compostela is the third most important holy city in Christendom, after Rome and Jerusalem. Because of its enormous significance to Christians over the centuries, all of the earliest western European roads led there via "The

Way." So popular was the pilgrimage in the Middle Ages that, in the 16th century, more than 200,000 pilgrims made the journey each year. Pilgrims today can enjoy a wealth of medieval art inside the cathedral, treasury, various cloisters, or ascend the cathedral towers to gain a fine panoramic view of the compact city. The entire old city of Santiago is designated as a UNESCO World Heritage Site.

Getting to Santiago de Compostela

The pilgrimage terminus city of Santiago de Compostela is located in the northwestern corner of Spain, about 30 miles (48 km) southwest of La Coruña. The cathedral, located at the Plaza de Obradoiro, is considered one of the finest architectural achievements in Europe and can be seen from miles away. Anyone in the city of Santiago knows the way to the famous plaza in the old city. Bus and train routes service the city regularly. Those wishing to hike, bicycle, or horseback ride

▲ Countless pilgrims came to Santiago Cathedral to fulfill a vow, seek the divine power of Saint James, or ask forgiveness of a past sin. Others were forced to make the trip.

along the various pilgrim routes, called the *Camino* ("The Way of Saint James"), should contact the Santiago Pilgrim's Office. The office will provide resources, such as route directions, maps, and guide books to the historical sights along The Way. The most popular route is the French Way, starting in the Pyrenees, but there are at least six other well-marked routes coming into Santiago from all directions. The Way in Spain is some 600 miles (965 km) long, most of it a footpath still untouched by cars, winding its way through fields and past monasteries. All Camino routes are demarked by the image of a clam shell.

Toledo

When much of northern Europe was being unsettled by the brutal Viking invasions in the 9th and 10th centuries, the brilliant development of Arab learning was in full bloom. Apart from China, the Arab nations were incomparably more advanced than any other civilization in the world. It is known that the Christian Renaissance in Europe owes its inspiration as much to contact with the Islamic cultures as it does to the revival of Greek learning. Indeed, most of Greek literature and philosophy reached the West not from Greek manuscripts, but from Arabic translations out of Córdoba and Toledo when the Moors controlled most

▲ The cathedral in the old section of Toledo ranks among the great cathedrals of Europe, both for its spectacular architecture and the priceless artwork contained inside.

of Spain. It was only in the last few centuries, in particular during the Industrial Revolution, did the West forge ahead scientifically. In the 12th century, Muslim science was way ahead, particularly in such fields as mathematics, medicine, and astronomy.

Toledo was originally a Roman outpost called *Toletum*. The first historian to mention it was Roman author Titus Livius, who described it as a "small fortified town." It later served as the capital city of Visigothic Spain, beginning with King Liuvigild, and continued to thrive after the Moors conquered Iberia in the 8th century. It was the capital of Spain from the Visigoth era, through the Moorish occupation, and continued after the Christian reconquest until 1560, a fact that explains its exceptional medieval architecture. While under control of the Moors, Toledo became one of the most important European centers of medieval learning. The Mosque of Cristo de la Luz still remains from this glorious era of scientific blossoming. Toledo is a unique city, where beautiful and harmonious buildings feature an array of architectural styles. Walking through the streets can feel like having stepped back into the Middle Ages.

In its medieval past, Toledo emerged as one of the cradles of European civilization through its Toledo School of Translators and its many houses of learning. The Toledo School of Translators made available great academic and philosophical works in Arabic and Hebrew by translating them into Latin, bringing vast stores of knowledge to Europe for the first time. By working together in unity, Toledo became a shining example of tolerance and coexistence between the Jewish, Muslim, and Christian inhabitants.

Toledo was famed for religious harmony.
Even after the reconquest of Spain from the
Moors in 1492, Toledo remained the historic,
artistic, and spiritual capital of Spain, especially to displaced Jews and Muslims.

The Juderia, Toledo's old Jewish Quarter, contains two synagogues, two of only three from the Moorish era in Spain that survived the expulsion (the other one is in Córdoba). After the expulsion of the Sephardic Jews from Toledo in 1459 CE, the *Sinagoga del Tránsito* was closed as a synagogue under the new Christian religious laws. Today, it is called Museo Sefardí and hosts the official acts, Jewish artifacts and numerous exhibits of its original Sephardic beliefs. The Synagogue of Saint Mary the White (*Sinagoga de Santa Maria la Blanca*) was founded in 1180, and remains a beautiful construction of the famed Toledo Mudéjar style. It has five wings separated by 28 horseshoe arches that support brick columns covered with cement and painted with limestone. After being taken over by the Christians, Cardinal Silicio declared it to be "a refuge for misled and repentant women."

Toledo is one of the greatest art cities not only of Spain, but of the civilized world. Of its principal religious edifices, the Toledo cathedral is a magnificent five-nave Gothic structure dominating the center of the city. Considered one of the finest cathedrals in Europe, it contains a marvelously vast interior with equally magnificent artwork by El Greco, Goya, Rubens, Velázquez, Titian, and Bellini. The cathedral also features numerous additional sections begun in 1227 by King Saint Ferdinand and Archbishop Jiménez de Rada. Also worth visiting is the Franciscan Monastery of San Juan de los Reyes, built in 1476 by Ferdinand and Isabella, to which a church and cloister is attached in the ornate Ogival style. The famous painter El Greco lived in Toledo for the last 37 years of his life. The Santa Cruz Museum contains 15 paintings by El Greco. The Museum of El Greco contains about 20 of his paintings, including portraits of the Apostles and his masterful work *View of Toledo*. With so much rich culture and spiritual history, it is easy to understand the origin of the term "Holy Toledo!"

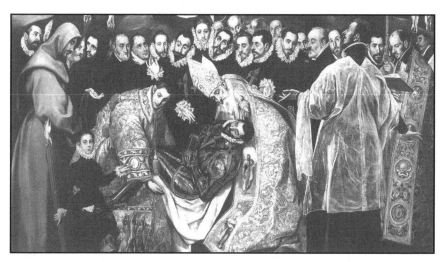

▲ "The Burial of the Count of Orgaz" by El Greco is one of Toledo's many treasures.

Getting to Toledo

Toledo has a privileged location along the natural turn of the Tagus River, situated on a circular hill with the cathedral centrally located in the old city. It has been continuously populated for some 3,500 years. Only an hour south of Madrid by car, bus, or train, Toledo is a city that is easily accessed from all parts of Spain. The three Tourist Information offices in Toledo offer excellent maps and resources for discovering this magnificent city.

CONCLUSION

Science at its best should leave room for poetry.
—*Richard Dawkins, Unweaving the Rainbow*

I T CAN BE ARGUED that the European nations have been more influential in the collective development of world civilization than any other grouping of nations. Throughout history, the people of Europe have asserted cultural and social change from their respective countries, mainly through military prowess and colonization. Beginning with Alexander the Great spreading Hellenistic culture to India in the 4th century BCE, to profit-minded European merchant sailors two thousand years later, Europeans had a reputation for a global outlook. In their heyday, imperial Englishmen took pride that "the sun never sets on the British Empire." European philosophy, religion, languages, commercial practices, and political models have influenced nearly every country around the globe. Although other civilizations such as Imperial China, the Maya and Inca high cultures, and Middle Eastern advancements made crucial contributions to world development, Europeans were the undisputed colonial masters. By "borrowing" the best the world had to offer and discarding all the rest, Europeans enriched their own lives, and conversely of those they conquered. It cannot be denied that Europe has long been a rich incubator of dynamic people and ideas.

Even with such far-reaching ambitions, the European psyche has been divided by some of the finest human accomplishments in history, along with some of the worst. From ushering in the tragedy of two World Wars in the last century, to producing some of the most advanced scientific minds civilization has ever known, the people of Europe represent the full range of human potential. Although Europe is the second smallest inhabited continent, it has contributed so greatly that half the planet attributes its roots to Western Civilization. For better or for worse, Europeans pride themselves on being a harbinger for change and development.

Given its critical role in human "progress," it is not surprising that a majority of the most "famous" sacred places worldwide can be found on European soil. The reader has likely noticed that there was no inclusion of battlefield sites, concentration camps, or any other places where terrible human atrocities occurred. Certainly Europe possesses more than its fair share of dark energy locations, which, in a strange way, can also inspire people. But in my subjective manner of choosing sacred sites for this book, I offer locations exclusively orientated towards the positive. A "sacred place" is defined in part by the best humanity has to offer as it strives to be both artistically and spiritually exceptional. It doesn't matter if we are not of the same religious persuasion of those who worship at the site to reap its benefits. If it matters to those who worship at the location, then it should matter to us. After all we, as advanced human beings, should know the importance of acceptance and diversity, even if what that sacred place represents doesn't fit into our own religious or philosophical constructs. If any religious denomination finds a location inspiring or enlightening, or if a person long ago performed actions that helped others, that site represents the best of humanity and made my list of "108 Destinations."

From the time I embarked on my 2004 European research trip to develop this book until late in 2006, when the final chapters were submitted to my exceptional editor Jeff Curry, some major changes have occurred in Europe. For starters, the Visočica Valley Pyramids were discovered in Bosnia. Also in the former Yugoslavia, two new European countries — Montenegro and Kosovo — have declared their independence. Another dozen countries, mostly from the former Soviet bloc, have been approved or are being considered for acceptance into the European Union (EU). Unlike static national boundaries on other continents, the ever-changing political landscape of Europe redefines itself seemingly every year. The dynamic aspect of Europe could be its greatest asset or its biggest downfall. The EU could easily become the largest world superpower, or it can remain divided by its myriad of cultural differences. With so many people in such a small geographical area, it is poised once again to influence the global stage, or it has the potential to unravel into petty divergences. Either way, Europe is a wonderful travel destination, filled with the history that has shaped most of our lives.

My sole objective in producing this travel book (and many others) is to inspire people to see the world, particularly to the destinations outlined in these chapters. I have always felt that travel is the best education one can receive, but travel to sacred places certainly raises the ante. No longer are people satisfied spending their holidays sipping mai tais by the hotel poolside. They want more from their vacations—they want a higher meaning in their excursions. If travel is food for the soul, then travel to sacred places is the sugar and spice. It gives travel added meaning. I truly believe we can better the world simply with our presence in foreign lands. Travelers are ambassadors of peace, whether we chose to accept the role or not. In a world filled with injustice, imbalance, and cruelty, just witnessing an alternative reality may be the most important first step in our own personal development. Perhaps some backpacker in India will give a child his first pen and that person will become the next Mohandas Gandhi. Or hopefully an affluent traveler, by discovering the locations outlined in this book, will make a contribution to preserve a sacred site that is being threatened. There are so many ways we can give back, and travel has to be one of the most exciting ways! Go out there and experience our beautiful planet filled with such amazing people, places, and things. You will undoubtedly return a much better person as a result.

Your Fellow Ambassador in Peace,

—Brad Olsen

San Francisco, CA

Winter Solstice, 2006

▲ EXTRA CREDIT: Who can identify this dolmen I am in? If you know it, write me a letter or email via CCC Publishing and I will send the first 10 people who answer correctly one of my books FREE! You must specifically name this European dolmen or send me a picture of you in it! Pick any book from my catalog and tell me where to send it—anywhere in the world.

ACKNOWLEDGMENTS

THIS WORK WAS GREATLY ENHANCED by the exceptional suggestions from the following editors: **Lead Editor Jeff Curry**, Edward Taylor, Martin Gray, Emiko Monobe, Shell Peczynski, and family members Elaine Olsen (mother), Marshall Olsen (father), his wife Susan, and Marsi Olsen (sister). Book design and direction thanks from Mark Maxam and book cover assistance by Eric Stampfli. Additional support came from my uncle Bud Hausman and his wife Bonnie, who let me work at their summer home in Wisconsin, Joe Firmage and the Many One organization, Michael O'Rourke, Justin Smith, Justin Wiener, and Peter Bartsch from the World Peace Through Technology Organization.

IN EUROPE, and in no particular order, I was assisted by the following people: Anna Grechsnt & John Maistre in MALTA; Daniela Lage in GERMANY; Rosina & Franz Lichtenberger in AUSTRIA; Fran Pell, Marshall & Susan Olsen, and Andrzej Fitrzyk in POLAND; Katja Manders, Hein & Isabel Kuiper, Mandy Soons, Martin DePee in THE NETHERLANDS; Bert Roeyen, Miet Waes in BELGIUM; Samantha Brickellin in ENGLAND; Maryse Gerbaud in FRANCE; Doug Lansky and family members Siggy, Sienna, and India in SWEDEN; Alf Hoyland in NORWAY; Lene Jorgensen in DENMARK; James Martinez in SPAIN; Zoe Coyle-Fitzgerald in IRELAND; Annamária Czene in HUNGARY; Tanya Serova in UKRAINE; and special thanks to Kirill Novosselski in RUSSIA, and Vera Ginzbourg.

SPECIAL PHOTO CREDIT THANKS TO: **Martin Gray and www. SacredSites.com**, Roy Tate, Berill Johnson, Jessica A. Eise, Carol Keiter, Orkney Tourism Board, Mercedes Windischmann of Kincsem Lovaspark Kft. and Meho Macic of www.BosnianPyramid.com

SPECIAL PROMOTIONAL THANKS TO: the Malta Board of Tourism, www.visitmalta.com & Virtu Ferries, www.virtuferries.com. Also the Austrian National Tourism Office 1-212-944-6880; www.anto.com. Rail Europe provided assistance with my rail pass and itinerary, please contact them for assistance with yours: 1-888-382-7245 www.raileurope.com

WWW.CCCPUBLISHING.COM   WWW.STOMPERS.COM
WWW.PEACETOUR.ORG   WWW.BRADOLSEN.COM

BIBLIOGRAPHY

Introduction

Adams, Russell B., Series Director, *Mystic Places: Mysteries of the Unknown*. Alexandria, VA: Time-Life Books, 1987.

Armstrong, Karen, *A History of God*. New York, NY: Ballantine Books, 1993.

Childress, David Hatcher, *Anti-Gravity & The World Grid*. Stelle, IL: Adventures Unlimited Press, 1995.

Dillard, Annie, "The Wreck of Time: Taking Our Century's Measure." *Harper's,* (New York), January 1998.

Judge, Michael, *The Dance of Time: The Origins of the Calendar.* New York, NY: MJF Books, 2004.

Metzner, Ralph, *The Unfolding Self.* Navato, CA: Origin Press, 1998.

Great Britain

Brennan, Janet, "Orkney's Mystery Mound." *Fate,* (Lakeville, MN), June 2004.

Clark, Kenneth, *Civilization*. New York, NY:Harper & Row, 1969.

Cowen, David & Arnold, Chris, *Ley Lines and Earth Energies.* Kempton, IL: Adventures Unlimited Press, 2003.

Dunford, Barry, *The Holy Land of Scotland*. Glenlyon, Scotland: Sacred Connections, 2002.

DuQuette, Lon Milo, *The Key to Solomon's Key*. San Francisco, CA: CCC Publishing, 2006.

Michell, John, *Sacred England*. Glastonbury, UK: Gothic Image Publications, 2003.

Pringle, Lucy, *Crop Circles: The Greatest Mystery of Modern Times*. London, UK: Thorsons, 1999.

Silva, Freddy, "Does Sound Create Crop Circles?" *Nexus,* (Mapleton, Australia), Sept.-Oct., 2005.

Solara, *11:11, Inside the Doorway.* Los Angeles, CA: Star-Borne Unlimited, 1992.

Steves, Rick, *Great Britain*. Emeryville, CA: Avalon Travel Publishing, 2004.

Whitehouse, David & Ruth, *Archaeological Atlas of the World,* San Francisco, CA: W.H. Freeman & CO., 1975.

Ireland

Bahn, Paul G., Editor, *100 Great Archaeological Discoveries*. London, UK: Barnes & Noble Books, 1995.

Brockman, Norbert C., *Encyclopedia of Sacred Places*. Oxford University Press: New York, NY, 1997.

Meehan, Cary, *Sacred Ireland*. Glastonbury, UK: Gothic Image Publications, 2002.

O'Brien, Henry, *The Round Towers of Ireland*. Originally published in 1834. Reprinted as *The Round Towers of Atlantis,* Kempton, Il: Adventures Unlimited, 2002.

Steves, Rick, *Ireland*. Emeryville, CA: Avalon Travel Publishing, 2004.

Tate, Karen, *Sacred Places of Goddess: 108 Destinations.* San Francisco, CA: CCC Publishing, 2006.

Wallace, Martain, *A Little Book of Celtic Saints*. Belfast, Northern Ireland: Appletree Press, 1995.

France and the Low Countries

Andrews, Richard & Schellenberger, Paul, *The Tomb of God.* London, England: Warner Books, 1997.

Doubleday, Nelson, Editor, *Encyclopedia of World Travel Volume 2.* Garden City, NY: Doubleday & Company, 1967.

Frank, Irene M., et. al. *To the Ends of the Earth.* New York, NY: Facts On File Publications, 1984.

Mohen, Jean-Pierre, *The Carnac Alignments: Neolithic Temples.* Paris, France: Monum, 2000.

Poux, Didier, *Cathar Country & the Cathar Religion.* Albi, France: Apa-Poux, 1995.

Steves, Rick, *Amsterdam. Bruges & Brussels.* Emeryville, CA: Avalon Travel Publishing, 2004.

Steves, Rick, *France.* Emeryville, CA: Avalon Travel Publishing, 2004.

Sullivan, Walter, et. al, *The World's Last Mysteries.* Pleasantville, NY: The Reader's Digest Association 1981.

Wilson, Colin, *The Atlas of Holy Places and Sacred Sites.* New York, NY: DK Publishing, 1996.

Central Europe

Flinn, John, "Bulgaria: Iron Curtain Lifted Slowly on Country Brimming with European Allure." *San Francisco Chronicle,* (San Francisco), July, 2006.

Hartt, Frederick, et. al. *Art: A History of Painting, Sculpture, and Architecture: Second Edition.* Englewood Cliffs, New Jersey: Prentice-Hall, 1985.

Osmanagic, Semir (Sam), *The First European Pyramid Discovered in Europe.* www.bosnian-pyramid.com

Remesova, Vera, *Graceful Infant Jesus of Prague.* Prague, Czech Republic: ArchArt, 2002.

Scarre, Chris, General Editor, *Past Worlds: The Times Atlas of Archaeology.* London, UK: Times Books Limited, 1988.

Eastern Europe

Bayly, C. A., et. al., *Light in the East.* Alexandria, VA: Time-Life Books, 1988.

Moloney, Norah, *The Young Oxford Book of Archaeology.* Oxford, England: Oxford University Press, 1995.

Wheeler, Mortimer, Editor, *Splendors of the East.* New York, NY: G.P. Putnam's Sons, 1965.

Wheeler, Tony, *West Asia on a Shoestring.* Hawthorn, Australia: Lonely Planet Publications, 1990.

Scandinavia

Doubleday, Nelson, Editor, *Encyclopedia of World Travel Volume 1.* Garden City, NY: Doubleday & Company, 1967.

Littmarck, Tore, *Gamla Uppsala: From Ancient to Modern Time.* Old Uppsala, Sweden: Parish Vestry, 2002.

Nordbok, AB, *The Viking.* Gothenburg, Sweden: Crescent Books, 1975.

Roesdahl, Else, *The Vikings.* London, England: Penguin Books, 1987.

Steves, Rick, *Scandinavia.* Emeryville, CA: Avalon Travel Publishing, 2004.

Sveen, Arvid, *Rock Carvings Jiepmaluokta, Alta.* Tromso, Norway: Kopinor, 2001.

Thue, Stein, Editor, *On the Pilgrim Way to Trondheim.* Trondheim, Norway: Tapir, 1998.

BIBLIOGRAPHY

Germany and the Alps

Belliveau, Jeannette, *An Amateur's Guide to the Planet*. Baltimore, MD: Beau Monde Press, 1996.

Bryson, Bill, *A Short History of Nearly Everything*. New York, NY: Broadway Books, 2003.

Fischer, Manfred, *Hall of Liberation at Kelheim*. Munich, Germany: Bayerische, 1999.

Steves, Rick, *Germany, Austria & Switzerland*. Emeryville, CA: Avalon Travel Publishing, 2004.

Greece

Ellingham, Mark, Series Editor, *Rough Guide Europe*. London, UK. Penguin, 1998.

Hamlyn, Paul, *Greek Mythology*. London, UK: Westbook House, 1964.

Hellander, Paul, coordinating author, *Greece*. Melbourne, Australia: Lonely Planet, 2006.

Howell, F. Clark, *Early Man*. Alexandria, VA: Time-Life Books, 1968.

Westward, Jennifer, Editor, *The Atlas of Mysterious Places*. London, UK: Weidenfeld & Nicolson, 1987.

Italy and Malta

Azzopardi, Aldo, *Malta: Gem of the Mediterranean*. Luqa, Malta: Plurigraf / Miller House, 2004.

Braca, Antonio, et. al., *Historical Information about Poseidonia*. Paestum, Italy: Paestum Museum, 2004

Cave, Ferruccio Delle, *Agrigento, the Valley of the Temples*. Vienna, Austria: Folio, 2004

De Camp, L. Sprague, *Great Cities of the Ancient World*, Garden City, NY: Doubleday, 1972.

Eiseley, Loren, Editor, *The Epic Of Man*, New York, NY: Life Books, 1961.

Flaherty, Thomas, Editor-in-Chief, et. al, *Pompeii: the Vanished City*, New York, NY: Time-Life Books, 1992.

Steves, Rick, *Italy*. Emeryville, CA: Avalon Travel Publishing, 2004.

Sullivan, Walter, et. al, *The World's Last Mysteries*. Pleasantville, NY: The Reader's Digest Association 1981.

Wright, Kevin J., *Catholic Shrines of Western Europe*. Liguori, MO: Liguori, 1997.

Spain and Portugal

Childress, David Hatcher, "The Search for the Ark of the Covenant" *World Explorer*, (Kempton, IL), Vol. 2, No. 2.

Frank, Irene M., et. al. *To the Ends of the Earth*. New York: Facts On File Publications, 1984.

Garcia, Vicenta Barbosa, *Granada*. Granada, Spain: Otermin Ediciones, 2003.

Ingpen, Robert, et. at. *Encyclopedia of Mysterious Places*. New York: Viking Penguin, 1990.

Steves, Rick, *Spain and Portugal*. Emeryville, CA: Avalon Travel Publishing, 2004.

TOUR OUTFITTERS TO SACRED PLACES

Many of the selected outfitters below specialize in one or more sacred site regions of Europe. Call for a free brochure and more information.

Adventure Center

1311 63rd Street, Suite # 200, Emeryville, CA 94608

800-227-8747

Specializes in affordable group travel to especially adventurous destinations.

Canterbury Tours, Inc.

PO Box 783, Pawling, NY 12564

800-653-0017

Leads pilgrimage groups to European shrines.

Catholic Pilgrimage Center

6278 N. Federal Highway, Suite # 284

Fort Lauderdale, FL 33308

800-952-2809

Features multi-country itineraries to Catholic destinations in Europe and the Holy land.

www.catholicpilgrimagecenter.com

Circle the Planet

800-799-8888

Lowest-cost tickets for round-the-world destinations and most European sacred sites.

www.circletheplanet.com

Deja Vu Tours

2210 Harold Way, Berkeley, CA 94704 USA

800-204-TOUR

Tours to sacred sites led by graduates of the Berkeley Psychic Institute.

www.berkeleypsychic.com

Global Exchange REALITY TOURS

2017 Mission Street # 303, San Francisco, CA 94110

800-497-1994

Educational, interactive, and inspiring excursions dealing with provocative themes, such as peace and conflict, human rights, revolution, history, culture, art, and the environment.
www.globalexchange.org

Global Tours
800-321-7798
www.globaltours-inc.com

Holy Pilgrimages
PO Box 177, Atkinson, NH 03811
603-362-4793
Small pilgrimage groups to European shrines.

Journeys Unlimited
500 Eighth Avenue, Suite # 904, New York, NY 10018
800-486-8359

Key Tours
11096B Lee Hwy. Suite # 104, Fairfax, VA 22030
800-576-1784
Specializes in tours to the Eastern Mediterranean region.
www.keytours.com

Luther Tours
888-458-8486
Specializes in tours of the various Martin Luther sites in Germany.
www.luthertours.com

Pilgrim Tours
800-322-0788
Tour outfitter to sacred Christian sites.
www.pilgrimtours.com

Power Places Tours & Conferences
116 King St., Fredericksted, Virgin Islands 00840,
800-234-8687
FAX: 340-772-1392
Tours led by modern-day luminaries to power places around the world.
www.powerplaces.com

Santiago Pilgrim's Office

981-542-527

Contact the Pilgrim's Office in Santiago, Spain for route directions, maps, accommodations, and guide books to the various historical sights along the Camino, or The Way of Saint James.

www.turgalicia.es

www.xacobeo.es

Tour Crafters

28085 North Ashley Circle, unit 202

Libertyville, Illinois, 60048

1-800-ITALY95 or

1-800-621-2259

Tours and hotels focusing on Italy, but also offering tours to France and other European destinations. Their focus is on art, food, and culture.

www.tourcrafters.com

Unitours

800-777-7432

www.unitours.com

World Explorers Club

PO Box 99, 403 Kemp Street, Kempton, IL 60946

815-253-9000

Tours/Expeditions/Conferences to more remote sacred places. Always led by an expert in the field or famous author.

www.wexclub.com

INDEX

Index

INDEX

317

SACRED PLACES NORTH AMERICA
108 DESTINATIONS

Travel along with author, photographer, and cartographer Brad Olsen as he reveals the many spiritual sites that abound in North America. "Pilgrimage is one way we can find ourselves and this book will provide a guide," raved the Twin Cities Wellness paper. The venerable Midwest Book Review said: "Sacred Places North America is a revealing, useful, and enthusiastically recommended guide." Spirituality and Health noted: "In this handy and helpful resource, Brad Olsen demonstrates his respect for sacred places." And the Orlando Sentinel reviewed: "He offers information on each site, juxtaposing local folklore and Native American legend with scientific theories or physical evidence to provide context." Read the critically acclaimed North America guide to 108 Destinations. Want to visit wondrous, exotic, incredibly gorgeous locales and experience a sense of mystical transcendence? You don't need a plane ticket, a passport, or even a psychedelic drug. In fact, there's probably such a place within driving distance of your home" observed Fearless Books.

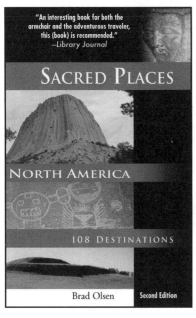

"An interesting book for both the armchair and the adventurous traveler, this (book) is recommended."
—Library Journal

SACRED PLACES

NORTH AMERICA

108 DESTINATIONS

Brad Olsen   Second Edition

■   Who were the first Europeans in North America: the Vikings, Celts, or ancient Phoenicians?

■   Why did Native Americans revere certain mountains?

■   Where are the most frequent sightings of Bigfoot and UFOs?

■   Why does attendance at Graceland increase every year?

■   Where do people of the New Age movement convene to experience Earth energy?

■   How did certain prehistoric civilizations mark seasonal equinoxes and solstices?

108 B&W Photographs / 66 Maps and Graphics

ISBN 1-888729-13-9   344 pages   USA $19.95 / Canada $24.95 2nd edition
Travel / Spirituality / History